SYSTEMATIC
APPROACHES *to*
a SUCCESSFUL
LITERATURE
REVIEW

Andrew Booth
Diana Papaioannou
Anthea Sutton

Los Angeles | London | New Delhi
Singapore | Washington DC

First published 2012

Reprinted 2013, 2014

SAGE Publications Ltd
1 Oliver's Yard
55 City Road
London EC1Y 1SP

SAGE Publications Inc.
2455 Teller Road
Thousand Oaks, California 91320

SAGE Publications India Pvt Ltd
B 1/I 1 Mohan Cooperative Industrial Area
Mathura Road
New Delhi 110 044

SAGE Publications Asia-Pacific Pte Ltd
3 Church Street
#10-04 Samsung Hub
Singapore 049483

Library of Congress Control Number: 2011925496

British Library Cataloguing in Publication data

A catalogue record for this book is available from the British Library

ISBN 978-0-85702-134-2
ISBN 978-0-85702-135-9 (pbk)

Typeset by C&M Digitals (P) Ltd, India, Chennai
Printed by Ashford Colour Press Ltd, Gosport, Hampshire

Contents

Solutions to Exercises – These can be found at www.sagepub.co.uk/booth

ONE

The literature review: its role within research

> **Learning Objectives**
>
> After reading this chapter, you should be able to:
>
> - Define a 'literature review' and rehearse arguments for its importance.
> - Describe some benefits from reviewing the literature in a systematic way.
> - Identify landmarks in the development of research synthesis.
> - Make an initial assessment of the extent to which reviews in your own discipline or topic area can be described as 'systematic'.

Introduction

Room without a (re)view?

Conducting any type of research project without conducting a literature review can be likened to travelling to a strange and exotic country but never coming out of your hotel room. How will you convince your friends back home that you truly sampled the delights of this exotic destination? Granted you may reach your destination, you may even achieve the occasional moment of insight but you will be starved of so many valuable moments of discovery. It may seem to an outsider that you have never even travelled at all!

Without a literature review, you will not be able to understand your topic fully. You will not be able to identify what has already been researched and what remains to be explored, and you will deny yourself valuable insights into those methods that are or are not appropriate for investigation of your topic. You will not only face the danger of reinventing the wheel but, even more critically, you will run the risk of 'reinventing the flat tyre'!

What is a literature review?

Fink (2005) succinctly defines a literature review as a 'systematic, explicit, and reproducible method for identifying, evaluating, and synthesising the existing body of completed and recorded work produced by researchers, scholars, and practitioners'. Particularly noticeable is the word 'systematic', a key concept for the title and content of this book. If criticism can be levelled at the growth in popularity of the term **systematic review** it is the unintended implication that there is an acceptable alternative, the unsystematic review! As we shall see all reviews share the requirement of original empirical research, namely to be systematic. Different types of review (Box 1.1) should differ only in the degree to which they are systematic – according to each review's role and function – and each type should help by telling you what exactly they have and have not done.

Box 1.1   Some common types of review

Critical review

Integrative review

Literature review

Mapping review/systematic map

Meta-analysis

Mixed studies review/mixed methods review

Overview

Qualitative systematic review/qualitative evidence synthesis

Rapid review

Scoping review

State-of-the-art review

Systematic review

Systematised review

Systematic search and review

Umbrella review

Note: These different types of review are defined and explained in Chapter 2. For the present it is sufficient to acknowledge that a plethora of terms exists for systematic approaches to a literature review.

Hart (1998) unpicks more detail of what a review process entails, focusing on the essential components, the documents themselves:

> the selection of available documents . . . on the topic . . . written from a particular standpoint to fulfill certain aims or express certain views on the nature of the topic and how it is to be investigated, and the effective evaluation of these documents in relation to the research being proposed.

If you are to perform this *effectively* then you will need to put in place processes to ensure that not only is the task completed in an *efficient* manner but also that it is fulfilled to the right *quality*. In the context of literature reviews, quality means 'appropriate breadth and depth, rigor and consistency, clarity and brevity, and effective analysis and synthesis' (Hart, 1998).

Why is the literature review so important?

Bem (1995) notes that 'authors of literature reviews are at risk for producing mind-numbing lists of citations and findings that resemble a phone book – impressive case, lots of numbers, but not much plot'. If we want to base our decisions on evidence it makes sense to use the best available evidence. By and large the best evidence for many decisions comes from a **systematic review** of *all* the evidence. Mulrow (1995) argues that reviewing in this way is a search for the whole truth, rather than just one part of it, and is thus a 'fundamentally scientific activity'. A specific and reproducible method is used to identify, select, and appraise all the studies of a previously agreed level of quality (either to include all studies or only those that meet a minimum quality threshold) that are relevant to a particular question. The results of the studies are then analysed and summarised. Synthesising evidence helps us to find out what we know and don't know about what works and what doesn't work. A good **research synthesis** can generally give us the most reliable estimate of the effectiveness of a specific intervention, and it can identify gaps in our knowledge that require further research. It can also give us a sense of the strength of the available evidence and the quality of the studies, thereby indicating how much confidence practitioners, service users, managers, policymakers, and the popular media should have in the results.

A research synthesis can also help us find out how well a policy, programme, technique or intervention works in different subgroups of users and inform us about its potential to cause harm. Some research syntheses can shed light on the pros and cons of different ways of organising or delivering services or policies. A research synthesis that includes considerations of cost can help shape our judgements about whether a chosen policy or course of action provides good value for money.

Yet another reason to synthesise the results of different studies of a given intervention is to learn whether findings are consistent across multiple studies. Light and Pillemer (1984) have written that 'disagreements among findings are valuable … [and that] conflicts can teach us a lot'. This is because we are able to see in what settings a particular social policy might succeed, under what circumstances an educational programme might work best, or what dose of a drug is most effective.

A good research synthesis frequently highlights weaknesses in the evidence and argues for further research. What should service users, policymakers, and others decide in the absence of evidence? Even when a research synthesis shows strong, unambiguous evidence to support one course of action, 'politics' may make that review's findings less influential than well-coordinated lobbying. As Chalmers, editor of the James Lind Library, and colleagues (2002) observe: 'Research synthesis sometimes yields unwelcome results that challenge strongly held opinions and other vested interests'. Yet even if the recommendations from a research synthesis are disregarded, its very existence allows more transparency about the role of other factors in decision making. No matter how well they are done, research syntheses are not a panacea for all problems, but they do offer a valuable aid to decision making.

Where does the literature review fit within the context of research?

The near ubiquitous presence of the literature review in so many disciplines and areas of policy development must not be allowed to mask the fact that there are essentially three contexts in which a literature review will be showcased:

1 As a component, or even entire ingredient, of a dissertation, thesis or other academic deliverable.
2 As a peer-reviewed publication, typically in a journal or, depending upon the discipline, as a book chapter.
3 As a report resulting from a funded research project or other commissioned research or consultancy.

Each of these contexts places specific additional requirements on the already polymorphic shape of a literature review. For example, where the literature review is intended to inform a dissertation or thesis, there may be a strong imperative to engage in conceptual innovation, to be reflexive about one's methods and to demonstrate a journey of personal growth through the methodology. A student is expected to demonstrate that they have acquired a 'knowledge about a particular field of study, including vocabulary, theories, key variables and phenomena, and its methods and history' (Randolph, 2009, w160). Furthermore they are required to provide evidence that they have become sensitised to the 'influential researchers and research groups in the field'. Of course these contexts are not mutually exclusive as the literature review from a thesis can subsequently be modified to become a 'legitimate and publishable scholarly document' (LeCompte et al., 2003).

Where the output is a peer-reviewed publication the challenge may be to funnel a wealth of data into the tight constraints of a journal's house style and word limits. Admittedly this situation has been eased somewhat by the relatively recent facility of online supplementary materials. Nevertheless there remains significant variation in how journals, and their parent disciplines, handle reviews, with some disparagingly refusing to even consider them while, in contrast, other journals make a virtue of annual review-type commissioned overviews and literature surveys.

Finally requirements for a funded research project or for consultancy may be evidenced in tight time constraints, in a quest for answers rather than issues, and in a tendency for commissioners to sidestep the methodology and cut straight to the results or findings. In particular, systematic reviews can yield much information of use to policymakers:

including information about the nature and extent of a problem, and the potential benefits, harms, uncertainties, and costs of interventions and policies. Policymakers may also want to know about the impact on different groups in various settings ... [and to] answer questions about how best to disseminate information and innovations; about a particular community's receptiveness to proposed interventions – whether the interventions are appropriate to local culture and context; and about the factors influencing study outcomes. (Sweet and Moynihan, 2007, w187)

Such distinctions are explicitly explored in Chapter 9 which deals with different types of presentation for different audiences and purposes. For the moment, it will be useful to flag the distinction made by Mays and others (Mays et al., 2005; Pope et al., 2007) between reviews for knowledge support and those for decision support. Reviews for knowledge support have as their endpoint the summarising and synthesis of research evidence (i.e. what currently exists and is known about a topic). They may usefully highlight gaps in the evidence base as a target for future research; seen in closest proximity within a thesis which may have the specific subsequent objective of addressing such a gap. Reviews for decision support seek to go further in bringing the existing evidence to bear on the particular individualised problem in hand. Gaps in the evidence base in this context lead to the supplementary question '... and what are we going to do about this issue or problem in the meantime?' Such questions are well-typified in a survey by Lavis and colleagues (2005) who found that managers were interested in reviews that addressed:

- decisions about continuing, starting/expanding, stopping/contracting or modifying a programme;
- how to fit programmes or services within an organisation or region (i.e. about governance, financial and delivery arrangements);
- how to bring about change.

In addition both managers and policymakers were interested in complex questions that combined all three of these questions as well as more general 'what do we know about x?' questions.

Within the healthcare field these knowledge support–decision support poles are unfairly characterised as being occupied by the **Cochrane Review** and the **health technology assessment**. In actuality, Cochrane Reviews are increasingly striving to contribute to decision making while health technology assessments may look beyond the immediate problem-focused timeframe to make recommendations for future commissioned primary research.

What types of research question are suitable for literature review?

An early principle to establish is that it is important for the literature review to be question-led. The question, together with the purpose of the review, the intended deliverables and the intended audience, will determine how the data is identified, collected and presented. It is tempting to consider that a literature review is only useful where a significant body of literature is already known to exist. However even where a researcher believes that they will be the first to examine a particular intervention, policy or programme they need to confirm this from the previously published literature to avoid the phenomenon of presenting islands without continents (i.e. falsely claiming innovation) (Clarke and Chalmers, 1998). A methodology from a proximate field may similarly provide an analogy that can save much development work.

However aside from such a circumstance it is generally true that most literature reviews are based on the assumption that at least one other researcher has at least considered, if not addressed, your question. The exact nature of your question will be shaped and influenced by the goal and focus of the review (Randolph, 2009, w160; Hart, 1998):

> *Effectiveness questions:* What effect does intervention X, compared with intervention y, have on outcome Z? What are the relative cost-benefits of x versus y?
>
> *Methodology questions:* What research methods have previously been used to investigate phenomenon X? What are the respective strengths and weaknesses of such methods?
>
> *Conceptual questions:* How has phenomenon X been identified and defined? Which theories have been used to explain phenomenon X? Which theory provides the best fit to findings from empirical studies? What are the main unresolved controversies? What are the underpinning epistemological and ontological foundations for the discipline?

Why review the literature?

Some practical reasons

One familiar phenomenon of this Internet age is the so-called **information explosion** (Major and Savin-Baden, 2010). Quite simply, with increasing numbers of articles being published and with larger quantities of these articles being freely accessible, it is becoming almost impossible to navigate around even the more specialised subject domains. At an individual level we face **information overload**. This occurs when we are overwhelmed by the volume of information that we are facing and are therefore unable to retrieve the information we need. Is there a solution to this situation? One possible way to succeed is by becoming **information literate** – put simply this means acquiring the skills covered in Chapters 4 to 9 in this book:

> An information literate person is able to recognise when information is needed and has the skills to locate, evaluate and use information effectively. (CILIP, 2009, w037)

Although technologies are always changing, database interfaces and search engines are continually being upgraded, and new topics continue to appear with regularity the skills of information literacy that you will be acquiring will stand you well, not simply for the duration of your project or dissertation but onwards through your career and working life.

Some theoretical reasons

There is broad and longstanding general agreement on the purposes of a literature review (Box 1.2), irrespective of your discipline (Cooper, 1989; Bruce, 1994, 1997; Hart, 1998; Galvan, 1999).

Box 1.2   Purposes for a literature review

- to place each work in the context of how it contributes to an understanding of the subject under review;
- to describe how each work relates to the others under consideration;
- to identify new ways to interpret, and shed light on gaps in, previous research;
- to identify and resolve conflicts across seemingly contradictory previous studies;
- to identify what has been covered by previous scholars to prevent you needlessly duplicating their effort;
- to signpost the way forward for further research; and
- to locate your original work within the existing literature.

REFLECTION POINT 1.1

Your reasons for conducting a review

Look at Box 1.2 and identify those purposes which are important to you for your literature review

Which of the points listed most accurately capture your reason(s) for conducting a literature review?

As well as the points we have mentioned, you may have a specific reason for reviewing the literature. In addition to 'taking stock' of what has gone before and identifying a niche for your own research, the literature may help you to design your own research. You may wish to advance a theory against which you might explore a specified hypothesis, to select tools, instruments or scales that are useful in conducting your research and identify research gaps which may signal unexplored topics or research questions. Some of these reasons for reviewing the literature are exemplified in the following brief history of research synthesis.

A brief history of research synthesis

It is impossible even to suggest a tentative date for the origins of research synthesis. Very early on in human history there would have been a need to record what had previously occurred, to compare experiences across cases and gradually to build up a knowledge base of what was now known and what remained unknown. Those who chronicle research synthesis prefer to identify specific landmarks and then to join these with a dotted line to reflect ongoing evolution and development of the methods (Macauley, 2001, w128).

Probably the best, and certainly the most cited, history of research synthesis comes from three of the science's foremost proponents, Chalmers, Hedges, and Cooper (2002), in 'A brief history of research synthesis'. Indeed the pervasive influence of research synthesis is attested to by the authorship of the article with Chalmers from clinical medicine, Cooper from psychology and Hedges from social policy. A more extensive treatment of the same topic is available in *Handbook of Research Synthesis and Meta-analysis* (Cooper et al., 2009). As you read this book you should bear in mind that, notwithstanding the fact that research synthesis began in a select number of disciplines, recent years have witnessed its spread to almost every area of academic activity (Moynihan, 2004, w138).

There is nothing particularly novel about the idea of research synthesis. In 1753, James Lind, the Scottish naval surgeon who was instrumental in the first **randomised controlled trial**, recognised the value of systematic methods for identifying, extracting and appraising information from individual studies as a protection against biased interpretation of research (Box 1.3). However at this period of time it was a particular challenge to identify, acquire and interpret the scattered body of published and unpublished research, Subsequently, developments in **information retrieval**, documentation and document delivery have contributed much to the practicality of research synthesis.

Box 1.3   The first systematic review?

On 20 May 1747, James Lind took 12 'similar' patients with scurvy and divided them into six pairs. He carried out different treatments for each pair. Six days later, Lind reported:

> The result of all my experiments was that oranges and lemons were the most effectual remedies for this distemper at sea. (w112)

Six years later, in *A Treatise of the Scurvy in Three Parts. Containing an inquiry into the Nature, Causes and Cure of that Disease, together with a Critical and Chronological View* of what has been published on the subject, Lind acknowledged the need to review existing literature systematically and to discard 'weaker evidence':

> As it is no easy matter to root out prejudices ... it became requisite to exhibit a full and impartial view of what had hitherto been published on the scurvy ...

---

by which the sources of these mistakes may be detected. Indeed, before the subject could be set in a clear and proper light, it was necessary to remove a great deal of rubbish. (w112)

Gathering the published research, getting rid of the rubbish, and summarising the best of what remains is essentially the science of research synthesis.

Other antecedents to modern research synthesis have been traced to seventeenth-century astronomers who found that combining data from related studies introduced greater precision to their individual observations (Petticrew, 2001). However a closer relative to current methods lay in the work of the statistician Karl Pearson. Recognising the limitations of the evidence on inoculations against fever, Pearson identified the need to bring together multiple small studies in order to arrive at a definitive opinion (Pearson, 1904). Three years later, Joseph Goldberger, a scientist in the United States, reviewed 44 studies of typhoid fever and then abstracted and pooled data from 26 of the 44 studies (Chalmers et al., 2002).

Similar work was undertaken within agriculture by Ronald Fisher and colleagues in the 1930s. However it was not until the 1970s that formal procedures for synthesising studies were labelled as **meta-analysis** by Gene Glass (1976) and other social science colleagues. Towards the end of that same decade Iain Chalmers and colleagues at Oxford's National Perinatal Epidemiology Unit compiled an authoritative two-volume compendium of controlled trials in perinatal medicine, *Effective Care in Pregnancy and Childbirth* (Enkin et al., 1989). This internationally recognised initiative laid a platform for significant achievements in collaborative synthesis of research, from which the **Cochrane Collaboration**, and its sibling the **Campbell Collaboration**, were launched.

In 1984 Light and Pillemer published *Summing Up: the Science of Reviewing Research*, a pioneering work in the recent history of research synthesis. 'Our broad goal,' they wrote, 'is to help readers organize existing evidence in a systematic way,

Table 1.1   Milestones in the history of research synthesis

Date	Milestones
1753	James Lind published first 'systematic review'
1904	Pearson published landmark review on effects of vaccines against typhoid
1976	Glass coined term 'meta-analysis'
1984	Light and Pillemer *Summing Up*
1987	Mulrow *The Medical Review Article: State of the Science*
1989	Enkin and colleagues *Effective Care in Pregnancy and Childbirth*
1992	Antman and colleagues illustrated value of cumulation of findings
1993	Launch of *Cochrane Collaboration* (w042)
1994	Establishment of the UK NHS Centre for Reviews and Dissemination
2000	Founding of *Campbell Collaboration*

whether a review is motivated by a scientific problem or the need for a policy decision.' They argued that the new methods of research synthesis applied to many fields, including health, education, and psychology:

> Without a clear picture of where things stand now, simply adding one new study to the existing morass is unlikely to be very useful ... For science to be cumulative, an intermediate step between past and future research is necessary: synthesis of existing evidence. (Light and Pillemer, 1984)

Three years later, Mulrow (1987) published an article entitled 'The medical review article: state of the science'. She delivered a damning indictment of the quality of 50 articles classified as 'review or progress articles' published in four leading medical journals (1985–1986). Only one of the 50 reviews 'had clearly specified methods of identifying, selecting, and validating included information'. In addition she observed that:

- 80 per cent addressed a focused review question;
- 2 per cent described the method of locating evidence;
- 2 per cent used explicit criteria for selecting studies for inclusion;
- 2 per cent assessed the quality of the primary studies;
- 6 per cent performed a quantitative analysis.

She concluded: 'Current ... reviews do not routinely use scientific methods to identify, assess, and synthesize information.' On the contrary, these reviews are often 'subjective, scientifically unsound, and inefficient' (Mulrow, 1987).

Mulrow's proposals for a more systematic approach to reviewing and summarising medical evidence were picked up in 1993 when Oxman and Guyatt assessed 36 published reviews and produced their own critique of their quality. They surveyed the reviews' authors about their levels of expertise, the time they had spent on their reviews, and the strength of their prior opinions. They concluded:

> Our data suggest that experts, on average, write reviews of inferior quality; that the greater the expertise the more likely the quality is to be poor; and that the poor quality may be related to the strength of the prior opinions and the amount of time they spend preparing a review article. (Oxman and Guyatt, 1993)

The rising popularity of **evidence-based health policy** and **evidence-based practice** in the 1990s led to recognition of the importance of research syntheses in other disciplines such as education (Evans and Benefield, 2001). However not everyone welcomed such a trend (Hammersley, 2001). Nevertheless, a similar political push for evidence-based policy and practice started to gain pace in other fields such as social care and management (see, for example, Davies et al., 2000; Nutley et al., 2002; Trinder and Reynolds, 2000). Governments began to fund initiatives committed to supporting research syntheses, particularly systematic reviews (Davies, 2000).

Many other organisations began producing research syntheses during the 1990s. Several funding bodies began requiring systematic reviews of existing research before considering applications for funding for further study. For instance, the UK Medical Research Council now asks a researcher to demonstrate that a systematic review has been undertaken before it will commission a new trial (Clark and Horton, 2010). This ensures that the question has not already been answered, and that the results of previous research are used in designing the new trial.

In 1999, Mulrow's survey was repeated using 158 articles from six major medical journals (McAlister et al., 1999) each with 'review', 'overview', or 'meta-analysis' in the title or abstract or claiming an intention to review or summarise the literature. It found that:

- 34 per cent addressed a focused review question;
- 28 per cent described the method of locating evidence;
- 14 per cent used explicit criteria to select studies for inclusion;
- 9 per cent assessed the quality of the primary studies;
- 21 per cent performed a quantitative analysis.

This snapshot from over a decade ago remains to be updated. However what we have witnessed in the ensuing years is an increasing popularity of derivative versions of the literature review, characterised under the expression in our title as 'systematic approaches'. More than anything this has emphasised that the degree to which any review is systematic lies on a continuum that runs from implicit expert commentary through to **gold standard** systematic review.

What is the place of theory in literature review?

Webster and Watson (2002) defined a successful literature review as one that:

> creates a firm foundation for advancing knowledge. It facilitates theory development [italics added], closes areas where a plethora of research exists, and uncovers areas where research is needed.

In fact the place of theory within literature review is contested, particularly given the fundamentally pragmatic drivers behind the science of systematic review, attested to by the brief history of research synthesis we have already considered. For example much evidence synthesis in the healthcare field is essentially atheoretical – at least in the sense of not acknowledging a specific theoretical contribution. As you move outwards to contiguous disciplines such as public health, health promotion and nursing, theory is more plentiful. This is similarly the case for such disciplines as social care, education, management and even information systems. Nevertheless such generalisations necessarily oversimplify a much more complex panorama.

Qualitative evidence synthesis, particularly using interpretive techniques such as **meta-ethnography** and **critical interpretive synthesis**, may be construed as essentially theory generating and **grounded theory** approaches have also been used within secondary research. Other techniques such as **realist synthesis** provide an opportunity to explore the application of mid-range **programme theory** to a mix of quantitative and qualitative data. Furthermore the specific systematic approach known as **concept analysis** explicitly seeks to define, expand, and extend the theoretical underpinnings of a target concept.

In actuality, the science of literature review offers multiple opportunities to engage and interact with theory (Table 1.2). Where the authors of component studies have themselves engaged with one or more theories, an evidence synthesis offers the opportunity to consolidate current thinking, even in creating a 'meta-model'. Where the source literature is fundamentally atheoretical, a literature review can be used to generate theory *de novo*. Alternatively it provides a rich test data set against which existing theories can be examined and modified. Finally, where the literature review does not possess full explanatory power for differences that exist between apparently similar mechanisms or contexts, an extraneous theory may be introduced alongside the data set in an attempt to investigate forensically such differences.

Table 1.2 Examples of the interplay of literature review and theory

Type of review	Reference	Interplay of literature review and theory
Concept analysis	Teamwork: a concept analysis. (Xyrichis and Ream, 2008)	Used Walker and Avant's approach to guide analysis (1995). Literature searches used bibliographic databases, Internet search engines, and hand searches (1976–2006). Based on analysis, proposed definition for teamwork, and identified essential ingredients for it to take place.
Creation of meta-model	Fostering implementation of health services research findings into practice: a consolidated framework for advancing implementation science (Damschroder et al., 2009, w060)	Used **snowball sampling** approach to identify published theories, evaluated to identify component constructs. Combined constructs across published theories with different labels to remove redundancy or overlap. Created Consolidated Framework for Implementation Research (CFIR) offering overarching typology for implementation theory development.
Meta-ethnography	Using meta-ethnography to synthesise qualitative research: a worked example (Britten et al., 2002)	Four papers about lay meanings of medicines arbitrarily chosen. Used Noblit and Hare's seven-step process for meta-ethnography (1988). Six key concepts identified leading to second-order interpretations (from chosen papers) and construction of four third-order interpretations (based on key concepts/second-order interpretations). Worked example produced middle-range theories as hypotheses to be tested by other researchers.

Type of review	Reference	Interplay of literature review and theory
Meta-narrative review	Storylines of research in diffusion of innovation: a meta-narrative approach to systematic review (Greenhalgh et al., 2005)	Identified 13 key meta-narratives from literatures as disparate as rural sociology, clinical epidemiology, marketing and organisational studies. Researchers in different traditions had conceptualised, explained and investigated diffusion of innovations differently. Reconciled seemingly contradictory data, systematically exposing and exploring tensions between research paradigms.
Review of theories	Healthcare professionals' intentions and behaviours: a systematic review of studies based on social cognitive theories (Godin et al., 2008, w089)	Systematically reviewed literature on factors influencing health professionals' behaviours based on social cognitive theories. Seventy-eight studies met inclusion criteria. Most used theory was Theory of Reasoned Action or its extension Theory of Planned Behaviour.
Review of use of theory	A systematic review of the use of theory in the design of guideline dissemination and implementation strategies and interpretation of the results of rigorous evaluations (Davies et al., 2010, w061)	Systematic review of use of theory in 235 evaluations of guideline dissemination and implementation studies (1966–1998). Classified theory according to type of use (explicitly theory based, some conceptual basis, and theoretical construct used) and stage of use (choice/design of intervention, process/mediators/moderators, and post hoc/explanation).
Realist review (as complement to effectiveness review)	Realist review to understand the efficacy of school feeding programmes (Greenhalgh et al., 2007, w098)	Effectiveness reviews rarely give detailed information on context, mechanisms, and outcomes of interventions and theories that underpin them. Described theory and processes in 18 trials of school feeding programmes.
Scoping review	Disseminating research findings: what should researchers do? A systematic scoping review of conceptual frameworks (Wilson et al., 2010, w204)	Searched 12 electronic databases to identify/describe conceptual/organising frameworks for use in guiding dissemination activity. Narrative synthesis undertaken. Thirty-three frameworks met inclusion criteria underpinned by three theoretical approaches (persuasive communication, diffusion of innovations theory and social marketing).
As precursor to grounded theory conceptual work	The place of the literature review in grounded theory research (Dunne, 2011).	Increasing recognition of the role literature review can play in grounded theory methodology

Summary

Like all science, research synthesis is evolving and uncertain. For example, the application of statistical methods for pooling and synthesising the quantitative results of different studies – meta-analysis – is steadily improving, though considerable challenges remain (Egger et al., 2002). While much early development was undertaken within the context of systematic reviews of evidence about healthcare interventions – drugs, therapies, technologies – the principles of research synthesis remain the same whatever the subject matter under review.

APPLY WHAT YOU HAVE LEARNT 1.1

How systematic is this review?

As already mentioned, disciplines differ in the extent to which they have adopted systematic approaches to research synthesis. We would like you to identify a review article from within your own subject area or discipline. (You may wish to use an approach similar to that employed by McAllister et al., (1999) namely search for the words 'review', 'overview', or 'meta-analysis' in the title or abstract.) We want you to make a preliminary assessment of the extent to which your chosen review demonstrates systematic features or principles. To do this we suggest that you construct a grid as in the following example and complete it with your own observations.

1 Features that make this review appear SYSTEMATIC	2 Features that make this review appear NON-SYSTEMATIC

Your observations will provide a backdrop for the discussion of the importance of systematic approaches to reviewing the literature in Chapter 2.

Key learning points

- All literature reviews should be systematic. They will mainly differ in the degree to which they are systematic and how explicitly their methods are reported.
- Research synthesis has a long pedigree and recent years have seen it spread across multiple fields and disciplines.
- Surveys of research syntheses consistently reveal poor reporting of review methods.
- Evidence-based policy and practice has provided a major stimulus to the science of research synthesis.

Suggestions for further reading

Lomas, J. (2007) Decision support: a new approach to making the best healthcare management and policy choices. *Healthcare Quarterly*, **10**, 3, 14–16.

Randolph, J. (2009) A guide to writing the dissertation literature review. *Practical Assessment, Research and Evaluation*, **14**, 13. (w160)

Steward, B. (2004) Writing a literature review. *British Journal of Occupational Therapy*, **67**, 11, 495–500.

Volmink, J., Siegfried, N., Robertson, K., and Gülmezoglu, A. (2004) Research synthesis and dissemination as a bridge to knowledge management: the Cochrane Collaboration. *Bulletin of the World Health Organisation*, **82**, 10, 778–83. (w199)

References

Antman, E.M., Lau, J., Kupelnick, B., Mosteller, F., and Chalmers, T.C. (1992) A comparison of results of meta-analyses of randomized control trials and recommendations of clinical experts. Treatments for myocardial infarction. *JAMA*, **268**, 2, 240–8.

Bem, D.J. (1995) Writing a review article for Psychological Bulletin. *Psychological Bulletin*, **118**, 2, 172–7.

Britten, N., Campbell, R., Pope, C., Donovan, J., Morgan, M., and Pill, R. (2002) Using meta ethnography to synthesise qualitative research: a worked example. *Journal of Health Services Research and Policy*, **7**, 4, 209–15.

Bruce, C.S. (1994) Research students' early experiences of the dissertation literature review. *Studies in Higher Education*, **19**, 2, 217–29.

Bruce, C.S. (1997) From Neophyte to expert: counting on reflection to facilitate complex conceptions of the literature review, In: Zuber-Skerritt, O. (ed.), *Frameworks for Postgraduate Education*. Lismore, NSW: Southern Cross University.

Chalmers, I., Hedges, L.V., and Cooper, H. (2002) A brief history of research synthesis. *Evaluation and the Health Professions*, **25**, 1, 12–37.

Clark, S. and Horton, R. (2010) Putting research into context – revisited. *The Lancet*, **376**, 9734, 10–11.

Clarke, M. and Chalmers, I. (1998) Discussion sections in reports of controlled trials published in general medical journals. Islands in search of continents? *JAMA*, **280**, 280–2.

Cooper, H.M. (1989) *Integrating Research: A Guide for Literature Reviews*, 2nd edn. Newbury Park, CA: Sage Publications.

Cooper, H.M., Hedges, L., and Valentine, J. (eds) (2009) *The Handbook of Research Synthesis and Meta-Analysis*, 2nd edn. New York: The Russell Sage Foundation.

Damschroder, L.J., Aron, D.C., Keith, R.E., Kirsh, S.R., Alexander, J.A., and Lowery, J.C. (2009) Fostering implementation of health services research findings into practice: a consolidated framework for advancing implementation science. *Implementation Science*, **4**, 50. (w060)

Davies, H.T.O., Nutley, S.M., and Smith, P.C. (eds) (2000) *What Works? Evidence-Based Policy and Practice in Public Services*. Bristol: Policy Press.

Davies, P. (2000) The relevance of systematic reviews to educational policy and practice. *Oxford Review of Education*, **26**, 3–4, 365–78.

Davies, P., Walker, A.E., and Grimshaw, J.M. (2010) A systematic review of the use of theory in the design of guideline dissemination and implementation strategies and interpretation of the results of rigorous evaluations. *Implementation Science*, **5**, 14. (w061)

Dunne, C. (2011) The place of the literature review in grounded theory research. *International Journal of Social Research Methodology*, **14**, 2, 111–24.

Egger, M., Ebrahim, S., and Smith, G.D. (2002) Where now for meta-analysis? *International Journal of Epidemiology*, **31**, 1, 1–5.

Enkin, M., Keirse, M.J., Renfrew, M., and Neilson, J. (1989) *Effective Care in Pregnancy and Childbirth*. Oxford: Oxford University Press.

Evans, J. and Benefield, P. (2001) Systematic reviews of educational research: does the medical model fit? *British Educational Research Journal*, **27**, 527–41.

Fink, A. (2005) *Conducting Research Literature Reviews: From the Internet to Paper*, 2nd edn. London: Sage Publications.

Galvan, J.L. (1999) *Writing Literature Reviews*. Los Angeles: Pyrczak Publishing.

Glass, G.V. (1976). Primary, secondary and meta-analysis of research. *Educational Researcher*, **10**, 3–8.

Godin, G., Bélanger-Gravel, A., Eccles, M., and Grimshaw, J. (2008) Healthcare professionals' intentions and behaviours: a systematic review of studies based on social cognitive theories. *Implementation Science*, **3**, 36. (w089)

Greenhalgh, T., Kristjansson, E., and Robinson, V. (2007) Realist review to understand the efficacy of school feeding programmes. *BMJ*, **335**, 7625, 858–61. (w098)

Greenhalgh, T., Robert, G., Macfarlane, F., Bate, P., Kyriakidou, O., and Peacock, R. (2005) Storylines of research in diffusion of innovation: a meta-narrative approach to systematic review. *Social Science and Medicine*, **61**, 2, 417–30.

Hammersley, M. (2001) On 'systematic' reviews of research literatures: a 'narrative' response to Evans and Benefield. *British Educational Research Journal*, **27**, 5, 543–54.

Hart, C. (1998) *Doing a Literature Review: Releasing the Social Science Research imagination*. Thousand Oaks, CA: Sage

Lavis, J.N., Davies, H.T.O., Oxman, A.D., Denis, J-L., Golden-Biddle, K., and Ferlie, E. (2005) Towards systematic reviews that inform health care management and policy-making. *Journal of Health Services Research and Policy*, **10**, Suppl 1, S35–48.

LeCompte, M.D., Klinger, J.K., Campbell S.A., and Menke, D.W. (2003) Editor's introduction. *Review of Educational Research*, **73**, 2, 123–4.

Light, R. and Pillemer, D. (1984) *Summing Up: The Science of Reviewing Research*. Cambridge, MA: Harvard University Press.

Major, C.H. and Savin-Baden, M. (2010) *An Introduction to Qualitative Research Synthesis: Managing the Information Explosion in Social Science Research*. London: Routledge.

Mays, N., Pope C., and Popay, J. (2005) Systematically reviewing qualitative and quantitative evidence to inform management and policy-making in the health field. *Journal of Health Services Research and Policy*, **10**, Suppl. 1, 6–20.

McAlister, F.A., Clark, H.D., van Walraven, C., Straus, S.E., Lawson, F.M., Moher, D., and Mulrow, C.D. (1999) The medical review article revisited: has the science improved? *Annals of Internal Medicine*, **131**, 947–51.

Moynihan, R. (2004) *Evaluating Health Services: A Reporter Covers the Science of Research Synthesis*. New York: Milbank Memorial Fund.

Mulrow, C. (1987) The medical review article: state of the science. *Annals of Internal Medicine*, **106**, 485–8.

Mulrow, C.D. (1995) Rationale for systematic reviews. In: Chalmers, I. and Altman, D. (eds) *Systematic Reviews*. London: BMJ Publishing Group.

Noblit, G.W., and Hare, R.D. (1988) *Meta-ethnography: Synthesizing Qualitative Studies*. Newbury Park, CA: Sage.

Nutley, S., Davies, H., and Walter, I. (2002) ESRC UK Centre for Evidence Based Policy and Practice: Working Paper 9. Evidence Based Policy and Practice: Cross Sector Lessons from the UK. Research Unit for Research Utilisation. Department of Management, University of St Andrews. August 2002: ESRC UK Centre for Evidence Based Policy and Practice; Research Unit for Research Utilisation.

Oxman, A.D. and Guyatt, G.H. (1993) The science of reviewing research. *Annals of the New York Academy of Science*, **703**, 125–33.

Pearson, K. (1904) Report on certain enteric fever inoculation statistics. *BMJ*, iii, 1243–6.

Petticrew, M. (2001) Systematic reviews from astronomy to zoology: myths and misconceptions. *BMJ*, **322**, 98–101.

Pope, C., Mays, N. and Popay, J. (2007) *Synthesizing Qualitative and Quantitative Health Evidence: a Guide to Methods*. Maidenhead: Open University Press, 13–15.

Randolph, J. (2009) A guide to writing the dissertation literature review. *Practical Assessment, Research and Evaluation*, **14**, 13. (w160)

Sweet, M. and Moynihan, R. (2007) Improving population health: the uses of systematic reviews. New York: Milbank Memorial Fund. (w187)

Trinder, L. and Reynolds, S. (eds) (2000) *Evidence-based Practice: A Critical Appraisal*. Oxford: Blackwell Science.

Walker, L.O. and Avant, K.C. (2005) *Strategies for Theory Construction in Nursing*, 4th edn. Upper Saddle River, NJ: Pearson Prentice Hall.

Webster, J. and Watson, R.T. (2002) Analyzing the past to prepare for the future: Writing a literature review. *MIS Quarterly*, **26**, 2, 13–23.

Wilson, P.M., Petticrew, M., Calnan, M.W., and Nazareth, I. (2010) Disseminating research findings: what should researchers do? A systematic scoping review of conceptual frameworks. *Implementation Science*, **5**, 91. (w204)

Xyrichis, A. and Ream, E. (2008) Teamwork: a concept analysis. *Journal of Advanced Nursing*, **61**, 2, 232–41.

TWO

Systematic approaches to the literature

Learning Objectives

After reading this chapter, you should be able to:

- Describe what is commonly meant by 'systematic'.
- Examine published reviews with a view to identifying their potential for bias.
- Distinguish between a traditional review and a systematic review.
- Describe the four components that help to characterise the exact nature of the main types of review.

Introduction

As discussed in Chapter 1 there is increasing recognition that all reviews should be 'systematic'. This is no surprise given that all research, whether primary or secondary, requires some type of 'system' whether in its conduct, analysis and/or the presentation. As Hammersley (2002, w102) states:

> Who would want reviews to be unsystematic, if by 'systematic' we mean no more than 'properly carried out, taking account of all the relevant evidence, and making reliable judgements about its validity and implications'? On this definition, to produce a systematic review is simply to do the job of reviewing well.

However, reviewers have not always recognised this important fact. Consider the following hypothetical recipe for a traditional literature review:

> Take a simmering topic, extract the juice of an argument, add the essence of one filing cabinet, sprinkle liberally with your own publications and sift out the work of noted detractors or adversaries.

Clearly such methods are open to accusations of significant bias, of systematic error (Hammersley, 2002, w102). Such bias may exist at the identification,

Table 2.1 Words associated with being 'systematic'

Systematic	Either	Unsystematic
Explicit	Creative	Implicit
Transparent	Comprehensive	Opaque
Methodical	Imaginative	Whimsical
Objective	Publishable	Subjective
Standardised	Stimulating	Variable
Structured	Topical	Chaotic
Reproducible	Well-written	Idiosyncratic

selection, synthesis and analysis stages of the review process. As Mulrow and colleagues (1997) highlight:

> Preparation of reviews has traditionally depended on implicit, idiosyncratic methods of data collection and interpretation.

This point is similarly recognised by Greenhalgh (2010) for what she labels the 'journalistic review':

> Remember the essays you used to write when you first started college? You would mooch round the library, browsing through the indexes of books and journals. When you came across a paragraph that looked relevant, you copied it out and if anything you found did not fit in with the theory you were proposing, you left it out. This, more or less, constitutes the *journalistic* review – an overview of primary studies which have not been identified or analysed in a systematic (standardised and objective) way.

A quick scan of these commentaries starts us building a continuum relating to how systematic a review might be. At one end we place words such as 'implicit' and 'idiosyncratic' while at the other we locate terms such as 'standardised' and 'objective' (Table 2.1). Increasingly however we should recognise that the negative connotations held by the word 'standardised', in the sense of stifling creativity and individual initiative, may be countered by engaging with an increasingly diverse toolkit of review techniques and methods.

REFLECTION POINT 2.1

What makes a review systematic?

This chapter has already used the term 'systematic review' on several occasions. No doubt you have encountered this term in your reading. Briefly reflect on what the term 'systematic' means to you, both in the context of literature reviews and more generally. Do you perceive this generally as a positive or a negative word?

The traditional narrative review, the systematic review and 'systematic approaches'

Frequently the **narrative review**, much maligned by such commentators as Greenhalgh (2010), Mulrow and others (1997), is referred to as a 'traditional review', 'conventional review', or, even more damning, as a 'non-systematic review'. At this point we should distinguish between reviews that do not claim to be systematic and, indeed, claim a virtue of allying themselves to the traditional model of review, and those that are simply unable to convince us that they are systematic through inadequate or incomplete reporting of methods. Indeed Mulrow (1994) observes how the absence of a clear and objective method section leads to several methodological flaws, which can bias the author's conclusions. These twin aspects of **quality of conduct** and **quality of reporting** (Shea et al., 2002) resurface throughout this book.

The availability of time, personnel and money may further constrain the quality of the final review product (see Chapter 3). A reviewer may be aware of what steps they need to take to improve the robustness of their review. However such measures may not be achievable within the resource constraints. In such a case a reviewer must select a model of review that is most appropriate to the purpose required. The reviewer should also be explicit about any limitations inherent to the chosen approach. For example, a **scoping review** that is required to provide a snapshot of a particular topic area prior to specifying a more specific systematic review question (Arksey and O'Malley, 2005) will not usually attempt **quality assessment**. Typically, therefore, such a review should report this limitation. In such a situation, the reviewer applies, in effect, **vote-counting** by acknowledging and documenting that each item of literature exists without making a judgement about whether it is of adequate quality.

In contrast, systematic reviews (or overviews) are:

> syntheses of primary research studies that use (and describe) specific, explicit and therefore reproducible methodological strategies to identify, assemble, critical appraise and synthesise all relevant issues on a specific topic. (Carney and Geddes, 2002)

When conducted well systematic reviews have been found to improve the reliability and accuracy of conclusions, clearly allying them to the scientific method:

> A research synthesis is ... the critical first step in effective use of scientific evidence. Synthesis is *not* a conventional literature review. Literature reviews are often position papers, cherry-picking studies to advocate a point of view. Instead, syntheses systematically identify where research findings are clear (and where they aren't), a key first step to establishing the conclusions science supports. Syntheses are also important for identifying contested findings and productive lines for future research (Rousseau et al., 2008, w164).

The results of systematic reviews are rarely unequivocal and require careful reading and interpretation (Hopayian, 2001). Furthermore an 'overview' may achieve a birds-eye view of a topic area at the expense of the loss of reassuring detail about context and implementation. Such loss of detail makes it much more challenging to make a decision about a particular instance or case. One further difference between narrative reviews and systematic reviews is that the former are designed to be a 'snapshot' of the available research at a particular point in time (i.e. **prevalent knowledge**) whereas many systematic reviews explicitly aim to monitor and capture new research evidence as it emerges continuously. Many systematic reviews incorporate approaches to accommodate **incident** (i.e. new) **knowledge** as it appears. They are therefore intended to be updated periodically to take into account the emergence of new evidence.

In his taxonomy of literature reviews, Cooper (1988a, 1988b) identifies four possible approaches:

1 exhaustive coverage, citing all relevant literature;
2 exhaustive coverage with selective citation;
3 representative coverage (discussion of works which typify particular groupings in the literature); and
4 coverage of pivotal works.

It is noticeable that all four models could be construed as 'systematic' in the broad sense of the word. Only the first two possess the characteristics of **exhaustivity** so often associated with the 'systematic review'. We should caution that selective citation, as embodied in the second model, is understandably regarded as a potential source of bias (Song et al., 2010, w123).

Clarification of terminology

Up to this point we have avoided a discussion of terminology preferring to use the umbrella concept of 'research synthesis' unless specifically referring to a particular type of review. One justification for this approach is that classification of review types is multidimensional depending upon such variables as the purpose of the review (e.g. the **mapping review**), the types of included study (e.g. systematic review of randomised controlled trials), the nature of included data (e.g. the qualitative systematic review), the type of question being addressed (e.g. the effectiveness review), the phenomenon being investigated (e.g. **meta-theory** or **meta-method**), and the underlying intent (e.g. **meta-ethnography** for theory generation or **realist synthesis** for theory verification). Other characteristics relate to the context of the review (e.g. the rapid evidence assessment) or to the underpinning 'philosophy' regarding subsequent use of the review (e.g. best evidence synthesis). This book will attempt to identify defining characteristics of each of these types of review wherever possible. However, as acknowledged elsewhere:

> Only a handful of review types possess prescribed and explicit methodologies and many of the labels used fall short of being mutually exclusive. In lieu of internationally recognized review definitions, [we acknowledge] that there is a lack of unique distinguishing features for the most common review types, whilst highlighting that some common features do exist. (Grant and Booth, 2009, w095)

We must also acknowledge that methodologists may benefit from a perverse incentive whereby invention of a new form of review that differs ever so slightly from its predecessors may result in a rich vein of citations. In the chapters that follow we focus on the techniques and ingredients of the review process in the hope that this will stimulate cross-fertilisation of techniques and act as a counter balance to methodological 'pigeon-holing'.

Towards a taxonomy

Many authors have attempted to produce a taxonomy of literature review types (Strike and Posner, 1983; Cooper, 1988a, 1988b; Grant and Booth, 2009, w095). Such a task is challenging because a review may be characterised across multiple domains. For example Cooper (1988b) categorises reviews according to (a) focus; (b) goal; (c) perspective; (d) coverage; (e) organisation; and (f) audience. Such an approach not only reveals the complexity of the review as both process and product but also provides a challenge in distinguishing, for example, focus and perspective.

Approaches to the synthesis of any body of literature can be broadly characterised as either **aggregative** or **interpretive** (Weed, 2005, w201). In the former the value of bringing together studies on a similar topic is that each additional study adds 'weight' to a shared finding. While this may appear like crude **vote counting** (Cabinet Office, 2003, w028) such approaches typically move beyond 'one paper, one vote' by assigning extra weight to size, quality, or both. Of course in order to bring studies together in this way one must make some assumptions about how similar studies are (**homogeneity**). In practice all studies are different (e.g. in the population studied, in how a procedure is implemented, in how an outcome is measured, etc.). The reviewer, and indeed the reader, has to make a judgement as to whether studies are more alike than different.

The implication of such aggregative approaches is that there may come a point at which sufficient studies have been identified to establish a finding beyond statistical doubt. Indeed some meta-analyses have demonstrated such a point in time, suggesting that subsequent studies possess a certain degree of 'redundancy' (Antman et al., 1992). Nevertheless, in theory at least, additional studies hold the potential to overturn a previous finding. Aggregative reviews therefore represent an ongoing attempt to identify studies that have previously been missed, particularly if their absence might reveal a previously neglected systematic bias.

In contrast, interpretive reviews seek to broaden our understanding of a particular intervention or phenomenon. Each study holds the potential to add one or more additional insights and to contribute to the overall picture. Of course such potential may be more limited in fields where a broad consensus exists and authors report the same type of insights. This is analogous to **theoretical saturation** within primary research (Dixon-Woods et al., 2005). In theory, such an occurrence should be less frequent than in primary research as, unlike interviewees, authors are not independent informants (Dixon-Woods et al., 2006). Indeed

Table 2.2   Interpretive or aggregative?

You will find it helpful to consider whether the overall intent of your intended review is interpretive or aggregative

Interpretive	Aggregative
Is my question going to develop and change as new insights emerge from the literature?	Is my question fixed and focused, allowing me to decide authoritatively whether studies are relevant or not?
If new papers fail to contribute new insights will I purposively move on to very different types of sources?	Will I keep searching until I am confident that I have exhausted all likely sources?
Is the main value of each new study in adding a different insight to what I am investigating?	Is the main value of each new study in adding weight to, or confirming, what has previously been found?
Is my principal focus on the 'exception to the rule'?	Is my principal focus on the mean or 'average' overall result?
Will my data be presented primarily as themes or models with accompanying commentary?	Will my data be presented primarily as tables and graphs with accompanying commentary?

authors purposively seek recognition for innovative insights. When faced with such circumstances a reviewer will make particularly strenuous attempts to sample from other fields or types of literature. Whereas aggregative reviews implicitly value the average result which adds strength to the overall result from multiple similar studies, interpretive reviews place particular value on identifying the **disconfirming case**. Interpretive reviews often make an explicit attempt to contribute to theory, either in theory generation or in validating existing theory (Walshe and Downe, 2005).

Occasionally 'integrative review' is used synonymously with the interpretive review. While this terminology remained appropriate for as long as quantitative and qualitative reviews were kept separate, integration of quantitative and qualitative data is increasingly a feature of what is now termed the **mixed-methods review**. In this text, we reserve the term 'integrative review' for only those cases where both types of data are brought together (Whittemore and Knafl, 2005), typically to produce a whole that is greater than the sum of its parts (Strike and Posner, 1983).

Why be systematic?

While many arguments can be advanced for the desirability of systematic approaches to reviewing the literature, we have identified at least three principal considerations, namely clarity, validity, and auditability.

Many systematic approaches are designed to improve the *clarity* of scholarly communication. An overarching structure makes it easier to navigate and interpret a review's contents. Clear methodology makes it easier to judge what the reviewers have and have not done. A focused question and explicit search strategies help to clarify considerations of scope and terminology. Stated inclusion and exclusion criteria allow readers to recognise why particular articles known to them have not been included. Data extraction offers access to the contents of included papers and tabulation makes it easier to locate the main characteristics and variables. Graphical, textual and tabular features combine with the intent to reveal rather than to conceal.

A second consideration appeals to the scientific requirement for internal *validity*. The review product needs to be defensible against the potential for bias. Several forms of systematic bias need to be considered in reviews (see Chapter 8). Among the most important is **selection bias**, that is a systematic bias in the primary research studies selected for inclusion in the review, as with a reviewer who only selects those studies that support his/her prior beliefs. However biases that impact upon the final set of included studies may also include **publication bias** (the tendency of investigators, reviewers and editors to differentially submit or accept manuscripts for publication based on the direction or strength of the study findings) (Gilbody and Song, 2000). Furthermore **language of publication bias** (studies finding an effect are more likely to be published in English, the international language of science, whilst a neutral or negative study may be published in lower impact journals in the language of the author) (Egger and Smith, 1998). Such biases may be almost imperceptibly introduced, for example, by an over-reliance on electronic databases (where a searcher may not know how or why particular journals have been selected for inclusion and, as a consequence, relevant primary literature may end up being overlooked). As a consequence, systematic approaches require that items are selected for inclusion on the basis of how relevant they are and how rigorous they are, not on whether they have a favourable outcome or whether their results are intrinsically 'interesting'. As a counter measure two reviewers may be involved in such stages as the selection of studies, the extraction of data and the assessment of study quality.

Finally an increasing emphasis on transparency and research governance has led to concerns with *auditability* – how do we know that the reviewer's conclusions are grounded in the data retrieved from the review process and not an argument fabricated to support a prior conclusion?

> Systematic research syntheses are important, too, as quality control. Peer-review serves more as a check on a primary study's published report. The original data themselves seldom are subject to scrutiny. (Rousseau et al., 2008, w164).

While many such considerations coincide with concerns of clarity and validity we can detect the presence of this specific imperative in such features as flowcharts of numbers of included studies, accompanying documents, and appendices relating to search strategies and sample data extraction forms, and the reassuring detail of Date Searched. Furthermore the twin concerns of clarity and auditability are addressed by an increasing number of reporting standards specifying how systematic reviews, along with other types of research outputs, are to be presented in peer-reviewed journals (see EQUATOR Network, w078).

A noticeable omission from such considerations is comprehensiveness or **exhaustivity**. While the early days of the systematic review process did stress the desirability of retrieving *all* studies on a clearly defined topic, this requirement has received decreasing emphasis over more recent years. There are two main reasons for such a change. First, there has been increasing recognition that even the most exhaustive (and exhausting!) of searches cannot hope to identify the entire universe of studies on the most specific of topics. Second, there is now greater acknowledgement that appropriateness or 'fitness for purpose' is now a more realistic aspiration for a review. This is particularly the case given a wider range of review types and increasing time and resource constraints with which to trade off rigour versus relevance (Bennett et al., 2005).

APPLY WHAT YOU HAVE LEARNT 2.1

Identify a systematic review

Identify a systematic review in an area of interest to you and also identify a conventional review in a similar or related topic. Place the two reviews side by side and briefly make a list of the differences between the two reviews.

Conventional or traditional review	Systematic Review

EXERCISE 2.1

Compare and contrast two reviews

Hopefully you have been able to complete the Apply what you have learnt (2.1) exercise on your own. However we have added a few comparisons and contrasts from two relevant studies (Turner and Muller, 2005, w137; Pirzadeh, 2010, w154) should you wish to verify your own observations.

Conventional or traditional review	Systematic Review

Introducing the SALSA framework

As Rousseau and colleagues (2008, w164) state:

> Systematic means comprehensive accumulation, transparent analysis, and reflective interpretation of all empirical studies pertinent to a specific question. Reliance upon any sampling or subset of the literature risks misrepresenting its diversity in findings, outcomes methods, and frames of reference. (w164)

It may be helpful to characterise review types according to the attention given to each of four critical steps in the review process, namely the Search, the Appraisal, the Synthesis and the Analysis (Grant and Booth, 2009, w095). These can be conceived pictorially as a 'graphic equaliser' whereby both the strength and quality of each step contributes to the overall 'signal' emitted by the review. A tentative foray into a new area, through perhaps a 'scoping review', is characterised by a broad-brush approach to finding the most notable studies in the field, minimal attempts at evaluating them for quality, a very rudimentary attempt at synthesis (perhaps through listing, tabulation or mapping) and an overview type of analysis profiling the quantity and distribution of the literature. In contrast a **gold standard** systematic review, such as those endorsed by the **Cochrane Collaboration** (w042), will prescribe a comprehensive search of the literature, checklist-driven quality assessment, complex synthesis using textual, numerical, graphical and tabular methods and sophisticated analysis (for example for differences between subgroups, the differential effects of study groups, and the likelihood of missing studies). Between these two extremes lie numerous variants with different levels of input at the four key stages (see Table 2.3).

Furthermore we embody these four stages within the mnemonic, **SALSA** (Search, AppraisaL, Synthesis and Analysis) (Grant and Booth, 2009, w095). This approach is anticipated by other authors: for example, Bruce (2001) refers to the important stages of analysis and synthesis:

> Reviewing the literature is a well-established academic tradition which is handed down, in many disciplines, to new generations of researchers through the experience of postgraduate scholarship. Completing a literature review is usually a significant intellectual achievement in its own right, requiring the *analysis and synthesis* of previous work in such a manner that new understandings of that work are uncovered, and the way is opened for new scholarship or research.

More recently Major and Savin-Baden (2010) highlight the importance of synthesis, analysis and interpretation. We see the last of these as encompassing the more imaginative and explorative aspects of the wide-ranging methods and tools that we include under analysis.

Systematic approaches

When we consider research to be 'systematic', we think of two principal aspects, that is methods and presentation (Box 2.1). The methods for a review comprise

Table 2.3 Types of review[1]

Type of Review	Description	Search	Appraisal	Synthesis	Analysis
Critical review	Aims to demonstrate extensive research and critical evaluation of quality. Goes beyond Mere description To include degree of analysis and conceptual innovation. Typically results in hypothesis or model	Seeks to identify most significant Items in Field	No. Evaluates by contribution	Narrative, Conceptual Chronological	Significant component: seeks to identify Conceptual contribution to embody Existing or Derive new theory
Integrative review	Utilises broadest type of research review methods allowing for inclusion of both experimental and non-experimental research in order to understand more fully a phenomenon of concern. Integrative reviews may combine data from theoretical as well as empirical literature.	Comprehensive search to identify maximum number of eligible primary sources, using two or more strategies. Purposive sampling may be combined with comprehensive search if appropriate	Reports coded according to quality but not necessarily excluded.	Tabular (matrices, graphs, charts, or networks) usually according to a framework	Creativity, critical analysis of data and data displays key to comparison and identification of important patterns and themes.
Literature review	Provides examination of recent or current literature. Can cover wide range of subjects at various levels of completeness and comprehensiveness. May include research findings	Possibly comprehensive	Possibly	Narrative	Chronological, conceptual, thematic, etc.
Mapping review/ systematic map	Maps out and categorises existing literature from which to commission further reviews and/or primary research by identifying gaps in research literature	As Time Allows	No	Graphical Tabular	Characterises quantity and quality of literature, perhaps by study design and other key features. May identify need for primary/secondary research
Meta-analysis	Statistically combines results of quantitative studies to provide precise effect of results	Exhaustive and comprehensive. May use funnel plot to assess completeness	May determine inclusion/exclusion and/or sensitivity analyses	Graphical Tabular Narrative	Numerical analysis
Mixed studies review/ mixed methods review	Combines methods that include review component (usually systematic). Specifically combination of review approaches e.g. quantitative with qualitative research or outcome with process studies	Sensitive search or separate quantitative and qualitative strategies	Generic appraisal instrument or separate appraisal processes with corresponding checklists	Narrative Tabular Graphical (to integrate quantitative and qualitative studies)	May look for correlations between characteristics or use gap analysis to identify aspects absent in one literature but missing in other

Table 2.3 (Continued)

Type of Review	Description	Search	Appraisal	Synthesis	Analysis
Overview	Attempts to survey literature and describe its characteristics	Depends on how systematic their methods are	Depends on how systematic their methods are	Depends on how systematic their methods are. Narrative Tabular	Chronological, conceptual, thematic, etc
Qualitative systematic review/ qualitative evidence synthesis	Integrates or compares findings from qualitative studies. Looks for 'themes' or 'constructs' in or across individual studies	Selective or Purposive	Typically to mediate messages not for inclusion/ exclusion	Qualitative, narrative synthesis	Thematic may include conceptual models
Rapid review	Assesses what Is already known about policy or practice issue, uses systematic review methods to search and critically appraise existing research	As Time Allows	As Time Allows	Narrative Tabular	Quantities of literature and overall quality/direction of effect of literature.
Scoping review	Preliminary assessment of potential sise and scope of available research literature. Aims to identify nature and extent of research evidence (usually including ongoing research)	As Time Allows. May include research in progress	No	Narrative Tabular	Quantity and quality of literature, perhaps by study design and other features. Attempt to specify viable review
State-of-the-art review	Addresses current matters. May offer new perspectives on issue or point out area for further research	Comprehensive (Current literature)	No	Narrative Tabular	Current state of knowledge, priorities for future investigation; research limitations
Systematic search and review	Combines strengths of critical review with comprehensive search process. Addresses broad questions to produce 'best evidence synthesis'	Exhaustive and comprehensive	Possibly	Narrative Tabular	What is known; recommendations for practice.

[1]Adapted from Grant and Booth, 2009

the *conduct* of the four steps of search, appraisal, synthesis and analysis while its presentation involves the *reporting* of these steps. As a review report typically describes both conduct and reporting it is, in truth, very difficult to separate these two aspects. So a reader attempting to critically appraise a review (or indeed an original research study) finds it difficult to establish whether a particular feature has actually been omitted or whether it has simply not been reported.

Box 2.1 What do we mean by 'systematic approaches'?

By 'systematic approaches' we refer to those elements of a literature review that, either individually or collectively, contribute to its methods being both explicit and reproducible. Systematic approaches are evidenced in both the conduct and presentation of the literature review and are epitomised in the formal method of 'systematic review'. Specifically such approaches include:

- systematic approaches to searching of the literature, as seen in the **scoping review** and the **mapping review**;
- systematic approaches to quality assessment (appraisal) of the literature, as seen in an **integrative review**;
- systematic approaches to synthesis of the literature, as seen in such techniques as **meta-ethnography**, **realist synthesis** and **thematic synthesis;**
- systematic approaches to analysis of the robustness and validity of review findings such as **subgroup analysis**, either qualitative or quantitative, or **sensitivity analysis**.

This section takes each of the four stages or steps of the review in turn and describes briefly how we might establish whether each stage has been conducted well.

Systematic approaches to searching

In conducting systematic searches we seek to cover a broad range of sources to be searched and to be thorough in searching each source. In practice, it is difficult for readers of reviews, other than professional information specialists or librarians, to identify whether obvious sources have been omitted either unintentionally or because of difficulties in access. However it can be useful to compare a list of sources used for one review with a corresponding list for a related topic. As you start to plan your own review you will find it helpful to compile an optimal list of sources to be searched from corresponding lists in similar reviews.

A further indicator of search quality is a list of included search terms, together with the search syntax used to combine these terms (e.g. AND, OR, etc.). A subject expert will be able to identify missing terms or variants that might have been expected to be included. An information specialist will be able to judge whether the syntax has been used appropriately or whether there is an unwitting hole in the search logic. At the very least, readers should be able to check for themselves whether the search strategy has included both subject terms (i.e. those used by the indexers of the database) and free text terms (i.e. those used by the authors and by practitioners in the topic area) (see Chapter 5).

Systematic approaches to appraisal

Systematic approaches to quality appraisal typically use an explicit tool or instrument in order to assess quality consistently across multiple studies. This tool may be a formal checklist or scale, perhaps one that has been independently validated. Equally a series of prompts may be used to ensure that each included study has been treated equally (Dixon-Woods et al., 2004). It should be clear whether the quality assessment is being used to exclude poor-quality studies or whether quality is simply used to discriminate between higher-quality studies (those with less likelihood of bias) and those of lower quality. If multiple assessors have been employed, it will also be helpful to indicate how consistently they have applied the quality assessment criteria. *A word of caution:* some assessment processes use numerical scales with scoring systems to achieve a spurious precision. Such tools go beyond the minimum requirement to sort studies into broad bands of quality. They either assign the same weight to every criterion regardless of its importance or arbitrarily allocate different, yet ultimately meaningless, weights to different study features (see Chapter 6).

Systematic approaches to synthesis

With many alternatives for synthesis, qualitative, quantitative and mixed methods, it is difficult to judge whether a synthesis is systematic simply on the basis of how well it fulfils technical performance criteria. Some basic rules of thumb will be useful, e.g. use of a fixed effects meta-analysis where there is sufficient homogeneity or of a random effects meta-analysis where studies are demonstrably different (Hedges and Vevea, 1998) or use of framework approaches to qualitative synthesis where concepts are secure and more grounded theory-type approaches where they are still evolving (Dixon-Woods et al., 2005). However, it is difficult to get beyond initial judgements of appropriateness. It is much more important to be able to follow an audit trail through from the original individual studies to the reviewer's interpretation of the synthetic findings. You should also recognise that 'averaging' processes such as meta-analysis, together with the natural human tendency to identify similarities more readily than differences, may lead the reviewer to generalise or oversimplify (Petticrew and Roberts, 2006). A systematic and explicit approach to synthesis should allow the reader to identify the disconfirming case, the exception to the rule (Noyes et al., 2008, w030). If this is not possible, it either suggests that the review has arrived at some artificially contrived homogeneity (i.e. it lacks in natural variation), or that the synthesis is lacking in sensitivity (see Chapter 7).

Systematic approaches to analysis

While you as a reader cannot immerse yourself in the volume of data produced for a large-scale literature review to the same extent possible for the reviewer, you should still be able to identify the main lines of questioning that underpin the analysis. You should, for example, be able to discern any differences that exist between different populations (e.g. age, gender or ethnic background). Qualitative differences may exist between what is being received or delivered in different settings. You may be able to identity differences in the objectivity of different ways of measuring a particular outcome or result. You will also want to identify differences in the quality of studies that come to different conclusions as a possible explanation for such differences. Whether or not the analysis is systematic is judged more by the criteria of **meaningfulness** than by technical performance *per se* (see Chapter 8).

Systematic approaches to presentation

Much supporting detail for a review is typically located in an appendix, but it is no less important for all that. Typically it is helpful to scrutinise at least one detailed search strategy, from one of the major databases for a topic. A full list of databases and other sources (e.g. websites) may be helpfully included in an appendix particularly if, for reasons of economy in the text, a statement such as 'and 19 websites were searched' has been included in the methods section. Non-standard or adapted quality assessment checklists and data extraction forms may be included in the appendices. Some authors use summary tables of included studies in the main body of their review and then include full reports as appendices or supplements. A table of excluded studies (i.e. studies that appear to meet the inclusion criteria but which, on closer examination, are excluded for good reasons) is frequently included in standards of reporting. Increasingly qualitative systematic reviews produce tables or maps linking individual themes or study findings to their original sources. The decision on what to present in order to demonstrate that you have been systematic is increasingly being standardised by guidelines for reporting such as the *Preferred Reporting of Items for Systematic Reviews and Meta-Analyses* (PRISMA) statement (PRISMA Statement (w158); Moher et al., 2009, w137) (see Chapter 9).

Linking findings to conclusions

One possible criticism is that, by anatomising the entire review process into its four constituent stages, the SALSA approach favours correct procedures over overall coherence (Box 2.2). In other words a reviewer could conceivably follow all these steps *and* describe the methods in clear detail *and yet* still produce a review that lacks overall coherence. To protect against this danger we must consider whether the searching described leads to identification of the right types of study to be appraised. Furthermore, the quality assessment needs to have been taken into account when constructing the synthesis so that important findings are not disproportionately underpinned by poor quality studies. It is worth noting that criticism has been levelled at systematic reviews of effectiveness for conducting formal quality assessment but of not then using the results (Moja et al., 2005). This presents the very real danger of quality assessment becoming simply a 'tick the box' exercise. Finally the synthesis must demonstrate a clear and auditable link between the findings and the subsequent analysis and reporting of conclusions. It can be valuable for you as reader to try to relate the conclusions of a review back to its originating question. All these points emphasise that we are not simply interested in whether a review is internally valid we are also interested in whether it is internally consistent.

Box 2.2   What does 'systematic' look like?

- A priori specification of planned review methods/protocol
- A clearly focused question
- Clear explicit criteria for inclusion and exclusion
- Documentation of search process: sources and strategies
- Use of tables and boxes to make methods explicit
- Use of tables to summarise study characteristics
- An explicit mechanism to handle quality assessment
- Exploration of assumptions, limitations and areas of uncertainty
- Use of tables and graphics to support interpretation of data
- Appendices including search strategies, sample data extraction and quality assessment tools
- Explicit Declarations of Interest

EXERCISE 2.2

How systematic is that review?

We provide a hypothetical abstract describing 'a structured review of the literature'. Look through the abstract in the light of what you have already learnt regarding the search, appraisal, synthesis, analysis (SALSA) framework. Which elements of this

Abstract provide evidence of a systematic approach? Once you have completed this exercise refer to the Worked Example on the companion website to evaluate your responses against our suggestions.

Performing X in Y: a structured review of the literature

Abstract

{Two brief sentences of Background}. A literature search was conducted across {list of Databases and Internet sources} of studies that evaluated X. Information on the type of activity, sample and setting, endpoints, and study design were extracted. Studies were classified based on a modification of the {Hypothetical Worthy} model. Four categories of activity were identified: actor, decision-support, involvement and systems. The search strategy and selection criteria yielded 21 articles. Eleven studies used an actor activity; of these, eight also employed a systems activity, and one also used an involvement activity. Two studies used a decision support activity, seven used an involvement activity, and one used a systems intervention. The overall quality of research was uneven in several areas: research design – nine studies were quasi-experimental in nature, endpoint measures were not consistent – three did not perform statistical analysis, and sample characteristics varied dramatically. In conclusion, the number of high-quality studies of X remains limited. Methodological limitations include measurement of an inappropriate surrogate measure when measurement of an endpoint would be more valid. Further research is needed to understand how each type of activity improves the quality of performing X in a Y setting.

Summary

This chapter has examined the relative advantages of systematic over more traditional approaches to reviewing the literature. It has identified the main stages in the review process. Systematic approaches to the literature hold the potential to demonstrate greater clarity, to possess more validity, and to manifest improved auditability. The key steps of search, appraisal, synthesis and analysis (SALSA) are a possible way of articulating differences between different types of review. A brief consideration of different ways of examining how each step can be made systematic reveals that the steps of *search and appraisal* rely primarily on *Technical Performance*. In contrast *synthesis* depends more upon *Appropriateness and Coherence* and *analysis* more on *Meaningfulness*. The greater clarity offered by more systematic approaches to the literature offers a realistic solution to the situation neatly encapsulated by Rousseau and colleagues (2008, w164):

> The lack of syntheses making it clear what the evidence supports translates into three dangers affecting scholars, educators and practitioners: the misuse of existing research, the overuse of limited or inconclusive findings, and the underuse of research evidence with substantive implications for understanding and working with organizations. (w164)

Key learning points

- Traditional approaches to review of the literature possess recognised shortcomings with regard to opaqueness of methods, the hidden presence of bias and a lack of accountability to the reader.
- Systematic approaches to the literature attempt to address known deficiencies by offering greater clarity, internal validity, and auditability.
- Different types of review can be characterised by the extent to which they undertake the four steps of Search, Appraisal, Synthesis and Analysis (SALSA).
- Each of the four SALSA steps can be assessed for the degree to which it has been carried out in a systematic way; along with consideration of internal coherence, these can be used to provide an overall assessment of how systematic an individual review might be.

Suggestions for further reading

Mulrow, C.D. (1994) Rationale for systematic reviews. *BMJ*, **309**, 597–9.

Petticrew, M. (2001) Systematic reviews from astronomy to zoology: myths and misconceptions. BMJ, **322**, 13, 98–101.

Petticrew, M.A. and Roberts, H. (2006) Why do we need systematic reviews? In: Petticrew, M.A. and Roberts, H. *Systematic reviews in the social sciences*. Oxford: Blackwell, 1–26.

References

Antman, E.M., Lau, J., Kupelnick, B., Mosteller, F., and Chalmers, T.C. (1992) A comparison of results of meta-analyses of randomized control trials and recommendations of clinical experts. Treatments for myocardial infarction. *JAMA*, **268**, 2, 240–8.

Arksey, H. and O'Malley, L. (2005) Scoping studies: towards a methodological framework. *International Journal of Social Research Methodology*, B, 19–32.

Bennett, J., Lubben, F., Hogarth, S., and Campbell, B. (2005) Systematic reviews of research in science education: rigour or rigidity? *International Journal of Science Education*, **27**, 4, 387–406.

Bruce, C. (2001) Interpreting the scope of their literature reviews: significant differences in research students' concerns. *New Library World*, **102**, 4/5, 158–66.

Cabinet Office (2003) Chapter 2: What do we Already Know? In: Cabinet Office. The Magenta Book: *Guidance Notes for Policy Evaluation and Analysis*. July 2003.

Carney, S.M. and Geddes, J.R. (2002) *Systematic Reviews and Meta-analyses. Evidence in Mental Health Care*. Hove: Brunner Routledge.

Cooper, H.M. (1988a) The structure of knowledge synthesis: a taxonomy of literature reviews. *Knowledge in Society*, **1**, 104–26.

Cooper, H.M (1988b) Organizing knowledge syntheses: a taxonomy of literature reviews. *Knowledge, Technology and Policy*, **1**, 1, 104–26.

Dixon-Woods, M., Shaw, R.L., Agarwal, S., and Smith, J.A. (2004) The problem of appraising qualitative research. *Quality and Safety in Health Care*, **13**, 223–5.

Dixon-Woods, M., Agarwal, S., Jones, D., Young, B., and Sutton, A. (2005) Synthesising qualitative and quantitative evidence: a review of possible methods. *Journal of Health Services Research and Policy*, **10**, 1, 45–53.

Dixon-Woods, M., Bonas, S., Booth, A., Jones, D.R., Miller, T., Sutton, A.J., Shaw, R.L., and Young, B. (2006) How can systematic reviews incorporate qualitative research? A critical perspective. *Qualitative Research*, **6**, 1, 27–44.

Egger, M. and Smith, G.D. (1998) Bias in location and selection of studies. *BMJ*, **316**, 7124, 61–6.

Gilbody, S.M. and Song, F. (2000) Publication bias and the integrity of psychiatry research. *Psychological Medicine*, **30**, 253–8.

Grant, M.J. and Booth, A (2009) A typology of reviews: an analysis of 14 review types and associated methodologies. *Health Information and Libraries Journal*, **26**, 2, 91–108. (w095)

Greenhalgh, T. (2010) *How to Read a Paper: The Basics of Evidence-based Medicine*, 4th edn. London: BMJ Books.

Hammersley, M, (2002) Systematic or unsystematic, is that the question? Some reflections on the science, art, and politics of reviewing research evidence. Text of a talk given to the Public Health Evidence Steering Group of the Health Development Agency, October 2002. (w102)

Hedges, L.V. and Vevea, J.L. (1998) Fixed and random effect models in meta-analysis. *Psychological Methods*, **3**, 4, 486–504.

Hopayian, K. (2001) The need for caution in interpreting high quality systematic reviews. *British Medical Journal*, **323**, 681–4.

Major, C. and Savin-Baden, M. (2010) *An Introduction to Qualitative Research Synthesis: Managing the Information Explosion in Social Science Research*. London: Routledge.

Moher, D., Liberati, A., Tetzlaff, J., Altman, D.G., and PRISMA Group (2009) Preferred reporting items for systematic reviews and meta-analyses: the PRISMA statement. *PLoS Medicine*, **6**, 7, e1000097. (w137)

Moja, L.P., Telaro, E., D'Amico, R., Moschetti, I., Coe, L., and Liberati, A. (2005) Assessment of methodological quality of primary studies by systematic reviews: results of the metaquality cross sectional study. *BMJ*, **330**, 7499, 1053. Epub 2005 7 April.

Mulrow, C.D., Cook, D.J., and Davidoff, F. (1997) Systematic reviews: critical links in the great chain of evidence. *Annals of Internal Medicine*, **126**, 5, 389–91.

Mulrow, C.D. (1994) Rationale for systematic reviews. *BMJ*, **309**, 6954, 597–9.

Noyes, J., Popay, J., Pearson, A., Hannes, K., and Booth, A. (2008) Qualitative research and Cochrane Reviews. In: *Cochrane Handbook for Systematic Reviews of Interventions Version 5.0.1* (updated September 2008) ed. by Higgins, J.P.T., Green, S. The Cochrane Collaboration. Bognor Regis: Wiley-Blackwell. (w043)

Petticrew, M.A. and Roberts, H. (2006) Why do we need systematic reviews? In: Petticrew, M. and Roberts, H. *Systematic Reviews in the Social Sciences: A Practical Guide*. Oxford: Blackwell Publishing.

Pirzadeh, L. (2010) Human factors in software development: a systematic literature review. Master's thesis, Chalmers University of Technology, Department of Computer Science and Engineering, Gothenberg, Sweden. (w154)

Rousseau, D.M., Manning, J., and Denyer, D. (2008) Evidence in management and organizational science: assembling the field's full weight of scientific knowledge through syntheses. *Academy of Management Annals*, **2**, 475–515. (w164)

Shea, B., Moher, D., Graham, I., Pham, B., and Tugwell, P. (2002) A comparison of the quality of Cochrane Reviews and systematic reviews published in paper-based journals. *Evaluation and the Health Professions*, **25**, 116–29.

Song, F., Parekh, S., Hooper, L., Loke, Y.K., Ryder, J., Sutton, A.J., Hing, C., Kwok, C.S., Pang, C., and Harvey, I. (2010) Dissemination and publication of research findings: an updated review of related biases. *Health Technology Assessment*, **14**, 8, 1–193. (w176)

Strike, K., and Posner, G. (1983) Types of synthesis and their criteria. In Ward, S. and Reed, L. (eds) *Knowledge Structure and Use*. Philadelphia: Temple University Press.

Turner, J.R. and Müller, R. (2005) The project manager's leadership style as a success factor on projects: a literature review. *Project Management Journal*, **2**, 36, 49–61. (w194)

Walsh, D. and Downe, S. (2005) Meta-synthesis method for qualitative research: a literature review. *Journal of Advanced Nursing*, **50**, 2, 204–11.

Weed, M. (2005) Meta interpretation: a method for the interpretive synthesis of qualitative research. *Forum Qualitative Sozialforschung/Forum: Qualitative Social Research*, **6**, 1, Art. 37. (w201)

Whittemore, R. and Knafl, K. (2005) The integrative review: updated methodology. *Journal of Advanced Nursing*, **52**, 5, 546–53.

THREE

Planning and writing a literature review

Learning Objectives

After reading this chapter, you should be able to:

- Describe the main stages of the review process and their associated milestones and deliverables.
- Produce a draft timetable for your own literature review.
- Identify the various skills required for successful completion of a literature review.
- Conduct a training needs audit for yourself and/or a review team identifying skills required and possible routes to acquire them.

Introduction

As for any type of research, a literature review should be planned and managed as a project (Lyratzopoulos and Allen, 2004). The existence of formal methods for conducting literature reviews can actually make project planning much easier. However, considerable skill lies in tailoring the generic plan to the specific needs of a particular review. As for any project, the reviewer, or review team, needs to consider the elements of time, quality, and money (Box 3.1). Balancing these three considerations within an agreed timescale for delivery, whether one year for a dissertation or thesis or a longer (or indeed shorter) period of time for a commissioned project, is key to the success of a literature review.

Box 3.1 Three key questions for planning a review

- How much time must I allocate to the critical path of activities that must be done (and that cannot be abbreviated)?
- What quality is required for processes that are key to the review but where actual methods allow flexibility or possible negotiation?
- Where might time (and by implication money) be saved by efficiencies; either by one reviewer multitasking or by members of a review team dividing up the workload?

With regard to *time*, a literature review typically embodies a **critical path** that represents a minimum time for completion. For example, all materials for the review have to be identified, acquired and read before the review can be completed, unless agreed otherwise with the commissioner or supervisor. In addition to this minimum time there are processes that will contribute to the reader's confidence in the review method where the time spent is a question of degree. How comprehensive will the search be?, Will there be formal processes for data extraction and quality assessment?, How thorough will the processes of synthesis and analysis be? Typically, all reviewers and students in particular struggle with two areas. These are:

- Knowing when to stop reading for the literature review. (Bruce, 1993)
- Allowing enough time at the end for editing.

For these reasons, it is always helpful to set clear deadlines. Allow a certain period of time for reading and documenting the literature review. If you have time, you can revisit it later. In addition, it is useful to allow time for your work to 'rest' so that you can come back to it with fresh eyes. To avoid a feeling of 'wasted time' you could use this downtime to ask a critical friend to check your English for spelling, grammar and style. Alternatively, this could be the time when you share your review with your supervisor, a mentor, or external advisors – in the meantime you could be getting on with some other task such as tabulating data or checking the format, consistency and completeness of all of your references.

Decisions on such matters have a bearing on the *quality* of the final review. If the methods have been pre-specified, for example in a review plan or protocol, there is little room for subsequent negotiation. Clearly, however, if a degree of flexibility is permitted then a decision, for example, to switch from a formal checklist-based process of quality assessment to a holistic judgement of quality based upon some general prompts will considerably reduce the time taken by the review.

While *money* may appear to be relevant only in the context of a commissioned review, it is equally present, although sometimes implicitly, in all types of review. For example the concept of the 'opportunity cost' (If I wasn't doing this what else might I be doing?) underlies both the absolute time and resource allocated to the review as a whole and the relative time spent on each component of the review process. In the context of a PhD excessive time spent on the review as a whole may delay subsequent primary research (Randolph, 2009, w160). Similarly a decision to postpone reading of a body of literature until all avenues for finding relevant studies have been exhausted may result in a review with an underdeveloped, stunted or truncated analysis phase. This third aspect, relating to resourcing of the review, determines such decisions as 'Can I be doing certain processes together or in parallel?', 'Is there something that I can be doing during "downtime" for another process?', and 'Can this process be divided up and apportioned clearly to different members of a review team?'

Once you have given attention to this 'TQM (Time-Quality-Money) of Review Management' you are in a position to consider the more detailed logistics of your review project. Aspects frequently overlooked include:

Access to databases

You may be conducting your review within an academic institution that carries a wider range of database resources than typically required for your discipline (e.g. health, management, education, social science). However you cannot assume that you have access to all databases required for your topic. You may need to negotiate ad hoc access to particular sources, identified by looking at the Methods sections of related reviews. Such access may be afforded direct to you and your team, in which case you will need to think not only about payment of any fees or subscriptions but also about orientation or training. Alternatively it may only be available via an intermediary from the hosting organisation and thus require payment for database access, for information specialist time for the actual searching and, not to be overlooked, information specialist time for preparing and planning the search strategy (Forward and Hobby, 2002).

Reference management software

The scale of managing references makes use of **reference management** software virtually essential for any substantive literature review project (Sayers, 2007). Again you may already have access to **reference management** software, either via your institution or via free software on the Internet. However you should be aware that institutional agreements often relate to 'cut down' versions of software geared to general student use and comparatively ill-equipped for the heavier demands of a major literature review.

Furthermore there may be restrictions relating to simultaneous usage of a **reference management** database, the number of copies of a database that may be made, whether you are permitted to have versions running both at the office and at home, and whether external collaborators may also access the system. For free versions on the Internet, you will need to explore the functions available, whether it is worth paying an additional premium for added functionality, and issues such as backup and security of data. Ultimately the bottom line involves asking questions such as, 'What is the worst case scenario if the system malfunctions?' and 'What would be the implications for my review?' Faced with such questions you will frequently find that money for more robust and secure systems is well spent in terms of risk management and resulting peace of mind.

Obtaining literature

Most institutional libraries hold a collection of key journal and book resources to support core subject areas. However, where you move beyond this coverage, you will typically need to access other journal articles through inter-library loan and document delivery services. Few information units, aside from those specifically created to support systematic reviews, are geared up for processing possibly hundreds of journal article requests. You therefore need to seek out those who manage local libraries to alert them of your likely needs and to negotiate preferential arrangements to handle bulk quantities of requests. For large-scale projects this may necessitate either yourself or a member of your team doing pre-checking of holdings of other libraries. It may even require employment of a temporary member of staff specifically for this purpose. You should also consider whether it might be more advantageous to arrange trips to specialist libraries, e.g. national libraries or specialist collections, for you to access materials in person. Your preparation for such visits will include researching opening hours, access arrangements and eligibility, photocopying facilities and transport times and costs.

Analysis software

While it is difficult to predict the exact form that your final analysis of data will take, you will usually be able to identify whether quantitative (i.e. **meta-analysis**) or qualitative (e.g. **thematic synthesis**) analysis will be possible. In the former case you will want to budget for meta-analysis software and possibly statistical support. For the latter you may wish to consider qualitative data analysis software. Again decisions as to whether you will use commercial proprietary or free software depend on such factors as how central the analysis will be to your final deliverable, the available resources and demand for such software from elsewhere in your organisation.

A final logistic consideration relates to projecting the likely size and scale of the literature. This can be attempted in several ways. For example. bibliographic databases with data mining or analytical facilities (Scopus (w170), Scirus (w169), PubMed Reminer (w159), Web of Knowledge (w200)) can supply statistics regarding the frequency of certain terms or phrases. For example Pubmed Reminer helps you to identify key authors, key journals, countries of publication as well as terms used most frequently by authors and/or database indexers (w159).

Table 3.1   Some Areas of Review Efficiency

- Could I use a **methodological filter** to reduce the numbers of studies to be sifted?
- Can I identify a likely **law of diminishing returns** so that certain databases can be prioritised on the basis of likely yield?
- Could someone eliminate **duplicate citations** retrieved from different bibliographic databases instead of repeated decisions on inclusion or exclusion for the same research study?
- Could I select studies (i.e. sifting from abstracts) from core databases in parallel to ongoing searching of additional databases?
- Could I request and obtain potentially relevant articles while study selection is still being completed?
- Could I read and/or check initial articles received for relevant citations as soon as they are received rather than waiting for the full set of retrieved studies to be assembled?
- Could I start data extraction and quality assessment in advance of obtaining all studies?
- Could I conduct data extraction and quality assessment as a combined single operation?
- Will I extract data via data extraction forms or direct into summary tables?
- Do I need to use more than one reviewer for sifting or selecting all included studies (or could I use a second reviewer for a random sample of records or until a predetermined level of agreement has been reached)?

Such decisions have two main purposes. First, they help to determine the original review plan or protocol together with associated milestones and deliverables. Second, they constitute a toolkit of 'rescue' techniques to be considered for bringing a review back on track (Table 3.1). This will be particularly critical if time, quality or money aspects of a literature review appear to be deviating from the original plan (see Chapter 10).

The literature review process

The Educational Research Funders' Forum (2005) defines literature reviews as follows:

> Systematic reviews take varying amounts of time according to the topic but usually take between nine months to a year to complete. The duration is gradually reducing as expertise and systems develop. (w069)

Typical timescales are provided for six-month, nine-month, and one-year versions of a literature review (Tables 3.2 to 3.5).

Table 3.2   Sample project timetable for six-month literature review project

Note: A six-month timescale is most appropriate for a literature review that does not require significant appraisal, synthesis, and analysis (e.g. for a scoping review, a mapping review of a well-defined and focused area, or for a rapid evidence assessment). Mapping/scoping reviews are primarily **descriptive** (What does the literature look like? Where are the gaps?) rather than analytical (What does the literature tell us?). A rapid evidence assessment makes little claim to in-depth quality assessment. Similarly a well-circumscribed conceptual analysis, perhaps to inform a subsequent framework analysis, may be achieved within six months.

Task	Timescale
First project team meeting	Months 0–1
Search	
Finalise scope	Months 0–1
Preliminary literature searches	Months 0–1
Identify and contact key organisations	Months 0–1
Second project team meeting/discussion	Months 1–2
Full literature searches and reference management	Months 1–2
Selection of articles	Month 2
Obtain articles	Month 2–3
Follow-up cited references	Month 3
Third project team meeting/discussion	Month 3
Appraisa**L**	
Quality assessment and selective data extraction	Months 3–4
Fourth project team meeting/discussion	Month 4
Synthesis	
Data synthesis	Month 5
Analysis	
Data analysis	Month 5
Fifth project team meeting/discussion	Month 5
Report writing	Month 6
Draft report	Month 6
Sixth project team meeting/discussion	Month 6
Final report	Month 6

Table 3.3   Sample project timetables for nine-month literature review project

Note: A nine-month timescale is most appropriate as a component of a large-scale (e.g. two or more years) project where findings from the literature review feed into subsequent primary research. Similarly it may be suitable for the literature review component of a thesis to inform the design of primary data collection and as a deliverable in an upgrade report. This timescale assumes that other tasks, e.g. applying for ethical approval, are taking place during the concluding phases of the literature review.

Task	Timescale
First project team/supervisor meeting	Months 0–1
Search	
Finalise scope	Months 0–1
Preliminary literature searches	Months 1–2
Identify and contact key organisations	Months 1–2
Second project team/supervisor meeting/discussion	Months 1–2
Full literature searches and reference management	Months 2–3
Selection of articles	Months 2–3
Obtain articles	Months 3–4
Follow-up cited references	Months 4
Third project team/supervisor meeting/discussion	Month 4
Apprais**aL**	
Quality assessment	Month 5
Synthesis	
Data extraction	Month 5–6
Fourth project team/supervisor meeting/discussion	Month 6
Data synthesis	Month 7
Analysis	
Data analysis	Month 7–8
Fifth project team/supervisor meeting/discussion	Month 8
Report writing	Months 8–9
Draft report	Months 9
Sixth project team/supervisor meeting/discussion	Month 9
Final report	Month 9

For comparative purposes you may find it helpful to consider the published one-year timeline for a typical Cochrane (systematic) Review (Green and Higgins, 2008, w043). Obviously within these generic templates there is considerable scope for variability according to:

1 the size of the literature to be reviewed;
2 the scope of the literature review;
3 the number of team members, and proportions of their time, available to the review;
4 the format and quality of the review deliverables.

Nevertheless these templates are a useful starting point. They may also provide a basis for negotiations with a review commissioner or a supervisor. Pai and colleagues (2004) provide a useful step-by-step guide to the review process. Nicholson (2007) suggests that you should produce a SMART plan to identify the specific, measurable, agreed, realistic and timed objectives of the review project. He advises that the person managing the review plans each phase carefully, identifies each strand of work, and sets realistic completion dates. Such a SMART plan would have the format provided in Table 3.5:

Table 3.4 Sample project timetable for 12-month literature review project

Note: 12 months is a typical timescale for a stand-alone literature review such as a systematic review with meta-analysis or a qualitative evidence synthesis (whether aggregative with many included studies or interpretive with in-depth analysis of 10 to 12 studies). In the latter case the aim is to complete search, appraisal, and data extraction as early as possible to maximise time spent on synthesis and analysis.

Task	Timescale
First project team meeting	Months 0–1
Search	
Finalise scope	Month 1
Preliminary literature searches	Months 1–2
Identify and contact key organisations	Month 2
Second project team meeting/discussion	Months 2–3
Full literature searches and reference management	Months 2–3
Selection of articles	Months 3–4
Obtain articles	Months 4–5
Follow-up cited references	Month 6
Third project team meeting/discussion	Months 6–7
Appraisa**L**	
Quality assessment	Months 6–7
Data extraction	Months 7–8
Fourth project team meeting/discussion	Month 8
Synthesis	
Data synthesis	Months 8–9
Analysis	
Data analysis	Months 9–10
Fifth project team meeting/discussion	Month 10
Report writing	Months 11–12
Draft report	Month 11
Sixth project team meeting/discussion	Month 12
Final report	Month 12

Table 3.5 Extract from a SMART plan for a review

What	By whom	By when	Cost	Status
Conduct scoping searches	Information specialist	01/09/2012	£180 (per day)	Not started/in progress/ completed

---

APPLY WHAT YOU HAVE LEARNT 3.1

Producing a draft timetable for your review

Produce a draft timetable for your own review. Include the phases of scoping and planning; searching and obtaining references; data extraction and quality assessment; synthesis and analysis; and writing up and disseminating.

Now try to identify milestones (i.e. time deadlines) or deliverables (specific outputs from each phase of the review process) and where they lie in your review timetable. These may include, but not necessarily be restricted to, a review protocol or review plan (scoping and planning); a search strategy for a principal database with sample search results (searching and obtaining references); a draft data extraction form with completed quality assessment for an included article (data extraction and quality assessment); tables of included study characteristics (synthesis and analysis); and a draft report or article (writing up and disseminating). If you are undertaking a dissertation or thesis, use the timescale that you produce for these deliverables to identify useful points at which to meet with your supervisor. If you are conducting a commissioned review or working with a review team, these will be critical points for a combination of internal and external team meetings. You may find it helpful to use the format for a SMART plan (Table 3.5).

Study skills and techniques

As a novice reviewer, or a scratch review team, you must not assume that you already have the prerequisite skills in order to plan and conduct a literature review. This is a particular pitfall given that most researchers have prior familiarity with what they consider to be 'reviewing the literature'. They may also consider that the methods by which reviews are conducted appear explicit and straightforward. To illustrate, many experienced librarians consider that they already have excellent information retrieval skills. However, typically, such skills are honed in identifying a few specific key references for a research paper or proposal. This is a considerably different scale of endeavour from conducting sensitive searches designed to minimise the chances of missing something relevant. Similarly, prior familiarity with critiquing a research paper (the so-called 'science of trashing papers' (Greenhalgh, 2010)) may be a useful starting point for quality assessment. However, it again falls markedly short, in terms of both scope and intensity, from the level of skills required for systematic approaches to reviewing. The Educational Research Funders' Forum (2005) identified a skills deficit stating:

> As systematic reviewing is still relatively new in education, only a limited number of researchers have participated in systematic review training. (w069)

Although this observation was written more than five years ago, this deficit still exists in fields where systematic approaches to literature review are still in their infancy. Review expertise is distributed differentially across disciplines. Most trained reviewers work in health with pockets of expertise in management, education and social care amongst others. Suggestions for building capacity in reviewing include funding research training, supporting on-the-job training with experienced researchers, and collaboration with other funders (Educational Research Funders' Forum, 2005, w069).

Generic study skills applied to review

The planning and conduct of a literature review requires key generic skills such as a methodical approach accompanied by good discipline in documenting methods and progress. Many review tasks, such as planning and executing a search strategy, extend over multiple occasions spread over many days. It is essential to document how far you have got, what remains to be done, and any false starts or blind alleys to be avoided in the future. You may need to re-execute an identical search strategy towards the end of an extended review to identify more recent materials. You may even need to re-examine search strategies to try to establish why an included study that you have subsequently identified was not retrieved from your original searches.

You will find that keeping a bench book or project diary for the duration of the review will yield dividends at later stages of the writing up process. It will also be helpful to create a dedicated project folder with sub-folders clearly labelled as follows: as Searches, Data extraction forms, Included studies, Review drafts, Reference management database, etc. Preferably this will be networked via an Intranet so that it can be shared amongst the review team. If this is not possible, then you should take regular snapshots of the folder contents and save them to external storage media such as hard drives or USB data sticks.

If your review is a more interpretive type of work, then a project diary will not simply be a procedural manual but will document reflectively major insights or decisions made along the way. In this way, it will assist you in documenting your review process and, subsequently, in justifying such decisions to a peer reviewer or examiner.

This emphasises that the review process is both a disciplined scientific process and a creative artistic one. Although review methods may appear unduly prescriptive, they can provide a frame or structure within which a more imaginative process of interpretation takes place. Data needs to be structured and ordered in such a way that aids pattern recognition and subsequent analysis. This may be likened to the meticulous care with which an artist assembles materials, organises their palette, and selects their vantage point before giving full rein to their creative energies. Such a blend of skills and attributes further attests to the considerable advantages to be gained by undertaking such a process as a review team rather than placing the onus on a single impossibly multi-faceted individual.

Acquiring skills in systematic searching

As previously mentioned, the requirement to conduct sensitive searches and thus minimise the chance of missing any relevant studies (Dickersin et al., 2004) is an exacting, yet natural extension, of skills in selectively identifying the key studies in a subject area. It is unlikely that a reviewer will be able to master all aspects of the literature search process so it is recommended that a librarian or information specialist be involved in every literature review (McGowan and Sampson, 2005). However, such involvement varies considerably in extent from advising on search terms or databases through tutorials on key databases through to being a fully integrated member of the review team (Beverley et al., 2003; Harris, 2005; Swinkels et al., 2006; Wade, 2006; Wilkinson et al., 2009).

Many academic or organisational libraries either run regular training or support sessions for literature searching or offer one-to-one support on an ad hoc basis. It is strongly recommended that you take advantage of such opportunities, perhaps bringing along your own attempts at searching to date. This will allow you to trial your own review topic or ask specific questions about your search strategy. In addition, many libraries, or indeed database providers, offer online tutorials or support documentation for key databases with such materials being increasingly accessible to all via the Internet. Those that will prove most useful include videos or screencasts walking you through the functions of a specific database source. Similarly, you will need to acquire, or at the very least to access, expertise in reference management. Again you should enquire about local provision through the library of your institution.

Developing skills in systematic appraisal

If you wish to be successful in conducting your literature review you will need to become familiar with the characteristics of the main types of study type to be included. For example, if you are planning a review of randomised controlled trials you will need to be able to recognise the key features of such a study, their likely limitations, and the consequent threats to validity that they may pose. This is equally true for reviews of other study designs such as case studies or those associated with qualitative research. A starting point is a checklist designed specifically for studies of a particular type; you can review each question to make sure that you understand the terminology, what is being assessed and where to find the design features in one of your included studies. You can also pilot the checklist for your review sharing your results with colleagues or with a mentor or supervisor. You can then follow up any identified gaps in your knowledge through targeted reading or by attending courses.

In preparing for your own detailed assessment of the quality of your included studies (Box 3.2) you will find it helpful to access books and articles that describe research methods or **critical appraisal** (Greenhalgh, 2010). You will also find it invaluable to read through published critiques of research studies performed by others. Above all you will find it a useful discipline to read through published research studies, focusing on their Methods sections and making notes of any limitations that you notice as you go. You can then read the authors' own sub-section or paragraphs on the limitations of their study (typically included in a well-written Discussion section) and compare their list with your own.

Box 3.2   Sources to help develop skills in quality assessment

Burls, A. (2009) What is critical appraisal? 2nd edn. (w027)

Critical Appraisal Skills Programme. (w054)

Greenhalgh, T. (2010) *How to Read a Paper: The Basics of Evidence-Based Medicine*, 4th edn. London: BMJ Books.

Katrak, P., Bialocerkowski, A.E., Massy-Westropp, N., Kumar, V.S.S., and Grimmer, K. (2004) A systematic review of the content of critical appraisal tools. *BMC Medical Research Methodology*, **4**, 22. (w116)

National Collaborating Centre for Methods and Tools (NCCMT) (2008) Compendium of critical appraisal tools for public health practice. McMaster University, Hamilton, Ontario – Public Health Agency of Canada. (w142)

Refining skills in systematic synthesis

To a large extent skills in systematic synthesis are the most difficult to anticipate. After all it is not until you start engaging with the specific contents of included studies that you will be able to assess what will or will not be possible in the way of synthesis. Nevertheless it is likely that, as a bare minimum, tabulation and an accompanying narrative commentary will be required for your review. You would do well to familiarise yourself with word processing packages, such as OpenOffice (w147) or Microsoft Word, particularly with features associated with referencing (including **cite-while-you-write**) and with production and layout of tables.

With such a variety of methods of synthesis, both quantitative and qualitative, to select from, you will find it helpful to read comparative overviews of multiple techniques (Dixon-Woods et al., 2004; Pope et al., 2007; Barnett-Page and Thomas, 2009, w011) (Box 3.3) so that you can assess their corresponding strengths and weaknesses and their suitability for your particular purpose. Try to find published reviews that seek to address a similar review question to your own (whether it relates to effectiveness, barriers and facilitators, attitudes, etc.). Look at the methods the authors have chosen and any observations that they make upon their experience of using such a technique.

As soon as you have a clear indication regarding advanced techniques that you may require, such as **meta-analysis** or **meta-ethnography**, you should investigate opportunities to attend formal courses in these methods. If this is not possible you should try to identify local expertise that you may be able to access during the course of your review, such as a resident statistician or qualitative researcher. Fortunately, many published worked examples exist to help you follow the steps of a specific technique. You can often access discussion lists for clarification of detailed points arising from your reading. You will also find it helpful to attend presentations by researchers who have used particular methods and to take the opportunity to ask for their observations and advice on the selection and subsequent use of their chosen method.

Box 3.3   Sources to help develop skills in synthesis

Dixon-Woods, M., Agarwal, S., Jones, D., Young, B., and Sutton, A. (2005) Synthesising qualitative and quantitative evidence: a review of possible methods. *Journal of Health Services Research and Policy*, **10**, 1, 45–53.

Major, C. and Savin-Baden, M. (2010) Exploring the relevance of qualitative research synthesis to higher education research and practice. *London Review of Education*, **8** 2, 127–40.

Oxman, A.D., Schünemann, H.J., and Fretheim, A. (2006) Improving the use of research evidence in guideline development: 8. Synthesis and presentation of evidence. *Health Research Policy Systems*, **4**, 20. (w148)

Popay, J., Roberts, H., Sowden, A., Petticrew, M., Arai, L., Rodgers, M., and Britten, N., with Roen, K. and Duffy, S. (2006) Guidance on the conduct of narrative synthesis in systematic reviews: a product from the ESRC methods programme. Version 1. (w156)

Pope, C., Mays, N., and Popay, J. (2007) *Synthesising Qualitative and Quantitative Health Research: A Guide to Methods*. Maidenhead: Open University Press.

Honing skills in systematic analysis

Of all the skills required for the review process it is those associated with analysis that are most difficult to acquire in a formal manner. Indeed novice reviewers often make the mistake of thinking that by assembling and 'cataloguing' their included studies they have concluded their review. Frequently when their data has been assembled in a clear and explicit way, a more experienced supervisor or mentor is able to identify previously neglected insights. Key, then, to the analysis stage of the review is a quest to maximise opportunities to identify patterns from the data. How this is achieved will be covered in more detail in subsequent chapters. For the moment it will suffice to flag up the three main types of 'pattern' to be explored, regardless of whether data is quantitative or qualitative. These are identification of similarities across studies, recognition of differences between studies, and isolation of subgroups of studies with reduced, heightened, or absent characteristics or effects. Such subgroups may be characterised in terms of their population, the properties of their intervention, or their outcomes and how they are measured, in terms of their setting or fidelity, or in terms of their study design or quality. A proficient reviewer will continually be alert to identification, exploration, and explanation of such patterns in the synthesised data.

It is true that some techniques will be suggested by their use in published examples of the methods that you are planning to use (Box 3.4). For example, once you have decided that your data is suited to synthesis through meta-analysis you will note from other published meta-analyses that this is frequently accompanied by such analytical techniques as the **funnel plot** (to detect possible **publication bias**) or **sensitivity analysis** (to establish the sensitivity of results to the presence or absence of particular studies). You will find that, while many such techniques may be helpful as interim methods of investigation and analysis, only a handful of these will be sufficiently informative to survive through to the subsequent phase of presentation and reporting.

Box 3.4   Sources to help develop skills in analysis

Egger, M. and Smith, G.D. (1998) Bias in location and selection of studies. *BMJ*, **316**, 7124, 61–6.

Egger, M., Davey Smith, G., and Altman, D.G. (eds) (2001) *Systematic Reviews in Health Care: Meta-analysis in Context.* London: BMJ Books.

Oxman, A.D. and Guyatt, G.H. (1992) A consumer's guide to subgroup analyses. *Annals of Internal Medicine*, **116**, 1, 78–84.

Song, F., Parekh, S., Hooper, L., Loke, Y.K., Ryder, J., Sutton, A.J., Hing, C., Kwok, C.S., Pang, C., and Harvey, I. (2010) Dissemination and publication of research findings: an updated review of related biases. *Health Technology Assessment*, **14**, 8, 1–193. (w176)

Polishing skills in writing and presentation

Writing and presentation is common to all areas of academic activity. You will have acquired many such skills in the course of your academic career. Again, the requirements for reviewing the literature differ not so much in their nature but more in their intensity and degree. Writing up will make demands on textual, tabular, graphic and numeric modes of presentation. Opportunities to polish these skills may present themselves through formal research training programmes, lunchtime sessions, and technical or software-specific training courses.

In particular you will need to expand your writing style from itemisation (e.g. 'Study A was conducted in a population of X') to narrative summary (e.g. 'Five of the eight studies were conducted in secondary schools with the remainder in training colleges. Six were from the United States with one from Canada and one from New Zealand'). Such synthetic principles assist in the all important identification of similarities, differences, and subgroups mentioned previously.

REFLECTION POINT 3.1

Personal skills audit

Having briefly reviewed the skills required in order to conduct a successful literature review, reflect on which of these skills you already possess and which you will need to acquire. How will you acquire such skills?

Review plans and protocols for planning your review

Although the phrases 'review plan' and 'review protocol' are, in theory, at least, interchangeable we tend to use the former for a more informal internal record of how a review will be conducted and the latter as a formal means of communicating this intent externally to others. All reviews should have a plan: a way of checking progress, managing both time and processes, and identifying checkpoints for meetings with a supervisor, mentor or other team members. Whether this is upgraded to a protocol will be determined by such factors as whether a project is accountable to external groups or funders and how important it is to demonstrate explicitly that a systematic approach is being followed. Related to this latter point comes the need to protect against **scope creep**, that is, the tendency for any review to expand the work required without due consideration of the costs and the implications for timely production, and other sources of potential bias (see Chapter 4).

According to the NHS Centre for Reviews and Dissemination (CRD, 2001):

> The protocol specifies the plan which the review will follow to identify, appraise and collate evidence.

Organisations such as the Cochrane Collaboration (w042) place a formal requirement to produce a review protocol on all intending reviewers. This statement of intent not only serves to 'stake a claim' for a review topic, thereby avoiding unnecessary overlap or duplication, but also represents a commitment to undertake the review within a two-year time period. The main strength of developing a protocol is that it encourages the reviewer to be explicit about how the review will be carried out. Rather like action plans and other project management tools (Baker et al., 2010), it fore-arms the reviewer by getting them to think through the different stages of the process at the beginning of the review and any associated problems or issues.

A protocol is also useful in promoting **transparency, transferability** and **replicability** (Boaz et al., 2002, w018). It outlines what the reviewer intended to do and makes it possible, at least in theory for the review to be repeated at a later date by others. Within the context of academic supervision, we find it helpful to require a review protocol from each dissertation student as an indication that they have given attention to both the feasibility of the topic and any anticipated challenges. In both contexts, the review protocol has a further purpose upon completion of the review, namely to assess the congruence between the intended deliverable and the final product. Indeed some academic submissions require the protocol to be submitted as an appendix to the final review; this may be considered good practice irrespective of mandatory requirements (see Chapter 4).

APPLY WHAT YOU HAVE LEARNT 3.2

Producing a draft protocol

Produce a first version of a review protocol for your own review. Share it with your supervisor, mentor, or review team. Annotate the review protocol with any substantive changes arising from their comments, carefully documenting any dates for changes.

Table 3.6 Common reviewer errors

Stage	Reviewer error
Search	Does not take sufficient time to define the best descriptors and identify the best sources to use in review literature related to the topic.
	Does not report the search procedures that were used in the literature review.
Appraisa**L**	Relies on secondary sources rather than on primary sources in reviewing the literature.
	Uncritically accepts another researcher's findings and interpretations as valid, rather than examining critically all aspects of the research design and analysis.
Synthesis	Reports isolated statistical results rather than synthesising them by chi-square or meta-analytic methods/*reports isolated themes or categories rather than examining the relationships between them.*
	Does not consider contrary findings and alternative interpretations in synthesising quantitative or *qualitative* literature.
Analysis	Does not clearly relate the findings of the literature review to the researcher's own study or the original review question.

Items in italics are added to make this checklist applicable to a wider range of review types than the original context of meta-analysis.

Avoiding Common Pitfalls

According to Gall et al. (1996) seven common mistakes are made when reviewing the literature. These mistakes may be mapped against the SALSA framework (see Table 3.6).

You will find it helpful to review these common pitfalls at various stages throughout the planning and conduct of your own review.

Summary

We have seen that a literature review may consume between six months and a year of academic activity. Furthermore, within the specific context of a thesis or a multifaceted project with subsequent primary data collection, you may have to return to the literature many times, often at significant intervals following completion of the original review. These requirements make it absolutely essential to employ a systematic approach to the planning and writing of your literature review. Far from being a luxury to be completed only if you have 'downtime' early in the project a review plan or protocol is a key deliverable from the review process. Aside from such pragmatic considerations, a review protocol performs a valuable function as a protection against **scope creep** and forms of systematic bias.

This chapter has focused on the planning of a review, a topic often omitted in published guidelines for the review process, and has provided useful frameworks for constructing a plan by which to tackle your own review. It has emphasised that, far from providing a shackle to your own creativity, attention to logistics early in the review process may provide you with more freedom to engage effectively with your data, thereby liberating your imagination for subsequent synthesis and analysis.

Key learning points

- A literature review requires careful planning, based around a minimum critical path, and reconciling the considerations of time, quality, and money.
- Attention must be paid to the training needs of the team as a whole and individual within the team.
- A protocol is not only a useful practical tool for management of the literature review but it also serves other valuable functions such as protecting against scope creep and communicating an intent to cover a particular topic area.

Suggestions for further reading

Boote, D.N. and Beile, P. (2005) Scholars before researchers: on the centrality of the dissertation literature review in research preparation. *Educational Researcher*, **34**, 6, 3–15.

Levy, Y. and Ellis, T.J. (2006) A systems approach to conduct an effective literature review in support of information systems research. *Informing Science Journal*, **9**, 181–212. (w124)

Randolph, J. (2009) A guide to writing the dissertation literature review. *Practical Assessment, Research and Evaluation*, **14**, 13. (w160)

Sayers, A. (2007) Tips and tricks in performing a systematic review. *British Journal of General Practice*, **57**, 545, 999.

Staples, M. and Niazi, M. (2007) Experiences using systematic review guidelines. *Journal of Systems Software*, **80**, 9, 1425–37.

References

Baker, P.R., Francis, D.P., Hall, B.J., Doyle, J., and Armstrong, R. (2010) Managing the production of a Cochrane systematic review. *Journal of Public Health*, **32**, 3, 448–50.

Barnett-Page, E. and Thomas, J. (2009) Methods for the synthesis of qualitative research: a critical review. *BMC Medical Research Methodology*, **9**, 59. (w011)

Beverley, C.A., Booth, A., and Bath, P.A. (2003) The role of the information specialist in the systematic review process: a health information case study. *Health Information and Libraries Journal*, **20**, 2, 65–74.

Boaz, A., Ashby, D., and Young, K. (2002) Systematic reviews: what have they got to offer evidence based policy and practice? ESRC UK Centre for Evidence Based Policy and Practice. Working Paper 2. Queen Mary University of London, ESRC. (w018)

Bruce, C. (1993) When enough is enough: or how should research students delimit the scope of their literature review? In: *Challenging the Conventional Wisdom in Higher Education: Selected Contributions Presented at the Nineteenth Annual National Conference and Twenty-First Birthday Celebration of the Higher Education Research and Development Society of Australasia Inc.*, HERDSA, University of New South Wales, Sydney, Australia, 435–9.

Dickersin, K., Scherer, R., and Lefebvre, C. (1994) Identifying relevant studies for systematic reviews. *BMJ*, **309**, 6964, 1286–91.

Dixon-Woods, M., Agarwal, S., Young, B., Jones, D., and Sutton, A. (2004) *Integrative Approaches to Qualitative and Quantitative Evidence*. London: NHS Health Development Agency. (w062)

Educational Research Funders' Forum (2005) Systematic literature reviews in education: advice and information for funders. NERF Working Paper 2.1 (January). (w069)

Forward, L. and Hobby, L. (2002) A practical guide to conducting a systematic review. *Nursing Times*, **98**, 2, 36–7.

Gall, M.D., Borg, W.R., and Gall, J.P. (1996) *Educational Research: An Introduction*. White Plains, NY: Longman.

Green, S. and Higgins, J.P.T. (eds) (2008) Preparing a Cochrane Review. In: Higgins, J.P.T. and Green, S. (eds) *Cochrane Handbook for Systematic Reviews of Interventions*, Version 5.0.1 (updated September 2008). The Cochrane Collaboration. Bognor Regis: Wiley-Blackwell. (w043)

Greenhalgh, T. (2010) *How to Read a Paper*, 4th edn. London: BMJ Books.

Harris, M.R. (2005) The librarian's roles in the systematic review process: a case study. *Journal of the Medical Library Association*, **93**, 1, 81–7.

Lyratzopoulos, G. and Allen, D. (2004) How to manage your research and audit work. *BMJ Career Focus*, **328**, 196–7.

McGowan, J. and Sampson, M. (2005) Systematic reviews need systematic searchers. *Journal of the Medical Library Association*, **93**, 1, 74–80.

NHS Centre for Reviews and Dissemination (2001) Undertaking systematic reviews of research on effectiveness: CRD's guidance for those carrying out or commissioning reviews. NHS Centre for Reviews and Dissemination, University of York, York (CRD Report 4: 2nd edn).

Nicholson, P.J. (2007) How to undertake a systematic review in an occupational setting. *Occupational and Environ Medicine*, **64**, 5, 353–8, 303.

Pai, M., McCulloch, M., Gorman, J.D., Pai, N., Enaroria, W., Kennedy, G., Tharyan, P., and Colford, J.M., Jr (2004) Systematic reviews and meta-analyses: an illustrated, step-by-step guide. *The National Medical Journal of India*, **17**, 2, 86–95.

Pope, C., Mays, N., and Popay, J. (2007) *Synthesizing Qualitative and Quantitative Health Evidence: A Guide to Methods*. Maidenhead: Open University Press.

Randolph, J. (2009) A guide to writing the dissertation literature review. *Practical Assessment, Research and Evaluation*, **14**, 13. (w160)

Sayers, A. (2007) Tips and tricks in performing a systematic review. *British Journal of General Practice*, **57**, 545, 999.

Swinkels, A., Briddon, J., and Hall, J. (2006) Two physiotherapists, one librarian and a systematic literature review: collaboration in action. *Health Information and Libraries Journal*, **23**, 4, 248–56.

Wade, C.A. (2006) Information retrieval and the role of the information specialist in producing high-quality systematic reviews in the social behavioural and education sciences. *Evidence and Policy*, **2**, 1, 89–108.

Wilkinson, A., Papaioannou, D., Keen, C., and Booth, A. (2009) The role of the information specialist in supporting knowledge transfer: a public health information case study. *Health Information and Libraries Journal*, **26**, 118–25.

FOUR

Defining the scope

Learning Objectives

After reading this chapter, you should be able to:

- Understand the importance of defining your scope in terms of the conception and delivery of a review.
- Focus your research question, using a framework to define the scope.
- Complete a review protocol for your own topic.
- Be aware of the challenges and pitfalls relating to defining the scope.

Introduction

The first step in the literature review process is to define the scope of your research. Typically you may have an idea for a broad area of research. Defining the scope allows you to focus your **research question**, which informs the subsequent literature review process. Essentially, defining the scope involves deciding on the 'who', the 'what', and the 'how' (Ibrahim, 2008) (Box 4.1).

Box 4.1   The three elements of defining the scope

WHO = who is the research question about?

WHAT = what must the researcher find out to answer the research question?

HOW = how will the study impact on the 'who'? (e.g. what is the outcome?)

Adapted from Ibrahim, 2008.

In short, defining the scope can take you from:

'I'd quite like to do some research on under-age drinking ...'

to:

'I'm going to do some research on the economic and social implications *[HOW]* of school age *[WHO]* drinking *[WHAT]*.'

This chapter explores how you can define the scope for your research question. We argue why it is an important step in the literature review process, and include resources and exercises on focusing your research question. We suggest that you use a framework to define your scope and show you how to write a review protocol. The chapter ends by exploring the challenges and pitfalls of this stage of the literature review process. As you read the chapter, you will find it helpful to have in mind your own research question, and to apply the exercises and case studies accordingly.

Why is defining the scope important?

A good **systematic review** is based on a well-formulated, answerable question (Counsell, 1997), and it is important to start with a clearly defined scope for any type of review, but particularly one that claims to be systematic. John Ruskin wrote in 1886: 'To be able to ask a question clearly is two-thirds of the way to getting it answered' (Booth, 2006). This still resonates. Most problems with the conduct of a literature review can be attributed to initial problems with the scoping process – 'Fuzzy questions tend to lead to fuzzy answers' (Oxman and Guyatt, 1988). If you ask too broad a question you may have no chance of answering it. Similarly you may, in fact, be asking a series of questions which need to be disentangled and separately articulated.

By clearly setting out the aims of your research at the outset, you are helping to determine all the following aspects of your review. For example, a good research question can inform your literature search, as it will be easier for you to identify the key concepts of the question and therefore your key search terms. This idea is explored more fully in Chapter 5. It will also inform your **inclusion criteria** (e.g. the selection of studies) as you will know exactly the type of study you are looking for. This is explored more fully in Chapter 6, but for now we present a brief example (Box 4.2).

Box 4.2   Example of a research question informing inclusion criteria

Research question: what are the economic and social implications of school age drinking?

Inclusion criteria

Study must include:

1 Subjects of school age (5–16 years) [WHO]
2 Drinking of any alcohol in any quantity [WHAT]
3 Economic and/or social implications [HOW]

You will also find that clearly defining your scope at the outset is invaluable in helping you to determine the resources required for your research (see Chapter 3).

Knowing exactly what your research does and does not include allows you to allocate the required time and money throughout the project. This helps you in writing a project plan or protocol, for your own use and for sharing with a wider project team. You will also be required to define your scope prior to securing any funding for which you may be applying.

How to define the scope: focusing your question

Defining the scope involves focusing your research question so that it contains explicit, specific information about your topic. It is here that you need to decide on the 'who', the 'what', and the 'how'. You can use a series of prompts to help you identify all the different elements of your question.

REFLECTION POINT 4.1

Considerations for focusing your question

Briefly reflect on how you would characterise your review question. Think initially in terms of your Who?, What?, and How?

WHO? – specific age groups? genders? occupations? socioeconomic groups? ethnic groups?, etc.

WHAT? – an intervention? an exposure? a hypothesis? a phenomenon?

HOW? – outcomes – how does the what affect the who? For example, for an educational intervention such as providing tuition on information skills – do the students who attend these tutorials gain higher marks for their assignments?

Focusing your question will typically be an iterative approach that develops during the initial or **scoping** literature searches (Khan et al., 2001). You may have a relatively clear idea of what area you want to research, and by carrying out some initial searches of **bibliographical databases** you can identify where the research gaps are, and where a literature review would be useful.

Frameworks for defining the SCOPE

At this stage, you may find it useful to use a formal structure to focus your question, as this will allow you to 'unpack' your question into its component concepts. Various frameworks are available to help you to do this, depending on your field of research, but for this chapter we concentrate on **PICOC** (Petticrew and Roberts, 2006) (Table 4.1).

Table 4.1 The Elements of PICOC

Population	Who or what is the problem or situation you are dealing with? In a human population, for example, which age, sex, socioeconomic or ethnic groups are involved? What are the technical terms, synonyms, and related terms?
Intervention	In what ways are you considering intervening in the situation? What sort of options do you have for tackling the problem? For example, this could be an educational intervention such as online tutorials on plagiarism (population = undergraduate students).
OR	NB: For non-intervention studies you may find it helpful to replace Intervention (a planned procedure) with **E**xposure (an unintentional occurrence or happening). For example, exposure to radio waves from mobile phone transmitters.
Exposure	
Comparison	What is the alternative? This is optional, when you wish to consider, for example, the effect of two or more interventions, comparing their outcomes possibly in terms of what they deliver and/or cost. So you may want information on the relative merits of: • buses versus trams for urban congestion; • natural versus chemical methods of agricultural pest control; • surgery versus drugs for an illness.
Outcome(s)	How is it measured? This may be more difficult to identify: you have a technical terminology for your problem and a range of management options, but what do you want to achieve? This stage does, however, focus your mind on what your desired outcome(s) might be and how you will assess the impact – e.g. what you are going to measure and how.
Context	What is the particular context of your question? Are you looking at specific countries/areas/settings?

Continuing with our previous example, Box 4.3 shows how a focused question might look using the PICOC model.

Box 4.3 Worked example of PICOC

Population = Children and adolescents/teenagers/young adults of school age – e.g. 5–16 years (Years 1–11 and international equivalents). Male and female. All school ages (when legally required to attend) – primary, infant, junior, secondary, high, grammar, comprehensive, state and public/private, home schooling.

Intervention/exposure = underage drinking of alcohol.

Comparison = none (not drinking alcohol).

Outcomes = economic and/or social impact. Impacts include, but are not limited to, future economic prospects (earning levels and growth), emotional development, educational and occupational achievement, antisocial and/or violent behaviour, sexual harassment, sexually transmitted diseases, teenage pregnancy, increased healthcare costs (including increased emergency admissions).

Context = Primary focus is on the UK, but international studies will be considered if the results can be applied to the local setting.

This example illustrates that time spent formalising the scope of your question is time well spent, as it also provides an opportunity to identify potential search terms and to consider the types of studies that you are going to include.

Other frameworks exist for defining the scope. Many of these have been developed to answer a specific type of question. PICOC itself is derived from the PICO (Population, Intervention, Comparison, Outcome(s)) formulation which was developed in the field of medicine to answer clinical queries (Richardson et al., 2002). SPICE (Setting, Perspective, Intervention/Interest, Comparison, Evaluation) or ProPheT (Problem, Phenomenon of Interest, Time) may be particularly useful for qualitative questions (Booth, 2004). Denyer and Tranfield (2009) have devised a management version of PICO, known as Context-Intervention-Mechanisms-Outcomes (CIMO) (Box 4.4).

Box 4.4   Context-intervention-mechanisms-outcomes (CIMO) framework

Context – which individuals, relationships, institutional settings, or wider systems are being studied?

Intervention. The effects of what event, action, or activity are being studied?

Mechanisms. What are the mechanisms that explain the relationship between interventions and outcomes? Under what circumstances are these mechanisms activated or not activated?

Outcomes. What are the effects of the intervention? How will the outcomes be measured?

Example of a focused question using CIMO: 'Under what conditions (C) does leadership style (I) influence the performance of project teams (O), and what mechanisms operate in the influence of leadership style (I) on project team performance (O)?' (Denyer and Tranfield, 2009)

APPLY WHAT YOU HAVE LEARNT 4.1

Using PICOC to focus your question

Now formulate your own research question using the PICOC model.

Population
Intervention OR Exposure
Comparison
Outcome(s)
Context

The review protocol

As with any project, your literature review should be carefully planned. It is good practice to write a review protocol in advance where you outline what you are planning to do. As with a research proposal for a primary research project, the protocol describes each step of the review process: 'A protocol is a written document containing the background information, the problem specification and the methodology of the review' (Khan et al., 2001).

The review protocol has three main functions:

1 Protection against **bias** – by clearly describing your methods you are ensuring rigour and minimising potential bias.
2 As a practical tool for conducting the methods of the review – by following your protocol closely you protect your review from deviating from the agreed methods. This is particularly useful when working within a wider project team as it ensures *that* all members will follow the same procedures. It can also be very useful when you are writing up your project – in writing a protocol you are effectively writing your Methods section in the future tense, so if you follow it closely you will only need to change it to the past tense for your final report.
3 Staking your claim to the topic – this is particularly important if your protocol will be published, for example if you are conducting a **Cochrane Review**.

The main components of a protocol are shown in Box 4.5.

Box 4.5   Components of a protocol

- Background
- Review question
- Search strategy (including search terms and resources to be searched)
- Study selection criteria and procedures
- Study quality assessment checklists and procedures
- Data extraction strategy
- Synthesis of the extracted evidence
- Project timetable

Table 4.2   Review protocol examples

Area of research	Topic
Computer science	Protocol for systematic review of within- and cross-company estimation models (w120)
Education	The impact of collaborative CPD on classroom teaching and learning (w049)
Healthcare	Skill mix in residential care (w010)
Information science	Impact of school library services on achievement and learning (w203)
Management	Sense-making and disconnection between intent and action (organisational behavioural) (w111)
Social care	Protocol guidelines for systematic reviews of home modification information to inform best practice (w024)

Examples of review protocols

You will find it useful to examine protocols from your own research area to see how a protocol looks in practice (see Table 4.2 for suggested examples).

APPLY WHAT YOU HAVE LEARNT 4.2

Examining a review protocol

Either examine one of the review protocols from Table 4.2 or one that you have identified yourself, and consider:

1 What are the key databases and sources within my discipline?
2 What methodological documentation does the author cite that may be of value for my own review?
3 What does the way that the review protocol is organised and presented tell you about the quantity and quality of the literature available in your field?

APPLY WHAT YOU HAVE LEARNT 4.3

The review protocol template

Fill in the blank version of the review protocol template (see Sage website) for your own review. You may find it helpful to refer to the instructions for completing the review protocol template (Table 4.3) and to consult the relevant chapters for each section of the protocol.

Table 4.3 Instructions for completing the review protocol template

Background
The background should set the context for your review, introducing the reader to your topic, without needing specialist knowledge to understand the area of research. This may include relevant current statistics and previous research, highlighting the importance for your review.

Objectives
Here you should outline the aims of your review and the research question(s) you are attempting to answer.

Criteria for inclusion and exclusion of studies
In this section, you should record how you will decide which studies to include and which to exclude. It is helpful to define this by key concepts such as study design, population, intervention, etc., as outlined in the following sections.

Types of studies
Which type of study design(s) are you going to include/exclude? For example: **randomised controlled studies**? **cohort studies**? **qualitative** studies? Surveys?

Types of populations
Revisit your focused question and record the type(s) of population you are going to include/exclude.

(Continued)

Table 4.3 (Continued) .

Types of interventions or exposure
Revisit your focused question and record the type(s) of intervention(s)/exposure(s) you are going to include/exclude.

Types of outcome measures
Revisit your focused question and record the type(s) of outcome you are going to include/exclude. If you have a broad outcome such as whether an intervention is 'effective' – you may want to define this further here. For example in the question: 'Is e-learning effective in teaching undergraduate students information literacy skills' – you may define effectiveness in terms of assignment marks and you would exclude any studies that did not measure this outcome. NB – it is possible to look at more than one outcome here.

Setting/context (where applicable)
If your research question applies to a particular setting or context, record which you will include/exclude here. For example, if you are only interested in studies taking place in a particular country, you can exclude studies from other countries. However, please be aware that this may limit your review too much, so you may have to look at any comparable settings also – e.g. Europe rather than the UK.

Search strategy for identification of studies (see Chapter 5 for more details)
Here you should record your methodology for finding studies under the following headings.

Electronic databases to be used – which sources will you search?

Other search methods – such as hand searching, reference checking, citation searching, etc.

Keywords and sample search strategy – here you should include initial ideas for search terms. You may also find it useful to provide an example search strategy from any scoping searches you have done.

Study selection

Method of review (see Chapter 6)
- Remember to include who will select studies and how they will do so. For example, if you are working within a project team you should state which project team members will be selecting the studies and how any disagreements would be resolved. If you are conducting all aspects of the review single-handedly, record that it is you who will be selecting the studies. It may be useful to record the process you will follow here – e.g. title sift, abstract sift, full-text sift, etc. (see Chapter 6 for further details).

Assessment of methodological quality (see Chapter 6)
- Here you will record how you plan to assess the methodological quality of your included studies. Remember to include details of any specific **checklists** that you will use.

Data extraction (see Chapter 7)
- What data will you extract? (variables, themes, etc.). If you plan to use/adapt an existing data extraction form you should record the details here. If you plan to design your own, state this intention here.

Data synthesis (see Chapter 7)
- What will your data look like – **qualitative** or **quantitative** or a combination?
- How you will synthesis it – using **narrative synthesis**, or **thematic synthesis**?

Timeframe (see Chapter 3)
List the stages of the review and outline how long each stage of the review will take you. This will help you set milestones by which you can assess your progress.

Task	Timescale
Literature search	
Study selection	
Data extraction	
Data synthesis	
Writing-up review	

You may find it helpful to construct a **Gantt chart** or similar if several stages will take place at the same time. Computer-based project management programs allow you to do this, such as Microsoft Project (w135). It is possible to use Excel for this purpose (w134). Free **open source software** is also available such as GanttProject (w087).

Defining the scope: challenges and pitfalls

As with any stage of a literature review, certain challenges and pitfalls may occur when defining the scope. These range from minor 'nuisance' complications, such as identifying duplicate and/or multiple citations, to more substantive challenges such as decisions regarding inclusion and exclusion criteria and **quality assessment** (Kennedy, 2007). In this section, we identify common problems to look out for when defining the scope for your own projects.

Comprehensiveness versus selectivity

A common challenge when defining the scope relates to knowing 'when to stop'. Debate centres on whether you should aim for comprehensiveness (in quantitative terms), **theoretical saturation** (in qualitative terms) or whether you should aim for a 'representative' approach. Another possibility is that you aim to cover key 'pivotal' works in your chosen field (as for a **meta-narrative** review or a **concept analysis**). Whichever approach you choose, and this may be influenced by the time and resources available (a completely comprehensive review may not be feasible) you should be explicit in your methods so that the reader is fully aware of the scope of your review, and the criteria for selection and relevance (Bruce, 2001).

Table 4.4   Types of review: scope

Type of review	Purpose	Example
Scoping review	To find out how much literature exists.	O'Malley, L. and Croucher, K. (2005) Housing and dementia care – a scoping review of the literature. *Health and Social Care in the Community*, **13**, 6, 570–7.
	To find out the characteristics of the literature.	The scope of this review focuses on **UK** studies of **housing and accommodation** related to dementia published since the **early 1980s**, with the aim of identifying gaps in existing knowledge.
Mapping review	Aims to identify gaps in the literature in order to commission further research.	Groves et al., 2006, w101.
		The scope of this review focuses on **Australian** research (although some international research has been included for context). The timeframe is from **1990** onwards, although the authors state that research prior to this has been included if appropriate.
Systematic review	Aims to be comprehensive	Edwards et al., 2002, w070.
	Scope should be well-defined and clearly stated.	The scope of this review was to find all **RCTs** of strategies to influence the response to a postal questionnaire. Note that although the authors are based in health research, the review is not restricted to medical surveys, it covers **any questionnaire topic in any population**. Studies in **all languages** were included.
	Systematic reviews tend to focus on the highest quality evidence available.	

The type of review you choose to write will help you to define your scope, as reviews differ in the degree to which they use and report systematic methods. Table 4.4 outlines three review types (scoping, mapping, systematic) and their respective purposes. For each review type it provides an illustrative example together with details of the scope covered.

REFLECTION POINT 4.2

Different reviews, different scopes

Consider the three types of review in Table 4.4 and note how the scope differs in each example given (for example the scope of the systematic review is more clearly defined than that for the more exploratory scoping and mapping reviews). Think about your own research question and how it may influence your choice of review type.

Scope creep

A major problem in the literature review process is **scope creep** – your research getting wider and wider until it is unmanageable. **Scope creep** is defined as:

> uncontrolled changes over time to a project's aims, direction, scale and/or timescale and, more specifically, the gradual unchecked expansion of the project's objectives. (Saunders, 2009, w167)

This can occur at any point during the review process, particularly when searching the literature. It is important to constantly refer back to your original scope to ensure the project does not go off track. There is a tension between what is interesting and what is useful – references you find may catch your attention, but may not be directly relevant to answer your research question. Of course, there may be situations where an amendment to the original scope is necessary. This can be managed by a **changes clause** (Matchar et al., 2006), particularly important when working on official contracts and/or as part of a wider research team.

Summary

Defining the scope is the first step in the literature review process. This involves focusing your research topic into an answerable question, clearly structured to show the 'who, what, and how' of your study. By setting out the aims of your research at this early stage, you are informing the rest of your project. A good research question helps your decision-making process in terms of literature searching and study selection. To focus your question, consider using a framework such as **PICOC** to define the key concepts of your research. It is helpful to complete a review protocol at this stage to help you carefully plan the process and adhere to it. Various tools can help you visualise the scope of your research, such as **concept mapping**.

Key learning points

1 Focus your question using a framework appropriate for your area of research.
2 Define your scope to inform the later stages of your review, such as identifying literature search terms and criteria for study selection.
3 Write a review protocol and constantly refer back to it during the process of your review.
4 Beware of **scope creep**!
5 Consider creating a **concept map** to visually define the scope of your literature.

Suggestions for further reading

Anderson, S., Allen, P., Peckham, S., and Goodwin, N. (2008) Asking the right questions: scoping studies in the commissioning of research on the organisation and delivery of health services. *Health Research Policy and Systems,* **6**, 7. (w005)
Coverdale, A. (2009) The use of mapping in literature review (PhD Wiki). (w052)
Durham University (2009) Template for a systematic literature review protocol. (w066)
Rowley, J. and Slack, F. (2004) Conducting a literature review. *Management Research News,* **27**, 4, 31–39. (w165)
Software Engineering Group, School of Computer Science and Mathematics, Keele University and Department of Computer Science, University of Durham (2007) Guidelines for performing systematic literature reviews in software engineering. (w175)

Tools for defining the scope

This tools section focuses on the various mapping processes that are available to help you to define the scope of your research question. The most commonly used mapping processes (**descriptive mapping, data mining, concept mapping,** and use of a **logic model**) are outlined with examples and links to resources, where available, that may be used to scope or to map the literature.

Descriptive mapping

Descriptive mapping is a way of defining the body of literature on a given topic, by allocating defined keywords to the studies found. It is a form of classification and can help to determine what research has been previously carried out as well as to identify research gaps (EPPI Centre, 2009, w074). Organisations such as the EPPI-Centre have devised purpose-specific sets of keywords (EPPI Centre, 2003, w073). Alternatively you could devise your own keywords tailored to the purposes of your own review.

Table 4.5   Example of a descriptive map

EPPI-Centre team (2003) A systematic map and synthesis review of the effectiveness of personal development planning for improving student learning. EPPI-Centre, w077, Appendix 3.1).

First author and date	Educational setting(s)	Discipline	Course/ qualification	Country	Main features of PDP intervention	Context of learner using PDP
Abbas (1997)	HEI	Education: teacher training	Physical science course	USA	Learning logs/ journals/diaries	Course
					Reflective practice	
					Cooperative learning between students	
					Cooperative learning between student(s)/ teacher(s)	
Alderman (1993)	HEI	Psychology	BA/BSc	USA	Goal setting	Course
					Learning logs/ journals/diaries	
					Learner training	
					Self-assessment/ evaluation	
Alvarez (2000)	HEI	Cosmology	Summer school course in astronomy	USA	Independent/ autonomous learner	Course
					Learning logs/ journals/diaries	
					Problem-based learning	
					Reflective practice	
					Self-assessment/ evaluation	
					Cooperative learning between students	
					Cooperative learning between student(s)/ teacher(s)	

This descriptive map from the EPPI-Centre, is presented as a table, and assigns keywords of the main intervention for each included study. The review aimed to identify empirical research on Personal Development Planning (PDP) processes in higher and related education. This section of the map is created from 157 included studies. Note that the 'Main features of PDP intervention' are categorised by a set of standardised keywords.

Data mining

Data mining refers to the process of analysing data to identify patterns and correlations. It can be useful at various stages of the review – including scoping and determining the review question, mapping the volume and distribution of the literature, and identifying terminology (useful to inform search strategy). Various projects have been undertaken to investigate automatic ways of doing this (Malheiros et al., 2007) – including ASSERT (Automatic Summarisation for Systematic Reviews using Text Mining, w141) (Ananiadou et al., 2007, w003).

Tools for data mining

Scopus (w170) is a multi-disciplinary database (see Chapter 5 for more details) allowing you to refine search results by source (e.g. journal), author, year, affiliation, or subject area. This allows you to identify quickly the characteristics of the evidence base for a particular topic area. Categories for refining results are ranked in order, allowing you to see the top journals and authors in your field. It also possible to add further categories, such as language, document type, keyword, and source type.

Web of Knowledge (w200): Web of Knowledge provides access to multi-disciplinary databases including Web of Science (see Chapter 5 for more details). Search results can be refined by several categories including subject area, document type, source title (e.g. journal), and several others. There is also an advanced option to 'analyse results', where results can be ranked by various fields (for example source Title), allowing you to identify quickly the most common journals in your topic area. This function is available for other fields, such as author, document type, etc.

PubMed ReMiner (w159) searches PubMed on your research topic and ranks your results so you can see which journals, authors, and terms appear most frequently.

ALI BABA (w001) allows you to search PubMed and presents the results visually as a graph. Note you will need to download ALI BABA to your computer in order to use it.

Note: other data mining tools specifically for PubMed include:

MScanner (w139) – provides rapid statistical classification on the MEDLINE database of biomedical literature.

GoPubMed (w093) – uses MeSH terms to increase search possiblities. Results are clustered with results grouped according to MeSH subject headings. An advanced statistics module provides summary statistics for top authors, etc.

ClusterMed (w041) – Like GoPubMed (w093), ClusterMed provides a variety of categories to narrow down your searches to find papers on the topic that you are seeking.

Concept mapping

Concept mapping (sometimes know as **idea webbing**) can be useful in making sense of the 'messy nature of knowledge', w002). Rowley and Slack (2004, w165) list many benefits for using concept maps when planning a literature review, including:

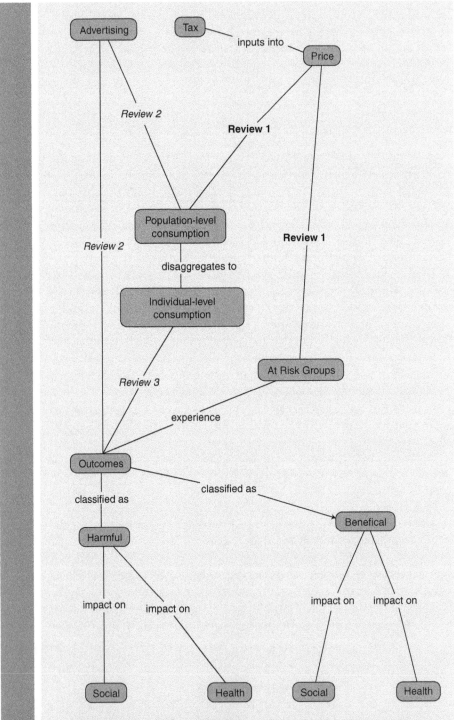

Figure 4.1   Example of a concept map

Booth, A., Meier, P., Stockwell, T., Sutton, A., Wilkinson, A., Wong, R., Brennan, A., O'Reilly, D., Purshouse, R., and Taylor, K. (2008) *Independent Review of the Effects of Alcohol Pricing and Promotion. Part A: Systematic Reviews.* Sheffield: University of Sheffield. (w020)

- identifying key concepts in a research area;
- identifying additional search terms;
- clarifying thinking about the structure of the literature review;
- understanding theory, concepts, and the relationships between them (Rowley and Slack, 2004, w165).

Tools for concept mapping

A **mind map** is a diagram used to represent words, ideas, tasks, or other concepts linked to, and arranged around, a central key word or idea. You can use free mind-mapping software to construct a **concept map**, including:

- FreeMind (w083)
- Freeplane (w084)
- SciPlore MindMapping (w168) (note this software is compatible with reference management software, such as Mendeley (w133)).
- XMind (w206)

Logic model

A logic model (also known as an impact model) is another type of concept map, originating from programme evaluation. Used widely in the field of health promotion, they are thought to be particularly useful in public health, by exploring complex relationships between practice (inputs and outputs) and outcomes (Baxter et al., 2010, w013).

Evaluation Support Scotland (2009) ESS Support Guide 1.2 – Developing a logic model (w080).

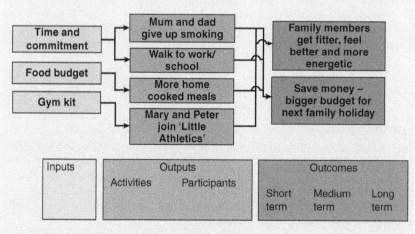

Figure 4.2   Example of a simple logic model

References

Alias, M. and Suradi, Z. (2008) Concept mapping: a tool for creating a literature review In: Canas, A.J. et al. (eds) *Concept Mapping: Connecting Educators.* Tallinn and Helsinki: The Second International Conference on Concept Mapping. (w002)

Ananiadou, S., Procter, R., Rea, B., Sasaki, Y., and Thomas, J. (2007) Supporting systematic reviews using text mining. Proceedings of the 3rd International Conference on e-Social Science, Ann Arbor, US. (w003)

Anderson, L.M., Shinn, C., Fullilove, M.T., Scrimshaw, S.C., Fielding, J.E., Normand, J., Carande-Kulis, V.G. and the Task Force on Community Preventive Services (2003) The effectiveness of early childhood development programs: A systematic review. *American Journal of Preventative Medicine,* **24**, 3S, 32–46. (w004)

Baxter, S., Killoran, A., Kelly, M.P., and Goyder, E (2010) Synthesizing diverse evidence: the use of primary qualitative data analysis methods and logic models in public health reviews. *Public Health,* **124**, 2, 99–106. (w013)

Booth, A. (2004) Formulating answerable questions In: Booth, A. and Brice, A. (eds) *Evidence Based Practice for Information Professionals: A Handbook.* London: Facet.

Booth, A. (2006) Clear and present questions: formulating questions for evidence based practice. *Library Hi tech,* **24**, 3, 355–68.

Bruce, C. (2001) Interpreting the scope of their literature reviews: significant differences in research students' concerns. *New Library World,* **102**, 158–65.

Counsell, C. (1997) Formulating questions and locating primary studies for inclusion in systematic reviews. *Annals of Internal Medicine,* **127**, 5, 380.

Denyer, D. and Tranfield, D. (2009) Producing a systematic review. In: Buchanan, D.A. and Bryman, A. (eds) *The Sage Handbook of Organizational Research Methods.* London: Sage, 671–89.

EPPI Centre (2003) Eppi-Centre Educational Keywording Sheet. EPPI Centre. 27 August 2010. (w073)

EPPI Centre (2009) Mapping and refining the review's scope. Social Science Research Unit, Institute of Education. (w074)

Grant, M.J. and Booth, A. (2009) A typology of reviews: an analysis of 14 review types and associated methodologies. *Health Information and Libraries Journal,* **26**, 2, 91–108. (w095)

Ibrahim, R. (2008) Setting up a research question for determining the research methodology. *ALAM CIPTA, International Journal on Sustainable Tropical Design Research and Practice,* **3**, 1, 99–102.

Kennedy, M.M. (2007) Defining a literature. *Educational Researcher,* **36**, 3, 139.

Khan, K.S., ter Rief, G., Glanville, J., Sowden, A.J., and Kleijnen, J. (2001) *Undertaking Systematic Reviews of Research on Effectiveness: CRD's Guidance for Those Carrying Out or Commissioning Reviews.* York: NHS Centre for Reviews and Dissemination, University of York.

Malheiros, V., Hohn, E., Pinho, R., Mendonça, M., and Maldonado, J.C. (2007) A visual text mining approach for systematic Reviews. In: ESEM '07: Proceedings of the First International Symposium on Empirical Software Engineering and Measurement, IEEE Computer Society, Washington, DC, USA, 245–54.

Matchar, D.B., Patwardhan, M., Sarria-Santamera, A., and Westermann-Clark, E.V. (2006) *Developing a Methodology for Establishing a Statement of Work for a Policy-Relevant Technical Analysis. Technical Review 11.* (Prepared by the Duke Evidence-based Practice Center under Contract No. 290-02-0025), Agency for Healthcare Research and Quality, Rockville, MD, AHRQ Publication No. 06-0026.

Oxman, A.D. and Guyatt, G.H. (1988) Guidelines for reading literature reviews. *CMAJ: Canadian Medical Association Journal,* **138**, 8, 697.

Petticrew, M. and Roberts, H. (2006) *Systematic Reviews in the Social sciences: A Practical Guide*. Malden, MA: Blackwell Publishing.

Richardson, W.S., Wilson, M.C., Nishikawa, J., and Hayward, R.S (1995) The well-built clinical question: a key to evidence-based decisions. *ACP Journal Club*, **123**, 3, A12.

Rowley, J. and Slack, F. (2004) Conducting a literature review. *Management Research News*, **27**, 6, 31–9. (w165)

Saunders, L. (2009) *The Policy and Organisational Context for Commissioned Research*. London: British Educational Research Association, TLRP 29 November 2010. (w167)

FIVE

Searching the literature

Learning Objectives

After reading this chapter, you should be able to:

- Translate your focused research question into its relevant search concepts.
- Understand what components can make a more systematic search.
- Devise a search strategy appropriate for searching identified sources.
- Identify appropriate sources of information to be searched.
- Use a number of techniques to make your search more systematic.
- Review and refine your search as necessary.

Introduction

Identification of evidence is a key component within any literature review and follows on from defining the scope of your review (Chapter 4). The purpose of the literature search is to identify information for your research topic. It also allows you to identify 'research gaps' enabling you to investigate a unique aspect of a topic. Literature searching can also help you to design the methodology for your own research by identifying techniques or methodologies most appropriate for your topic from the literature (Hart, 2002).

Searching the literature systematically entails more than seeking a quick answer from one or two selected articles. For whatever type of literature review you undertake, demonstrating that you have thoroughly searched for the evidence included in your review ultimately enhances the credibility of your review findings and conclusions.

Systematic literature search techniques optimise **sensitivity**; that is they maximise the chance of retrieving relevant items for your review. Of course, the downside to this approach is that whilst you reduce the risk of missing a relevant item, the number of irrelevant records you have to look through may increase. In contrast, whenever you are looking for a known item, you utilise techniques that optimise **specificity**; that is where you are unlikely to have to spend much time looking at irrelevant articles but there is a higher likelihood that you have missed some relevant ones.

This chapter covers the processes and methods that can make a literature search more systematic. A 'toolkit of techniques' is provided, from which you can select, depending on your topic and the degree to which you require your review to be systematic. The chapter draws upon methods used in a type of literature review called a **systematic review**. As discussed in Chapter 2, systematic reviews are types of literature review that aim to identify *all* the available evidence so as to reduce the effect of **bias** on the review findings. Methods for literature searching to identify evidence for systematic reviews of healthcare interventions were the first to be developed (Centre for Reviews and Dissemination, 2009, w036; Higgins and Green, 2008, w043); however, extensive guidance has also been developed for identification of evidence for systematic reviews of non-health topics such as the social sciences (Petticrew and Roberts, 2006). Similarly, whilst the guidance on systematic searching for health topics tends to focus on retrieval of quantitative evidence, now methods for identifying evidence for qualitative systematic reviews have been documented (Booth, 2009).

This chapter does not intend to teach you how to undertake a literature search for a systematic review. Rather by examining the ways in which systematic reviews identify evidence, it shows you how you can 'borrow' techniques to make the way in which you search the literature for your review more systematic, whatever the topic area. Depending on the purpose of your review, some techniques will be more appropriate than others. Nevertheless, carrying out a literature search in a more systematic manner will result in more comprehensive retrieval of literature; and therefore more meaningful and credible review findings that are less prone to **bias**.

The chapter starts by describing the five different stages in the search process and the different methods or techniques to systematically identify the evidence for a literature review. The next section considers the search methods in different types of literature reviews such as scoping, mapping, and systematic reviews (including qualitative reviews). This is followed by a practical section that demonstrates how to translate the clearly formulated research questions from Chapter 4 into a **search strategy**. Lastly, tools for the search process are examined. Throughout the chapter, examples from within different disciplines are referred to; however, it is useful to consider each section in the light of your own literature review topic.

Stages in the literature searching process

A systematic search necessitates the use of multiple approaches or techniques which may comprise some (but not always all) of the following major search strategies for locating references: (a) consultation with experts in the topic area, (b) searches in **subject indexes**, (c) browsing, (d) citation searches, and (e) footnote chasing (Wilson, 1992). This is not an exhaustive list and the approaches are not mutually exclusive; however, we will examine their use in the five distinct phases of the search process (see Table 5.1).

Table 5.1 The stages of the search process

Stage	Description	Steps
Stage 1	Initial search of the literature: **scoping search**	• Search for existing reviews and familiarise yourself with the topic and volume of literature by a scoping search on select databases • Determine which databases are to be included in the full search • Identify key search terms for each database • Develop and document a **search strategy**
Stage 2	Conduct search	• Search all databases using the identified search terms and the key search principles: **free-text** terms and tools, **thesaurus** terms, operators and limits • Conduct a search for unpublished or **grey literature** search • Consider the appropriateness of a **methodological filter** • Ensure if search is modified, this is documented
Stage 3	Bibliography search	• Search the reference lists and bibliographies of all papers for additional studies • Identify any key citations and conduct citation searches • Consider **hand searching** of relevant journals
Stage 4	Verification	• Check indexing of any relevant papers that have apparently been missed by search strategies • Revise search strategies if necessary • Consider contact with experts to determine if all relevant papers have been retrieved
Stage 5	Documentation	Record details such as the sources searched, search strategies used, and number of references found for each source/method of searching

---

Box 5.1   An important reminder

Remember, this chapter is not telling you that in order to carry out a systematic search you have to use every single one of these techniques! It is true that by using all the techniques described in this chapter, there is less risk of missing a relevant study for your review. However, you have to weigh up these techniques in relation to the purpose of your review. The approaches used in different types of literature review are covered later in the chapter.

Stage 1: Scoping search

To begin with it is helpful to undertake a **scoping search**. This is a preliminary search that identifies any existing reviews and gives an indication of the existing quantity and quality of **primary studies** relevant to the objectives of your review. The scoping search is ideally performed on a selection of core **electronic databases** (see Sources section) relevant to your topic area. Therefore, if your topic is multidisciplinary, then your scoping search will want to purposively sample from a range of subject disciplines. The scoping search process starts by using the brainstorming terms for each of the concepts included in the focused question as devised in Chapter 4.

Key sources or databases for a scoping search

Consider which are the key sources or databases that would be useful for a scoping search for your research question.

Results from the scoping search can help you to focus or refocus your literature review. Whilst viewing the titles, abstracts, subject headings and keyword descriptors of relevant citations, you can refine your search strategy to make it as comprehensive (i.e. sensitive) as possible. The scoping process, therefore, enables you to begin developing the search strategy to be used in conducting the search itself (Stage 2). After completing the scoping search, you will have identified key search terms for each database and drawn up a list of databases to search. It is important at this stage to document your search strategy, as this will help you in writing up your methodology. See the 'Stage 5: documenting your search' section of this chapter for information on the search details to document.

Pearl-growing is one way of starting off the development of your search strategy. This refers to identifying a known highly relevant article (the pearl) to isolate terms (both **free-text** and **thesaurus** – these different ways of searching are examined later in Stage 2 of the search process) on which a search can subsequently be based. If no initial article is available, you can conduct a precise search, such as a title search, to identify a key reference. This procedure may be repeated several times until no further relevant terms are identified. The technique assumes that articles on the same topic are indexed on a database in the same way (this may not always be the case). Figure 5.1 describes an example of using the process of pearl growing to identify relevant articles for the research question, 'What is the

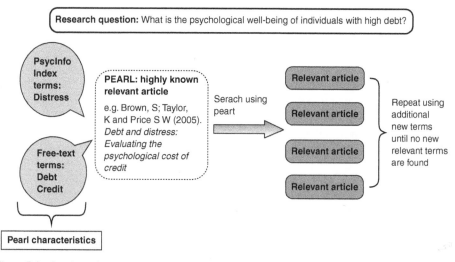

Figure 5.1   Pearl growing

psychological well-being of individuals with high debt?' A relevant article by Brown et al. (2005) yields the free-text search terms 'debt' and 'credit'. In addition, the article/pearl is indexed in the PsycInfo database under the term 'Distress'. These terms can then be used to search for further articles that are likely to be relevant and match our research question.

Stage 2: Conduct the search

By this stage, you should have a fairly well-defined list of search terms. These need to be organised into a search strategy. During Stage 2, you will probably need to modify your defined search strategy on each database that you have chosen to search. In addition, you will need to consider other potential sources of studies for your review such as reference list checking and contact with experts (see Stages 3 and 4). Some methods of searching to assist with Stage 2 are described in the following paragraph:

Free text searching

Electronic databases typically allow **free-text** searching. This approach uses **text-words** found in fields such as the title and abstract. The drawbacks of this approach are well-documented, such as the problems associated with different spellings (e.g. organisation or organization) and different terminology (e.g. young person, adolescent, teenager, youth, child, children, etc.). Fortunately, many databases offer features such as **truncation** ('*' or '$') and **wildcard** ('?') symbols. Searching on teenage*, for example, would retrieve records containing the words, teenage, teenager, teenagers. Check the help pages on each database you are searching to find out if these techniques are available and the relevant symbols you should use.

Thesaurus searching

A **thesaurus** (or **controlled vocabulary**) is a list of terms produced by librarians and database indexers. The terms are called subject headings or descriptors. They are used to apply consistent subject headings to articles which describe the same concept, but in a variety of ways. For example, the term 'reiki' translates to the MeSH term 'therapeutic touch' on the MEDLINE (w131) database. In ASSIA, the index term 'prisons' is used for 'jail', 'gaols', or 'penitentiaries'. Such preferred terms also take into account plurals and variable spellings. Some, although not all, databases, provide a thesaurus. Examples of databases with thesauri are MEDLINE (w131) and the Cochrane Library (w044) which both use thesauri called MeSH, Embase (EMTREE), ASSIA, ERIC (w079). See Figure 5.2 for an example of thesaurus searching. Most thesauri are arranged hierarchically, with:

- Broader, more general subject headings at the top,
- Narrower, more specific subject headings indexed underneath them,
- Related terms with similar definitions may also be indexed under the same broader subject heading.

Typically, a thesaurus allows you to select subject terms from a hierarchical vocabulary; related terms are also suggested which may be worth searching in their

Population interested in = Teenagers
ASSIA Thesaurus term = Adolescents
[+} indicates there are narrower terms below the term.

Adolescents [+]   (Use For Teenagers)
Broader Terms= Children [+]
Narrower Terms=

- Autistic adolescents
- Behaviour disordered adolescents
- Blind adolescents
- Conduct-disordered adolescents
- Deaf adolescents
- Developmentally-disabled adolescents
- Disadvantaged adolescents
- Emotionally-disturbed adolescents
- Gifted adolescents [+]
- Hearing-impaired adolescents
- Hyperactive adolescents
- Learning-disabled adolescents
- Low-intelligence quotient adolescents
- Reading-disabled adolescents [+]
- Runaway adolescents [+]
- Sexually-abused adolescents
- Sick adolescents
- Special-needs adolescents
- Violent adolescents
- Visually impaired adolescents

Figure 5.2   Example of thesaurus searching

own right. A thesaurus may contain the actual term for which you intend to search; if not, you can search the thesaurus to find its closest match (see Figure 5.2). Your chosen thesaurus term can then be used as one of your search terms to retrieve records to which the selected thesaurus term has been assigned as a descriptor.

Thesaurus searching is a very effective way of searching a database, but some concepts may be absent from thesauri. For example, new concepts (e.g. 'credit crunch') and those specific to a particular country's administration (e.g. county councils in UK local government) may not appear in a globally used thesaurus. In such instances, a textword or free text search should also be carried out. An optimal and comprehensive search strategy will combine both free text and thesaurus terms. Remember thesauri terms vary between databases which will mean your search strategy will need to be revised for each database.

EXERCISE 5.1

Thesaurus searching

Using an appropriate database for your discipline (see Table 5.4 for subject coverage), find appropriate thesaurus terms for the following concepts:

Database	Concept	Thesaurus Term
ASSIA	Neighbourhood watch	
	Lifelong learning	
	Foster care	
ERIC (w079)	Computer based learning	
	English as a foreign language	
	Peer harassment	
LISA	Outreach librarian	
	Information retrieval	
	Dewey	
MEDLINE (w131)	Prozac	
	Shingles	
	Cost effectiveness	

HINT – if you are not sure, view the scope note/description of thesaurus terms to make a judgement on their relevance to the concept.

Boolean, adjacency and proximity operators

Once you have devised a focused question and brainstormed terms for each concept within your search strategy, **Boolean logic** can be used to combine terms together appropriately. Whilst sounding complicated, the use of **Boolean logic** to devise a search strategy is really very simple and easy to learn. Hart (2002) explains **Boolean logic** as a way of 'adding to, subtracting from and multiplying your search terms in order to expand (add), narrow (subtract), or include terms (multiply or combine) to your search'. In practical terms, this means using the **Boolean operators: AND, OR** and **NOT** to define how you want the databases to combine your individual search terms together. When constructing a search, remember the following rules:

1 OR is used to combine terms within the same concept together (e.g. child* OR adolescent* OR teenage*), thus expanding the search.
2 AND is used to combine different concepts together (e.g. child* AND inequalit*), thus narrowing the search by combining terms.
3 NOT is used to exclude irrelevant terms (e.g. NOT letter*), thus narrowing the search by removing terms.

To get a clearer idea of how AND, OR, and NOT are used within search strategies, take a look at the search strategies in the 'Translating your search question' section of this chapter.

Many databases allow you to specify how closely two or more words are positioned relative to each other by using operators to specify that terms must be near each other (**proximity**) or directly next to each other (**adjacency**) (see Figure 5.3 for examples). Again, you should check the help pages of databases to clarify which operators a particular database uses.

ADJ# (where #= number of words), two or more words within the same field in any order (MEDLINE (w131), Embase, PsycInfo via OVID)

NEXT finds adjacent terms (The Cochrane Library, w044)

NEAR/# (where #= number of words), two or more words within the same field in any order (The Cochrane Library, w044))

SAME finds two or more words in the same sentence (Web of Knowledge)

"exact phrase": use inverted commas to search for an exact phrase (ASSIA)

Figure 5.3 Examples of proximity and adjacency operators

Limits

Most databases will provide a **limit function**, with the most common way of limiting a search being by publication year and/or language. Ideally, searching should not be limited to the English language; however, resources for translation are frequently limited and this will often prevent you pursuing such an option for a thesis or dissertation.

Another way of restricting a search is by limiting to specific publication and/or study types which will often prove effective. MEDLINE (w131) for example, allows you to limit searches by publication type (PT), while the Citation Indexes (Web of Science) offer the option of limiting to various document types, including 'article' and 'review'. ERIC (w079) allows limitation to documentation types such as 'dissertations' and 'opinion papers' and 'journal articles'. If you do decide to limit by publication type, be sure that you know how each publication or document type has been defined.

Searching the grey literature

As well as searching the published literature, it is useful to attempt to find and include possibly relevant but not fully published studies within a systematic literature review. **Grey literature** is defined as 'Information produced on all levels of government, academics, business and industry in electronic and print formats not controlled by commercial publishing, i.e. where publishing is not the primary activity of the producing body' (GreyNet, 2008). This literature is referred to as the grey or fugitive literature owing to the fact it is sometimes difficult to identify and obtain.

The rationale of searching the grey literature is to minimise [g]**publication bias**. McAuley and colleagues (2000) examined a random sample of systematic reviews in a range of disease areas. Thirty-three per cent of the systematic reviews contained both grey and published studies. Generally, published studies showed larger effects of the intervention when compared with grey literature, thus demonstrating that the exclusion of grey literature from systematic reviews can lead to exaggerated estimates of intervention effectiveness (McAuley et al., 2000). Within the social sciences, the need for searching the grey literature is even more apparent since a vast quantity of evidence exists in practitioner journals, books, and reports from public, private and voluntary sector bodies as well as official publications (Grayson and Gomersall, 2003, w096);Young et al., 2002). The proliferation of new material which had been enhanced by the Internet makes searching for evidence difficult (Grayson and Gomersall, 2003, w096).

Sources of grey literature in all its forms include research registers for ongoing research, e.g. in the UK: UK Clinical Research (UKCRN) Study Portfolio (w195) and Current Controlled Trials (w059), governmental or quasi-governmental organisations for reports and guidance (National Institute for Health and Clinical Excellence (NICE) (w143)), specialist library catalogues or databases for reports (Health Management Information Consortium (HMIC)), Social care online (w173), conference abstracts for ongoing or unpublished literature (conference proceedings indices, conference websites in your chosen field), dissertations and theses (Dissertation Abstracts, Index to theses (w108)) and appropriate websites in the field of interest, for example in social research from the Joseph Rowntree Foundation (w114) .

Stage 3: Bibliographic searching

Checking bibliographies and reference lists

Since electronic searching may still miss important published studies, particularly when concepts are hard to define or where the level of indexing has been superficial, further steps need to be taken to ensure identification of studies. One simple way of doing this is to examine the bibliographies or reference lists of all relevant retrieved studies to check that nothing has been missed. It may also be useful to check the reference lists of existing reviews. Several studies have demonstrated the importance of reference list checking for identification of further studies for inclusion in reviews (Brettle and Long, 2001; Greenhalgh and Peacock, 2005; McNally and Alborz, 2004; Papaioannou et al., 2010; Stevinson and Lawlor, 2004).

Citation searching

Citation searching focuses on following a chain of references that cite one or more earlier studies. The citation search begins by identifying an influential article on a given topic. Next, a database with the facility for citation searching (e.g. Social Science Citation Index, SSCI) is used to locate all articles referred to by this key article. Once additional materials have been located, this process can be repeated (**snowballing**) using the new materials as the starting point for additional citation searches. As such, citation searching is extremely useful for tracing the development of a body of literature. In contrast to most other search strategies, both recall and precision tend to be high for well-constructed citation searches. Again, this technique has been shown to identify studies missed from the main bibliographic search (Brettle and Long, 2001; McNally and Alborz, 2004; Papaioannou et al., 2010).

Author searching

Where a particular author has been influential or prolific in your area of interest, **author searching** may be useful and allows searches to be conducted on specifically named authors. Whilst useful to identify literature, author searching can result in a biased sample of references, perhaps reflecting only one line of argument.

Hand searching

Some topics may be concentrated in a few key journals or may be inconsistently indexed or not indexed at all by the databases being searched. This may require **hand searching** of key journals in the field, examining the contents pages of individual journals (electronically or by hand). A **Cochrane Review** of studies compared the results of hand searching with the results of searching one or more electronic databases (Hopewell et al., 2009). Hand searching found between 92 per cent to 100 per cent of the total number of reports of randomised controlled trials and was particularly useful in finding trials reported as abstracts, letters, and those published in languages other than English as well as articles in journals not indexed in electronic databases. In areas where the research question is less well-defined, hand searching has also been shown to be useful (Armstrong et al., 2005). However, hand searching is very time consuming and should be used sparingly. Greenhalgh and Peacock (2005) found that in searching for a systematic review of complex evidence, 24 papers identified from hand searching made the final report. It took a month to complete the hand-search, and thus an average of one paper per nine hours of searching was included in the review. They also found that other supplementary methods such as reference list checking and citation searching proved much more fruitful and less time intensive for their diffuse topic (Greenhalgh and Peacock, 2005).

Stage 4: Verification

Consultation with experts

Consultation involves locating references by corresponding with others. It tends to be a low-recall strategy, since it is limited by the knowledge, memory, and biases of correspondents. Conversely, it is generally high in precision because the references provided have been pre-screened for relevance. A major advantage of consultation is the ability to locate unpublished materials. Internet technology (e.g. e-mail, discussion groups) has greatly increased the utility of consultation as a search technique. Consulting experts in your topic area (perhaps your supervisor or tutor) provides validation that relevant studies have been found and instils confidence that the efforts to identify such studies have been wide-ranging and encompassing (Ogilvie et al., 2005; Petticrew and Roberts, 2006). For example, contact with experts yielded two additional unique studies for inclusion in a review of the student experience of e-learning that might otherwise have been missed (Papaioannou et al., 2010).

Indexing and revision

If you subsequently discover that you have missed one or more relevant articles for your review in Stage 2, it may be necessary to consider revising your search strategy. First, you need to find out if the articles that were missed are actually indexed within your selected databases. If they are indexed, examining the descriptors and **free-text** terms assigned to the missed articles will help to identify terms that you can incorporate within your revised search strategy. If the articles that were missed are not indexed, it may be necessary to use additional search techniques such as browsing of contents pages, citation searching or checking of reference lists.

Stage 5: Documenting your search

Whilst you may not use all the search techniques discussed in this chapter so far, all literature reviews should provide an accurate account of the process that was undertaken to identify evidence for the review. By describing exactly what sources were searched and with which search terms, as well as recording other techniques used to locate evidence (e.g. checking of reference lists), you will fulfil two criteria of a systematic search: transparency and reproducibility. In this way, readers know exactly what you did to find the evidence for your review and also, in theory, should be able to repeat the process for themselves.

It is a good idea to document your search process as you go along so that you are easily able to write up the literature search methodology for your review. Details to record include the sources searched, search strategies used, and number of references found for each source/method of searching. Many databases allow you to save your search strategy online and to generate an electronic copy of the strategy (typically as a text file to be copied and pasted into a Word document). The **PRISMA** (Preferred Reporting Items for Systematic reviews and Meta-Analyses) statement (w158) (Moher et al., 2009, w137) aims to help authors improve the reporting of systematic reviews and meta-analyses. The 27-item checklist included in the PRISMA statement (w158) contains two items relating to the documentation of the literature search in a systematic review or meta-analysis (Box 5.2). Chapter 9 discusses additional items included in the PRISMA statement (w158).

Box 5.2   Items from the PRISMA statement relating to searching

The PRISMA statement is a published reporting standard for systematic reviews and meta-analyses. These two items from the PRISMA statement specifically deal with reporting the literature searching methods.

Item 7: Information sources

Describe all information sources (e.g. databases with dates of coverage, contact with study authors to identify additional studies) in the search and the date last searched.

Item 8: Search

Present full electronic search strategy for at least one database, including any limits used, such that it could be repeated.

Source: the PRISMA Statement (w158)

Other standards have been proposed for the reporting of literature searches, including the STARLITE mnemonic (sampling strategy, type of study, approaches, range of years, limits, inclusion and exclusions, terms used, electronic sources) (Booth, 2006, w179).

EXERCISE 5.2

Case study of the search process

Table 5.2 provides details of the methods of identifying literature for a systematic litera-ture review looking at 'Childhood disadvantage and health inequalities' (Attree, 2008, w009). A total of 11,224 primary data sources (e.g. articles, book chapters, reports, etc.) were retrieved. Consider Table 5.2 and then try to answer the following questions.

Questions:

1 How would you rate this search in terms of the number and types of sources searched? Is this adequate?
2 What disadvantages are there in the author's search approach?
3 What aspects of the search process in the case study might be applied to your own review?

Types of literature reviews

Remember that systematic approaches to reviewing the literature do not neces-sarily require that you conduct a full-blown systematic review-style search! The search techniques you choose and the breadth of approach will depend on the type of literature review you undertake, which in turn will be guided by the review's aim. For example, a **systematic review** aims to be exhaustive and

Table 5.2   Anatomy of the search process

Focused review question	Description of review	Details of the search process used in this review
Setting: living in disadvantage **Population:** children and young people **Intervention:** resources and strategies to help children and young people **Comparison** – none **Evaluation:** through qualitative evidence of the children and young people's perspective	The objective of this systematic review was to identify, critically appraise and synthesise qualitative studies of children's accounts of living in disadvantage. Nine studies were identified in which the main sources of support described by disadvantaged children and young people were their families, friendships, and social networks in neighbourhoods. Conflicts existed between the different sources of support, which could also be a sources of psychosocial stress. Informal sources of support alone are likely to prove inadequate for disadvantaged children and young people.	Stage 1: initial search of the literature (scoping search) A pilot search was carried out in ASSIA to test the sensitivity and specificity of the search strategy prior to the main search. Stage 2: conduct search • Searches were carried out in 17 electronic databases, including IBSS, Ingenta, PsychINFO, ASSIA, and the Social Science Citation Index. • Conducted a search for grey literature: Dissertation Abstracts International (US), Index to theses (UK) (w108), SIGLE (w172), HMIC and Zetoc. • Comprehensive search strategy used including terms for the setting, population, intervention and type of study* Stage 3: Bibliography search • Reference lists of identified studies were scanned • Selected journals were hand searched Websites such as Google (w091), BUBL (w026), SOSIG (w177) were searched using key terms Stage 4: Verification • Experts in poverty and health inequalities research were consulted • Research networks were contacted resulting in number of useful leads.

comprehensive in its identification of literature and thus adopts an exhaustive search process. In the systematic review example in Table 5.3, Webb and colleagues (2009) searched seven electronic databases, checked reference lists of included studies, and contacted experts in order to identify studies for a systematic review of workplace interventions for alcohol-related problems. In comparison, a **scoping review** may seek to provide a preliminary assessment of the potential scope and size of the available and size in a topic area and thus adopt a less exhaustive approach. In our example of a scoping review (Table 5.3), the review authors limited their approach to identifying evidence for the review by searching only key databases within the field (although in this instance this was still 10 databases!) and searched for ongoing research. It is interesting to note that although the authors did not use additional methods to identify evidence such as reference list checking and contact with experts, the search approach used was well-documented, transparent, and thus entirely reproducible.

Table 5.3 also explores the appropriate literature searching methods for different types of review. Each review type is defined and guidance is suggested on the types of literature search methods to be used. These are categorised as 'definitely use' (e.g. essential for this type of review), 'consider using' (e.g. this may or may not be appropriate, depending on your review question and scope), and 'not essential' (not usually a necessary method for this type of review). Note that it is difficult to stipulate what methods should be used within a type of review as this will largely be determined by the topic area of your review and the aim of the review. Try to think about what each technique may bring to your literature search, both in terms of positive aspects and negative aspects – this will help you weigh up which techniques to use.

Table 5.3   Types of review

Type of review	Search methods			Example
	Definitely use ✓	Consider using ?	Not essential X	
Scoping review: – Aims to identify key research in the topic area. – May restrict the number of sources searched to key ones in topic discipline(s). – Often involves an assessment of ongoing research.	– Database searching	– Grey literature – Ongoing research	– Reference list checking – Citation searching – Hand searching – Contact with experts	Kavanagh et al. (2005). A scoping review of the evidence for incentive schemes to encourage positive health and other social behaviours in young people (w117). This review undertook comprehensive searching of 10 databases covering the disciplines relating to the topic area. In addition, there was a thorough attempt to identify ongoing research/projects. This search is well-documented and the process for identifying evidence is transparent.
Mapping review: – Several examples exist of exhaustive, comprehensive searching in mapping reviews. – It would be reasonable to use any/all of the techniques (as guided by your topic area and/or aim of review).	– Database searching – Grey literature – Reference list checking – Citation searching	– Grey literature – Hand searching – Contact with experts – Ongoing research		Graham–Matheson et al. (2006) A systematic map into approaches to making initial teacher training flexible and responsive to the needs of trainee teachers (w094). This review undertook several different approaches to identify evidence including comprehensive database searching, hand searching of journals, contact with experts, citation searching and reference list checking. This search is well-documented and the process for identifying evidence is transparent.

(Continued)

Table 5.3   (Continued)

Type of review	Search methods			Example
	Definitely use ✓	Consider using ?	Not essential X	
Systematic review: – Exhaustive, comprehensive searching – use all search techniques available.	– Database searching – Grey literature – Reference list checking – Citation searching – Hand searching – Contact with experts – Ongoing research			Webb et al. (2009). A systematic review of work–place interventions for alcohol–related problems. This review demonstrates a systematic literature search both in practice and in the reporting. A variety of sources were searched and search terms were adapted for each database. The search strategies used for each database are presented. Additional search methods were also used; networking with colleagues and checking the reference lists of the studies found in the electronic searches. Searches were limited to papers published between 1995 and 2007. This paper presents the search method in a flowchart diagram and well as describing the search within the text. This is commonly seen in systematic reviews.
Qualitative systematic review: – May employ selective or purposive sampling. – Database searching may be limited to key databases. – More emphasis may be placed on using other search techniques (such as citation searching and contact with experts).	– Database searching – Grey literature – Reference list checking – Citation searching – Contact with experts	– Hand searching – Ongoing research		Duggan and Banwell (2004). Constructing a model of effective information dissemination in a crisis (w064). This review demonstrates an extensive search of a variety of sources, including electronic databases, web resources, and other sources of grey literature. In addition, hand searching of a key journal was carried out and checking of the reference lists of relevant papers. A full search strategy is an omission from the paper.

Translating your search question

Using a variety of topics and databases, this section presents some worked examples of how to derive a search strategy from a focused research question.

EXERCISE 5.3

Examining search strategies

Look at each search strategy in turn, and consider the following:

- How would you rate the search strategy? Have the concepts of the research question (e.g. population, intervention/exposure, outcome(s), etc.) been successfully translated into search terms? Are there any other search terms that you might have included?
- What types of searching (e.g. thesaurus searching, **free-text** searching) have been used and are these appropriate?
- Which search tools have been used (Boolean operators, truncation, etc.)? Have these been used successfully?

NB – please note that these example searches were conducted in July 2010, so re-running the search at a later date may produce a different number of results.

Research question A

Is the location of schools near to electromagnetic fields from electricity pylons liable to have adverse health effects on schoolchildren?

Suggested search strategy (superimposed boxed text added):

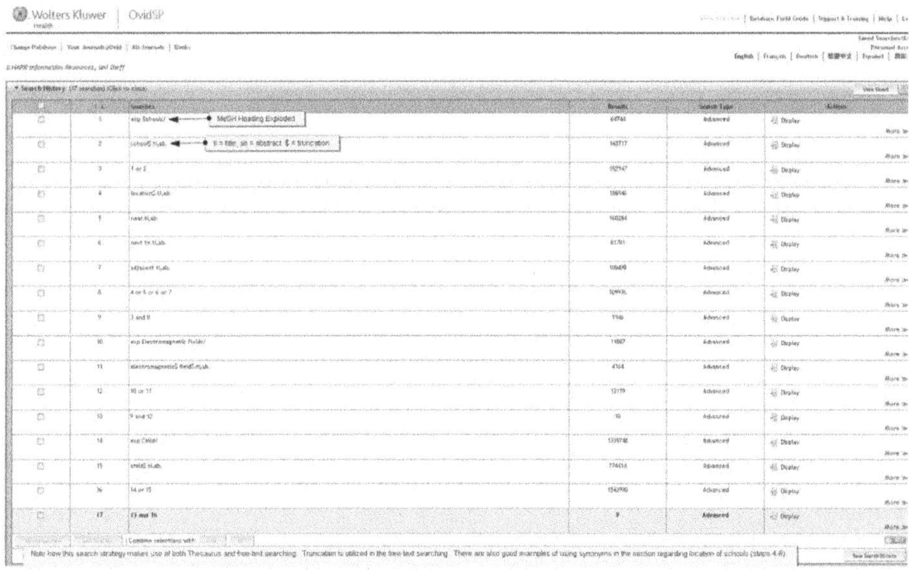

Figure 5.2

Research question B

Do ICT interventions improve primary schoolchildren's performance in solving maths problems?

Suggested search strategy:

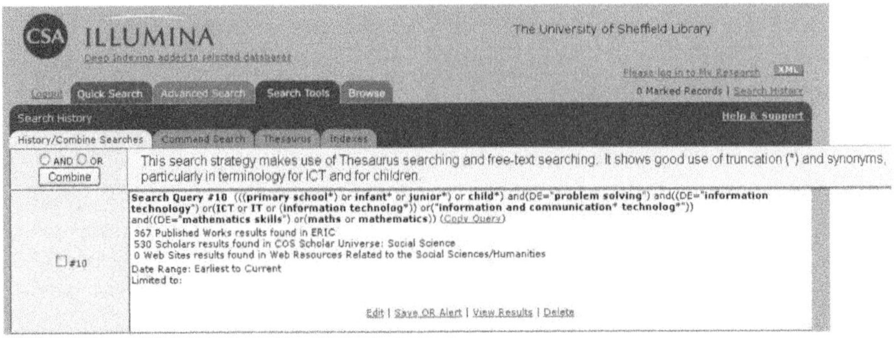

Figure 5.3

The screen shot and its contents are published with permission of ProQuest LLC. Further reproduction is prohibited without permission.

Research question C

Is the provision of solar-powered cars likely to result in benefits to society in an industrialised nation?

NB – this search has focused on environmental and financial benefits.

Suggested search strategy:

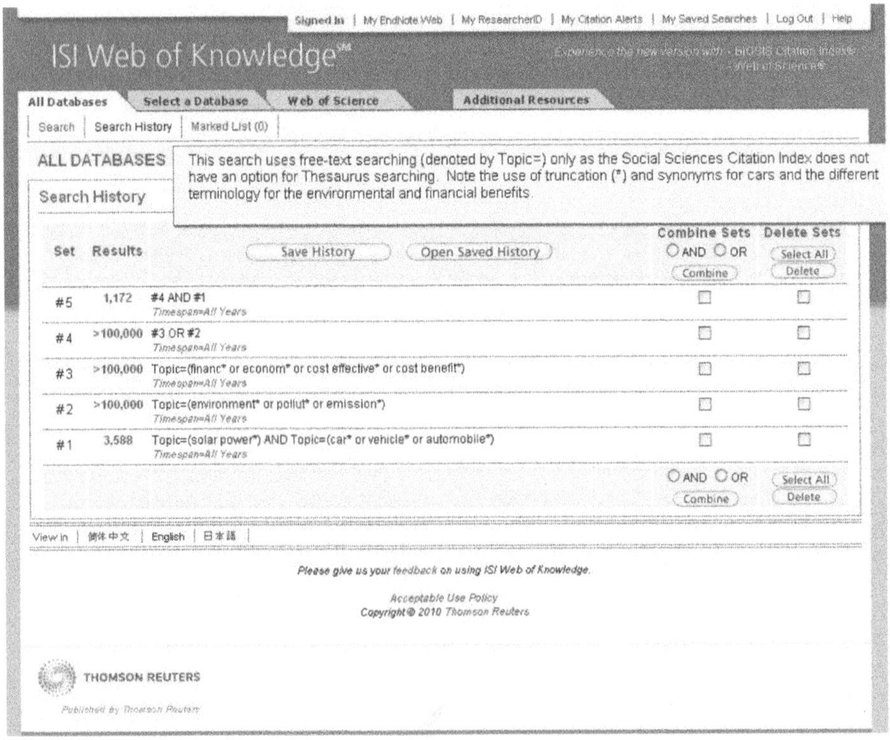

Figure 5.4   (Web of Science® via the Thomson Reuters Web of Knowledge℠)

Research question D

Is early discharge of stroke patients from hospital into the community more effective than standard hospital care?

Suggested search strategy (superimposed box text added):

Figure 5.5

Note how this search demonstrates the use of a search filter (Steps 9–40) (Scottish Intercollegiate Guidelines Network, 2010) (see accompanying tools section of this chapter), in this case to limit the search to retrieve systematic reviews only. Steps 1–3 are the population terms (stroke patients) and steps 5–6 are the intervention (hospital (early) discharge). The search makes use of **thesauri** and **free-text** searching and truncation ($).

APPLY WHAT YOU HAVE LEARNT 5.1

Start to plan your literature search

Practise yourself by working through the following questions.
Think ...

- about the purpose of your review – how systematic does your search need to be to fulfil the purpose of your review?
- about your focused question – what types of databases may index articles on your topic area? What terms might describe each of the concepts in your focused question?
- do you know of any key citations or authors in your topic area? (Hint: ideally these papers should have been published between five and ten years ago in order to have accrued sufficient impact.)

Decide on the following ...

- database sources to search, including sources of unpublished or grey literature;
- additional searching techniques: reference list checking, contact with experts, citation searching;
- brainstorm search terms for each concept within your focused question – think of all the synonyms;
- identify thesaurus terms for your search terms;
- include free-text terms where appropriate;
- combine your search terms using an appropriate operator.

APPLY WHAT YOU HAVE LEARNT 5.2

Pearl growing and author searching

In the grid provided list three or four key citations that might be regarded as useful 'pearls' in your topic area. List authors or institutions that might have conducted research studies in your topic area.

Candidate pearls: Candidate authors or institutions for author searching:

1   1
2   2
3   3
4   4

Sources to search

List the different sources that would be useful to search for your chosen review topic area. Check your list with a local librarian/information specialist.

Databases

1
2
3
4
5
6
7
8
9
10

Grey literature

1
2
3
4
5

Journals

1
2
3
4

Experts

1
2
3

At the end of Chapter 4, Defining the scope, you will have defined your research question as concepts and brainstormed **synonyms** for each concept. The next stage is to identify **thesaurus** and **free-text terms** for each synonym within a concept. Once you have derived a set of terms for each concept, you need to assemble your search strategy using the steps outlined in Box 5.3.

Box 5.3   Assembling your search strategy

1   Combine terms within the same concept (e.g. all population search terms) using OR; and terms for different concepts (e.g. population AND intervention terms) with AND.
2   First combine Population AND Intervention/Exposure terms to refine your strategy.
3   If your search result set is unmanageable, combine Population AND Intervention/ Exposure AND Outcome terms.
4   If your search result set is unmanageable, combine Population AND Intervention/ Exposure AND Outcome terms AND Comparison terms.

NB: If your search does not fit a 'PICOC' question (see Chapter 4), carry out the same process with the headings for the method you used to define your question (e.g. SPICE), brainstorming terms, and combining together in a similar way.

**Tip, if you're struggling to assemble a search, take a look at the examples in the Translating your search question section for guidance.

Summary

Systematically searching the literature ensures you identify relevant studies for your research question. The breadth and type of approach you take will be dependent on the type of review being undertaken and the topic area of your review. This chapter has outlined the five key stages in the literature search and techniques to be used to make your literature search more systematic. Identifying the evidence for your review may include: scoping searching; conducting the search proper; further search techniques such as reference list checking; citation searching and hand searching; search verification and search documentation. Database tools such as **thesaurus** searching, **free-text** searching, **Boolean operators** and application of limits will help in the development of a search strategy for electronic databases. The sources to search will be informed by your subject area, and may include electronic databases, national registries of ongoing research, websites and conference proceedings. Central to the process of systematically reviewing the literature is your research question and your search approach must be fit for purpose (e.g. according to review type) and designed to identify the studies to answer your research question. It is good practice for all types of literature review to report the ways in which they have identified evidence in a transparent manner so that it is possible for someone else to reproduce the process from the methods described.

Key learning points

1 Pre-plan your search and carry out a scoping search.
2 Ensure that you are clear about the search parameters, such as whether you are aiming for sensitivity or specificity.
3 Select the most appropriate sources to search.
4 Take into account limitations of the literature, such as inconsistent terminology and problematic indexing, and brainstorm alternative search terms.
5 Select the most appropriate search techniques for the sources that you have chosen (e.g. is it appropriate to use search filters?).
6 Employ more than one search approach (e.g. citation searching as well as traditional database searching).
7 Evaluate your search results, modify your search strategies accordingly and be sure to document the search process!

Suggestions for further reading

Aveyard, H. (2010) How do I search for literature? In: Aveyard, H. (ed.) *Doing a Literature Review in Health and Social Care: A Practical Guide*, 2nd edn. Maidenhead: Open University Press: 68–88.

Beverley, C.A. (2004) Searching the library and information science literature. In: Booth, A. and Brice, A. (eds) *Evidence Based Practice for Information Professionals: A Handbook.* London: Facet Publishing, 89–103.

The Campbell Collaboration Library of Systematic Reviews (2010). (w030)

Centre for Reviews and Dissemination (2009) Section 1.3.1: identifying research evidence for systematic reviews. In: *Systematic Reviews: CRD's Guidance for Undertaking Reviews in Healthcare*, 3rd edn. York: Centre for Reviews and Dissemination. (w036)

Chartered Society of Physiotherapists (2005) CSP Guide to Searching the Literature. (w038)

The EPPI-Centre (2010) *Searching for Studies.* (w076).

The Open University (n.d.) Searching the literature. (w146)

Lefebvre, C., Manheimer, E., and Glanville, J. (2009) Searching for studies. In: Higgins, J.P.T. and Green S. (eds) *Cochrane Handbook for Systematic Reviews of Interventions.* Version 5.0.2 (updated September 2009). Oxford: Cochrane Collaboration. (w043)

Petticrew, M. and Roberts, H. (2006) How to find the studies: the literature search. In: Petticrew, M. and Roberts, H. (eds) *Systematic Reviews in The Social Sciences: A Practical Guide*. Malden, MA: Blackwell Publishing, 79–124.

Ridley, D. (ed.) (2008) Sources of information and conducting searches. In: *The Literature Review: A Step-by-Step Guide for Students*. London: Sage, 29–43.

Tools for successful searching

While many resources are available to help with the process of literature searching this tools section focuses on those which may be most useful in the context of a literature review project. These include various database sources and specialist sources of **grey literature**, **search filters** and software for **reference management**. However, to emphasise that a literature review is typically a cooperative endeavour we start, close to home, with your local librarian or information specialist.

Your local librarian/information specialist

Carrying out a systematic literature search may appear daunting. There are many choices to make regarding how broad to make a search, what databases to search, and what search techniques to use. So don't forget to ask a specialist! If you have access to an academic library, make use of the librarian or information specialist. They'll be able to advise you on how best to search the literature according to your topic area and purpose of your review.

Sources

Table 5.4 lists some common electronic databases (by subject area) together with sources of grey literature. Most electronic databases provide a free guide to searching on the database, providing hints, tips, and sometimes tutorials on searching as well as explaining the individual features of the database.

Table 5.4   Electronic databases: subject specific

Database	Coverage
Health	
Allied and Complementary Medicine Database (AMED)	Professions allied to medicine
	Alternative and complementary medicine
	Palliative care
BIOSIS	Biology and biomedical sciences (including botany, zoology, microbiology, biomedical science, ecology, biotechnology, biophysics, biochemistry and agriculture)
British Nursing Index	Nursing and midwifery
Cinahl	Nursing and allied health
The Cochrane Library (w044) includes:	
Cochrane Database of Systematic Reviews (CDSR)	Cochrane systematic reviews and protocols
Cochrane Central Register of Controlled Trials (CENTRAL)	Controlled trials included in Cochrane systematic reviews
Centre for Reviews and Dissemination Databases (w035) includes:	
Database of Abstracts of Reviews of Effects (DARE)	Abstracts of systematic reviews including quality assessment of reviews.
Health Technology Assessment database (HTA)	Health technology assessments from around the world
NHS economic evaluation database (NHS EED)	Health economic papers including economic evaluations

Database	Coverage
Embase	Biomedical and pharmacological sciences, as well as general medicine
MEDLINE (w131)	General medical and biomedical sciences. Includes medicine, dentistry, nursing, allied health
PsycInfo	Psychology and related fields
Social sciences	
ASSIA	Social sciences, includes sociology, psychology and some anthropology, economics, medicine, law and politics
Campbell Library (w030)	Systematic reviews of the effects of social interventions produced by the Campbell Collaboration. Includes Social Welfare, Crime and Justice, Education
International Bibliography of Social Sciences	Social sciences including economics, sociology, politics and anthropology
Sociological abstracts	Sociology and related disciplines
Social Science Citation Index	Social sciences
Social care	
Social care online (replaced Caredata) (w173)	Social work and community care
Social services abstracts	Social work, human services, and related areas
Social work abstracts	Social work and human services
Education	
Australian Education index	Education (Australia)
British Education Index	Education (Europe)
Education Resources Information Centre (ERIC) (w079)	Education (US emphasis)
Information studies	
Library, Information Science Abstracts (LISA) Library, Information Science and Technology Abstracts (LISTA) (w125)	Library and information sciences
Computer sciences	
Computer and information systems abstracts	Broad coverage of computer sciences
IEEE/IET Electronic Library (IEL)	Electrical engineering, computer science and related technologies
Business and management	
Emerald management reviews	Management
Multi-disciplinary	
Web of science	Comprises: • Arts and humanities citation index • Science citation index expanded • Social sciences citation index • Conference proceedings citation index – science *NB – these indexes can either be searched individually or simultaneously.*
Scopus (w170)	• Chemistry, physics, mathematics, engineering • Life and health sciences • Social sciences, psychology, and economics • Biological, agricultural, and environmental sciences
Google Scholar (w092)	Search tool dedicated to academic content

Table 5.5   Grey Literature

General sources:

- GreySource, which contains a selection of online grey literature in a variety of subject areas (w099)
- Touro College Libraries, contains a number of online grey literature sources including sources for Humanities, Business, Jewish Studies , Education and Psychology, Mathematics and Science, Health Sciences and the Social Sciences (w193)

Ongoing research: Research registers	Databases
<ul><li>UKCRN (w195)</li><li>Current Controlled trials (w059),</li><li>Medical Research Council (MRC) Register</li></ul>	<ul><li>System for grey literature in Europe (SIGLE, w172), 1980–2005 only.</li><li>Social care online (w173)</li><li>Dissertation abstracts</li><li>Index to theses (w108)</li></ul>

Conference abstracts	Websites – examples
<ul><li>Index of conference proceedings received (lists conference proceedings newly acquired by and available from the British Library)</li><li>Web of Science indexes international conference proceedings and has two conference proceedings databases: (i) Science (ii) Social sciences and humanities</li><li>British Education Index includes conference proceedings index</li><li>Topic specific conferences: check websites to find a record e.g. cancer: ASCO, ESMO; e.g. library: UMBRELLA</li></ul>	<ul><li>Social research: Joseph Rowntree Foundation (w114)</li><li>Social sciences: European Research papers (w174)</li><li>Mental health research: Sainsbury Centre for Mental Health (w132)</li><li>Education research: Higher Education Academy (w068)</li><li>Economics Research/working papers (w067)</li><li>Criminology, University of Toronto, CrimDoc (Criminology Library Grey Literature, w053)</li></ul>

Search filters

Search filters or **methodological filters** are standardised search strategies designed to retrieve studies of a particular methodology type e.g. **randomised controlled trials**, systematic reviews, economic evaluations. By using search filters, you can also restrict your search to the particular outcomes in which you are interested. For example, you may want to limit your search further to studies reporting costs of an intervention. Search filters can limit to the types of question (for example, in healthcare studies diagnosis, aetiology, prognosis or therapy) or types of article, (for example, reviews, economic evaluations, guidelines or qualitative research). Good sources of search filters are the Scottish Intercollegiate Guidelines Network (w171), the McMaster Hedges Project (w130), and the InterTASC Information Specialists' Sub-Group (ISSG) (w110).

Reference management

Reference management was mentioned earlier in the context of managing your review (Chapter 3). It refers to any systematic means of organising your references. Manual reference management involves recording reference details on index cards and storing articles in a filing system.

Electronic reference management involves the use of specialist software, such as Reference Manager (w161) and Endnote (w071). There are also online reference management systems that host a reference management library on the web, meaning that access to a shared computer network drive is not necessary if multiple users wish to share a reference database. Examples are RefWorks (w162) which is a subscription-only service whereas Connotea (w047), Mendeley (w133) and CiteULike (w040) are free to use.

Reference management can greatly assist the process of a systematic literature review. All references retrieved in the search can be accounted for during the systematic literature review ensuring a transparent process.

Electronic reference management software allows references to be directly imported from individual databases (using specially designed filters). From this bank of references, you are able to keyword, sort and search references; as well create in-text citations and the reference list for your final report.

References

Armstrong, R., Jackson, N., Doyle, J., Waters, E., and Howes, F. (2005) It's in your hands: the value of handsearching in conducting systematic reviews of public health interventions. *Journal of Public Health*, **27**, 4, 388

Attree, P. (2008) *Childhood Disadvantage and Health Inequalities: A Systematic Review of the Qualitative Evidence*. Lancaster: Lancaster University. (w009)

Booth, A. (2001) Cochrane or cock-eyed? How should we conduct systematic reviews of qualitative research? Paper presented at the Qualitative Evidence-based Practice Conference, Taking a Critical Stance.Coventry University, May 14–16, 2001. (w019)

Booth, A. (2006) 'Brimful of STARLITE': toward standards for reporting literature searches. *Journal of the Medical Library Association*, **94**, 4, 421–9. (w179)

Booth, A. (2009) Searching for studies (Chapter 5). Cochrane Qualitative Methods Group Handbook. Adelaide: Cochrane Qualitative Research Methods Group (w021)

Brettle, A.J. and Long, A.F. (2001) Comparison of bibliographic databases for information on the rehabilitation of people with severe mental illness. *Bulletin of the Medical Library Association*, **89**, 4, 353–62. (w023)

Brown, S., Taylor, K., and Price, S.W. (2005) Debt and distress: evaluating the psychological cost of credit. *Journal of Economic Psychology*, **26**, 5, 642–3.

Centre for Reviews and Dissemination (2009) *CRD's Guidance for Undertaking Reviews in Healthcare*, 3rd edn. York: Centre for Reviews and Dissemination. (w036)

Dixon-Woods, M., Fitzpatrick, R., and Roberts, K. (2001) Including qualitative research in systematic reviews: opportunities and problems. *Journal of Evaluation in Clinical Practice*, **7**, 2, 125–33.

Duggan, F. and Banwell, L. (2004) Constructing a model of effective information dissemination in a crisis. *Information Research*, **9**, 3. (w064)

Graham-Matheson, L., Connolly, T., Robson, S., and Stow, W. (2006) A systematic map into approaches to making initial teacher training flexible and responsive to the needs of trainee teachers. Technical report. Research Evidence in Education Library. London: EPPI-Centre, Social Science Research Unit, Institute of Education, University of London. (w094)

Grant, M.J. and Booth, A. (2009) A typology of reviews: an analysis of 14 review types and associated methodologies. *Health Information and Libraries Journal*, **26**, 2, 91–108. (w095)

Grayson, L. and Gomersall, A. (2003) A difficult business: finding the evidence for social science reviews. Working Paper 19, Economic and Social Research Council, UK Centre for Evidence Based Policy and Practice, London. (w096)

Greenhalgh, T. and Peacock, R. (2005) Effectiveness and efficiency of search methods in systematic reviews of complex evidence: audit of primary sources. *British Medical Journal*, **331**, 1064–5. (w097)

GreyNet (2008) Grey Literature Network Service International Conference on Grey Literature (Luxembourg, 1997 – expanded in New York, 2004). GreyNet, Grey Literature Network Service. Amsterdam: GreyNet. (w099)

Hart, C. (2002) *Doing a Literature Search: A Comprehensive Guide for the Social Sciences.* London: Sage.

Higgins, J.P.T. and Green, S. (2008) *Cochrane Handbook for Systematic Reviews of Interventions*, Version 5.0.1. Oxford, Cochrane Collaboration. (w043)

Hopewell, S., Loudon, K., Clarke, M.J., Oxman, A.D., and Dickersin, K. (2009) Publication bias in clinical trials due to statistical significance or direction of trial results. Cochrane Database of Systematic Reviews (w107)

Jones, K. (2001) Mission drift in qualitative research, or moving toward a systematic review of qualitative studies, moving back to a more systematic narrative review. *The Qualitative Report*, **9**, 1, 95–112. (w113)

Jones, M.L. (2004) Application of systematic review methods to qualitative research: practical issues. *Journal of Advanced Nursing*, **48**, 3, 271–8.

Joseph Rowntree Foundation Website. 2010. (w114)

Kavanagh, J., Trouton, A., Oakley, A., and Harden, A. (2005) *A Scoping Review of The Evidence for Incentive Schemes to Encourage Positive Health and Other Social Behaviours in Young People.* London: EPPI-Centre, Social Science Research Unit, Institute of Education, University of London. (w117)

McAuley, L., Tugwell, P., and Moher, D (2000) Does the inclusion of grey literature influence estimates of intervention effectiveness reported in meta-analyses? *Lancet*, **356**, 9237, 1228–31.

McNally, R. and Alborz, A. (2004) Developing methods for systematic reviewing in health services delivery and organization: an example from a review of access to health care for people with learning disabilities. Part 1. Identifying the literature. *Health Information and Libraries Journal*, **21**, 3, 182–92.

Moher, D., Liberati, A., Tetzlaff, J., Altman D.G., and PRISMA Group (2009) Preferred reporting items for systematic reviews and meta-analyses: the PRISMA statement. *PLoS Medicine,* **6**, 7, e1000097. (w137)

Ogilvie, D., Hamilton, V., Egan, M., and Petticrew, M (2005) Systematic reviews of health effects of social interventions. 1. Finding the evidence: how far should you go? *Journal of Epidemiology and Community Health*, **59**, 9, 804–8.

Papaioannou, D., Sutton, A., Carroll, C., Booth, A., and Wong, R. (2010) Literature searching for social science systematic reviews: consideration of a range of search techniques. *Health Information and Libraries Journal*, **27**, 2, 114–22.

Petticrew, M. and Roberts, H. (2006) *Systematic Reviews in The Social Sciences: A Practical Guide.* Malden, MA: Blackwell Publishing.

Scottish Intercollegiate Guidelines Network (2010). Search Filters. (w171)

Stevinson, C. and Lawlor, D.A. (2004) Searching multiple databases for systematic reviews: added value or diminishing returns? *Complementary Therapies in Medicine*, **12**, 4, 228–32.

Webb, G., Shakeshaft, A., Sanson-Fisher, R., and Havard, A (2009) A systematic review of work-place interventions for alcohol-related problems. *Addiction*, **104**, 3, 365–77.

Wilson, P. (1992) Searching: strategies and evaluation. In: White, H.D., Bates, M.J. and Wilson, P. *For Information Specialists: Interpretations of Reference and Bibliographic Work*, Norwood, NJ: Ablex, 153–81.

Young, K., Ashby, D., Boaz, A., and Grayson, L. (2002) Social science and the evidence-based policy movement. *Social Policy and Society*, **1**, 215–24.

SIX

Assessing the evidence base

| Learning Objectives |

After reading this chapter, you should be able to:

- Understand the different roles and challenges of assessing the evidence base for quality and relevance.
- Undertake relevance assessment and select studies to include in your literature review.
- Understand key concepts in quality assessment (validity and reliability) and their importance within literature reviews.
- Understand the concept of applicability or generalisability.
- Identify appropriate quality assessment resources, undertake quality assessment and be able to present the results of quality assessments.

Introduction

Assessing the **evidence base** is the point in the review process that focuses on the particular value that individual studies hold for your research question and the practical application of research. After searching the literature (Chapter 5), you will have identified a potential evidence base for your review, which often can be large in size. From this list of references, you need to systematically select those that are *relevant* for your research question and exclude those that are not relevant. Once you have a list of included studies for your literature review, you need to plan how you will assess the evidence base. Assessing the evidence base in literature reviews depends on the type of review being undertaken. So, at one end of the scale, assessing the evidence base might involve briefly characterising the literature, for example in a mapping review. At the other end of the scale, assessment might involve a detailed examination of the methods and conduct of each study included in the review.

You may have heard of the terms **critical appraisal** or **quality assessment** (often used synonymously). Essentially, **critical appraisal** or **quality assessment** focuses on 'whether we can believe a study', and this is often referred to as **internal validity**. Systematic reviews carry out **critical appraisal** or **quality assessment** as a standard procedure, and extensive multi-disciplinary guidance exists on how this is done (Centre for Reviews and Dissemination, 2009, w036; EPPI Centre, 2010, w075; Higgins and Green, 2008, w043). Another concept to throw into the mix is assessment of generalisability or **applicability**, also known as **external validity**. Often this process is considered alongside **quality assessment**, but its focus is slightly different. Put simply, we assess the **generalisability** or **applicability** of an individual study by asking 'Is the study relevant to us?' Typically issues concerning **internal validity** are presented in the Results section of a review, whilst **external validity** is considered in the Discussion/Recommendations/Conclusion (see Chapter 9 for how to write up your review); however many reviewers prefer to assess both in a single process.

This chapter discusses how to assess the evidence base, focusing on the processes of quality assessment. The chapter starts by discussing how to select relevant studies for a literature review. Then, the chapter considers how to begin to assess the evidence base and how the depth of assessment depends on the function of and type of literature review. The next section introduces the need for quality assessment and outlines the different properties assessed in the studies included in your review: validity, reliability, and generalisability/applicability. Next, an overview of different study designs is provided, focusing on the implications of study design features. This is followed by a section on 'doing' quality and relevance assessment, including presenting results and challenges of the process. Lastly, some tools for assessing the evidence base are provided. Throughout the chapter, examples from within different disciplines are referred to; however consider how each section might apply to your own literature review topic.

Assessing the relevance of studies to your research question

At this stage, you will have completed your literature search (Chapter 5), and as a result will have a list of potential candidate studies for your literature review from which you need to select those that are relevant to the research question you formulated in Chapter 4. In some instances, depending on the quantity of research in your topic area, this can be a very long list of studies. It can seem rather daunting as you are overloaded with an abundance of information.

Applying a systematic method to selection of studies from the results of your literature search allows you to exclude studies that are not relevant to your review whilst ensuring that you do not miss studies that are relevant. This is important to help reduce **selection bias** within the review i.e. the review findings should be based upon *all* relevant studies. Having a clear idea of what is relevant to your review is essential. Chapter 4 discussed formulating explicit **inclusion criteria** and **exclusion criteria**, and it is at this stage where, if you devised an appropriately focused research question, the process of selecting studies is made much easier. You simply look at your inclusion and exclusion criteria and assess how each study identified from the literature fulfils each in turn. If a study does not fulfil every single inclusion criteria or meets any of the exclusion criteria, it is not included in your reviews – it is that simple!

Steps in the selection process

Experience suggest that the most efficient way of screening studies for inclusion in a literature review is to first examine the *titles* of articles from your literature searches. You are able to tell frequently from the title of an article whether or not it is relevant. After screening titles, you can move on to look at the *abstracts* of any studies where it was not possible to judge relevance from the title alone. Finally, you would examine the *full-text* of studies obtained on the basis of the relevance of their abstracts to your inclusion criteria. When it comes to excluding studies examined at the full-text stage, it may be useful to record reasons for exclusion of each study for the sake of transparency and subsequent reporting. Some literature reviews provide a list of excluded studies together with reasons in an appendix. This allows for transparency and justification for decisions made in the study selection phase. It also allows you to anticipate queries as to why a particular study was excluded from your review.

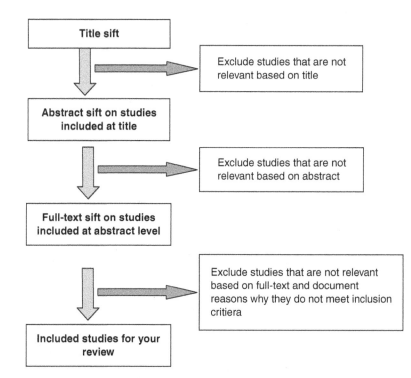

Figure 6.1 Process of selecting studies

Using reference management software for study selection

The Tools section in Chapter 5 discusses the different types of reference management software available to help you manage the literature review process. One function of reference management software is the ability to tag or apply keywords to records in the database. For example, you can tag all the references that have been selected for inclusion in your review at the abstract stage by tagging them with the keyword 'include abstract'. This function allows you to retrieve a list of included studies in the review, as well as providing an audit trial of decisions made in the study selection process. This means you should be able to know exactly which studies have been included or excluded and at what stage (title, abstract, or full-text examination). Chapter 9 discusses the importance of providing an account of the study selection process.

REFLECTION POINT 6.1

Studies for inclusion

If you are unsure about whether to include a study in your review what can you do?

You could: Ask for a second opinion – you could involve your supervisor/mentor. Alternatively hand a colleague your inclusion and exclusion criteria and ask them to apply these to the study in question.

APPLY WHAT YOU HAVE LEARNT 6.1

Study selection

Now, revisit your inclusion and exclusion criteria from Chapter 4 and write them down in the grid provided. Keep this grid handy whilst you go through your study selection process.

Tool for focusing your question e.g. PICO, SPICE, etc	Inclusion	Exclusion
e.g. Population		
e.g. Intervention/exposure		
e.g. Comparator		
e.g. Outcome (s)		
e.g. Context		

Assessing your included studies – first steps

Once you have selected the articles for your review, the next stage is to assess the evidence base in more detail. Here you are seeking to become immersed in, and familiar with, each study so that the ways in which to analyse and present the data start to become clear. Consider that at this point, you will have produced a list of studies judged to have met all your review inclusion criteria (i.e. correct population, outcomes, and study design) and so you know that each included study will provide its own findings that answer your research question in some way. You need to examine each study in detail, taking all the meaningful information from each included study (**data extraction**), before you start pulling together and synthesising the information. For whichever type of literature review you are undertaking, at this stage you are reading, becoming familiar with, digesting, reflecting upon and, perhaps unknowingly, making judgements on each study included in your review. All these processes are involved in *assessing the evidence base*.

The depth to which you assess the evidence base will depend on the type of review and its aim. For example, a systematic review generally involves an in-depth quality assessment of included studies. This is because a key component of systematic reviews is to reflect upon the credibility of the review's findings. In such cases, it is essential that you are aware of how weaknesses or flaws of included studies may impact upon the review's findings. However, for a mapping review, where the aim is to map out and categorise existing literature as well as identifying gaps in the literature (Grant and Booth, 2009, w095), the function of assessing the evidence base is to identify its key characteristics such as study design, country of publication or general direction of study findings allowing a rich picture of the existing literature to be described.

All literature reviews involve, and benefit from, some form of assessment of the evidence base, which helps to guide the subsequent stages of synthesis and writing up.

If nothing else, at this stage you will be familiarising yourself with the intricacies of each study and will start to spot where findings from studies agree or differ from one another. More importantly, you will start to suggest possible reasons for study similarities or differences. For example, what does an individual study contribute to your review? Does it add strength to an argument; a conflicting argument; a new argument, perspective or theory or, perhaps, nothing new?

To begin with, it is useful to ask yourself what you need to find out from your included studies to help you fulfil the aim of your literature review. Table 6.1 presents four types of review (introduced in Chapter 2) and looks at their aims in relation to how they might assess the evidence base. For each review type, there are some suggestions for 'key questions' to consider when assessing the evidence base. Therefore, answers to each question will help to shape how you will proceed with your review. Hopefully, you can identify how many of the questions apply to each particular review type. For example, in a systematic review most, if not all, of the questions in Table 6.1 are appropriate.

Table 6.1   Assessing the evidence base in different types of reviews

Type of review	Key questions to ask when assessing the evidence base	Practical application	Review example
Scoping review	Are there any previous reviews?	Identifies previous reviews on your topic area to avoid duplication.	*A scoping review of the evidence for incentive schemes to encourage positive health and other social behaviours in young people (Kavanagh et al., 2005, w117).*
	How much evidence exists on my research question?	If there is a significant volume of evidence, you might want to consider refining your scope. Too little evidence and you might want to broaden your question.	
	What type of evidence is available?		
		'Firms up' the research question by looking at what kind of evidence is out there. For example, if your review is limited to randomised controlled trials (RCTs) but your scoping search finds no such evidence, you may need to consider other types of research design. Similarly, if you have limited your research question to only UK studies but found none in your scoping search, you may wish to widen to include research undertaken outside UK	
Mapping review	Where is evidence plentiful?	Focus for subsequent literature reviews	A systematic map into approaches to making initial teacher training flexible and responsive to the needs of trainee teachers (Graham-Matheson et al., 2005, w094).
	Where is evidence lacking i.e. gaps?	Avoid for literature reviews, consider as an area for primary research (e.g. strengthens argument for the need of novel research in a master's or PhD thesis focus)	
	How can I describe the evidence?		
	Are there relationships or key themes occurring?	Key features of evidence base might include study design, country of publication, populations or subgroups, nature of intervention or exposures analysed (are they similar or differ greatly)	
		Directional (i.e. A affects B)	
		Studies in agreement	
		Conflicting studies	
Systematic review	How can I describe the evidence?	Key features of evidence base might include study design, country of publication, populations or subgroups, nature of intervention or exposures analysed (are they similar or do they differ greatly?)	Webb, G. et al. (2009) A systematic review of work-place interventions for alcohol-related problems. *Addiction*, **104**, 3, 365–77
	Are there relationships or key themes occurring?		
	How credible is the evidence?	Directional (i.e. A affects B)	
	How applicable is the evidence to my situation/scenario?	Studies in agreement	
		Conflicting studies	
	Where is evidence lacking i.e. gaps?	Quality of the study conduct and design: subgroup analyses	
		Generalisability of research	
		Areas for future research	

Type of review	Key questions to ask when assessing the evidence base	Practical application	Review example
Qualitative systematic review	How can I describe the evidence? What themes or constructs are present between or within individual studies? What is the quality of the evidence?	Key features of evidence base e.g. participants, settings (are they similar or differ greatly?) Interpretation of a phenomenon – broaden understanding Does this mediate the findings?	Constructing a model of effective information dissemination in a crisis (Duggan and Banwell, 2004, w064).

APPLY WHAT YOU HAVE LEARNT 6.2

Assessing the evidence base for your review

Consider the types of review in Table 6.1 and think about what questions you might want to ask when assessing the evidence base for your review:

Your review question: Which key questions do you need to ask for your review? What is the practical application of your questions?

Assessing the evidence-base in detail

For some literature reviews, a systematic exploration of study strengths and weaknesses is required to assess their impact on both the findings of that individual study and the findings of the literature review as a whole. The remainder of this chapter considers quality assessment and its role in the literature review process.

REFLECTION POINT 6.2

When is an article worth reading?

Before introducing quality assessment in more detail, when you come across a research study in a journal, consider:

1 How do you decide whether an article is worth reading?
2 What makes an article believable?

In addressing Reflection point 6.2 you will probably find that your factors can be divided into three distinct groups:

- *Applicability* – the topic of the study, how important it is to you at the moment, the similarity of the setting to the one in which you work, the level at which it is written, the professional group or discipline for whom it is written, etc.

- *Extrinsic factors* – those external factors which are assumed, but may not always be associated with the quality of the article: who wrote it, where they work, what their job or qualifications are, whether you have heard of them, who paid for the study, in which journal it is published, whether the authors have written on the subject before.
- *Intrinsic factors* – factors that relate to the study itself: the appropriateness of the study design to the question being asked, the suitability of the sample, the methods used to recruit the sample, methods used to obtain the results.

Quality assessment asks you to discard prejudices that you may have regarding the extrinsic factors. It asks you to make an initial judgement about the general relevance of the study, to then look exclusively at the intrinsic factors using a structured checklist, before finally returning to consider issues that relate to its suitability to your own practice. In this way it aims to make the process as objective and explicit as possible. On this basis, you can judge if a paper is worth reading, and if it is believable.

Assessing the quality of included studies – what is it and why do we do it?

Quality assessment, sometimes referred to as **critical appraisal**, aims to discover if first the methods, and consequently the results of the research, are valid. It is:

> the process of assessing and interpreting evidence by systematically considering its validity, results and relevance. (Parkes et al., 2001, w149)

Generalisability or applicability is often considered alongside quality assessment, and reflects on how research findings (if at all) impact on practice. Considering how the research is applicable or generalisable to practice defines the difference between **critical appraisal** and simply 'critical reading' of research (Booth and Brice, 2004).

Every study included in your literature review has weaknesses or flaws. Each weakness or flaw needs to be identified to determine first, its potential impact on the findings of an individual study and second, its implications for the findings of your review as a whole. It is important that you are aware of both the strengths and flaws of included studies so that you can take these into account when presenting and discussing your review findings.

It is important to consider which study flaws may be considered 'fatal' and which are 'non-critical'. All studies have weaknesses but by considering their impact upon the study findings, you can determine which are critical and which are not. Remember that undertaking research is fraught with difficulties. Several things can 'go wrong' or not as originally planned in research studies (for example poor recruitment to a study). It is all too easy to become very scathing about studies when you are assessing their quality! Sackett (1997) refers to this as **critical appraisal** 'nihilism' i.e. no paper is ever good enough. However, the function of **quality assessment** is not 'pursuit of some "holy grail" of perfection' (Petticrew and Roberts, 2006). Assessing the **evidence base** focuses on the practical application of research, and similar pragmatism is required when you are performing **quality assessment**. Therefore, if a particular flaw has minimal or limited impact on the findings of a study, is it really that important?

However, quality assessment is not simply used to identify study flaws. Using such a structured formal approach allows you to explore the detailed contents of a paper both in terms of its methodology and findings. It is therefore basically a type of 'acclimatisation' or 'sensitisation' to a study; the journey of discovery for the reader being its important feature (Booth, 2007). By critically examining published research, we become more aware of how others have conducted research. This also means, we can become better at designing and conducting our own research studies. For example, if a study has been carried out using an inappropriate study design, it might prove useful to repeat the research using a stronger study design. If a study has been carried out but failed to recruit enough subjects, it might be useful to repeat with a larger sample to determine results.

Lastly, quality assessment is helpful in identifying between-study differences; the technical term is **heterogeneity** and this is discussed further in Chapter 7. For example, smaller studies tend to overestimate findings in comparison to larger studies (Higgins and Green, 2008, w043).

Study designs – is there a hierarchy of evidence?

Before looking at quality assessment in more detail, it is useful to understand the different types of study design used in research. Some research designs are better able to answer certain questions. Therefore, early on in the process of quality assessment, you need to consider: 'Is this the most appropriate study design to answer this research question?' If you are not familiar with study designs, take a look at the resources available on the Oxford Centre for Evidence-based Medicine website (Centre for Evidence Based Medicine, 2009, w033).

The ability of study designs to answer research questions is given particular attention in health research; where the randomised controlled trial (RCT) is considered the **gold standard** study design to answer questions on the effectiveness of an intervention. The idea of the 'best study design for a research question' has been used prescriptively within such research, where so-called **hierarchies of evidence** have been developed. These hierarchies rank study designs in order of robustness for answering a type of question, for example, for effectiveness of an intervention, randomised controlled trials are normally considered at the top of the scale, in terms of robustness with case studies at the bottom. Of course, all study designs combining multiple well-conducted examples in a single systematic review will always be considered superior to the findings of an individual well-conducted study.

One of the most cited examples of a published hierarchy is the 'Levels of Evidence' produced by the Oxford Centre for Evidence Based Medicine (Chalmers et al., 2009, w034). This hierarchy allows the reader to select a particular type of research question and to identify the order of study design by robustness.

However, there are problems with classifying research designs in this way. First, hierarchies can give a false impression that a poorly conducted randomised controlled trial may provide better evidence than a well-conducted observational study. Second, it is often not straightforward to determine which research design is the most appropriate since the choice may be limited by practical and ethical considerations. For example a researcher may believe that it is not ethical to randomise subjects. Third, hierarchies of evidence are limited in addressing questions on the rigour of qualitative research where different designs have different attributes (Taylor et al., 2007). Finally, most hierarchies are health research focused, and their value is contested by researchers within other disciplines (Hammersley, 2001; Taylor et al., 2007).

Whatever your discipline, you will find it invaluable to be aware of different types of study design, the flaws or biases to which they are prone and, particularly, their effect on study findings. However, in a multi-disciplinary setting, it may be more helpful to consider when particular studies may be reasonably used and what the strengths or weaknesses are. Thus, this section takes a broad look at the three 'families' of study design: descriptive, analytic experimental, and analytical observational.

Studies can be broadly classified into **descriptive** or **analytic** designs. Descriptive study designs focus on describing or giving us a picture of what is happening in a population (for example **cross-sectional surveys** and **qualitative studies**). **Analytic** studies try to quantify relationships between factors (Centre for Evidence Based Medicine, 2009, w033) for example, the effect of an Information and

Table 6.2   Cross-sectional versus longitudinal

Study design feature	Implications		Studies that often use this feature
Cross-sectional: records outcomes or examines relationships between variables at one point in time only i.e. snapshot in time.	• Cheap and simple to set up Ideal for pinpointing the prevalence of a particular, e.g. what number of higher education students visit their public library?	• Cannot determine a cause and effect relationship between two variables.	Survey
Longitudinal: records observations over a period of time (can be several years)	• Changes over time are recorded in a population or outcome so more plausible to determine a cause and effect relationship.	• More complicated to set up and more costly than cross-sectional studies. Causality may only be determined if confounding factors are controlled for.	Cohort study Randomised controlled trial

Communication Technology (ICT) intervention on maths ability. Analytic studies can be further classified according to whether researchers simply measure the effects of an exposure (i.e. they do not manipulate the intervention or exposure in any way). In contrast, experimental analytic studies manipulate an intervention or exposure, for example in **RCTs** by allocating subjects to different intervention or exposure groups. The key characteristic of experimental studies is that they are designed to control bias in scientific research. Experimental studies may be **cross-sectional** or **longitudinal; prospective** or **retrospective**, contain one or more groups of participants (including random or non-random allocation to groups within a study) and may be **blind** or **open-label**. Each feature of an experimental study design has implications for the research, as explored in Tables 6.2 to 6.6.

Table 6.3   Prospective versus retrospective

Study design feature	Implications		Studies that often use this feature
Prospective: forward-looking and observe for outcomes. Typically a group or cohort of individuals is identified and followed for a long period of time.	• Able to determine cause and effect and provide 'real' incidence rates. • Can uncover unanticipated outcomes or associations.	• Can be prone to large loss of study participants **(attrition).** • The outcome of interest must be common or the study will fail to recruit enough participants to make the findings meaningful.	Cohort study Randomised controlled trial
Retrospective: identify a group of individuals who have had a particular outcome and then look back in time to record details about what interventions or exposures they received	• Able to determine cause and effect; particularly useful when an outcome is rare	• Looking 'backwards', particularly when asking study participants to remember events or details in the past makes retrospective studies particularly prone to **recall bias.**	Case control studies Cohort studies – occasionally

Table 6.4   One group versus more than one group

Study design feature	Implications		Studies that often use this feature
One group of study participants	• Fewer participants need be recruited to the study	• Between-group comparisons cannot be made • Confounding factors may not be taken into account as easily	Survey Cohort study Case control study
Two groups of study participants	• Between-group comparisons to be made • Confounding factors can be taken into account more easily • Groups can be balanced.	• Requires extra participants to be recruited	Survey Cohort study Case control study RCT

Table 6.5   Random versus not random allocation

Study design feature	Implications		Studies that often use this feature
Non-random allocation	• Not always possible or ethical to randomise participants to different groups (for example in a study investigating smokers and non-smokers)	• Because participants may have chosen which study group they are in (or the researcher has done so for them), this significantly biases the outcomes • For example if there were two groups of children: Group 1 in the top set for maths, and Group 2 in the bottom set for maths, and a study investigated performance in physics, the two groups of children are not similar	Cohort study Case control study
Random allocation	• Allows equal balancing of confounding factors • Limits bias in terms of participant selection of an intervention or exposure	• Not always possible or ethical to randomise participants to different groups	RCT

Table 6.6   Blind versus open-label studies

Study design feature	Implications		Studies that often use this feature
Blinding: an individual is not aware of what intervention or exposure they're given. Individuals who can be blinded in a study include the participants, the researchers and the analysts, and so a study can be single, double or triple blind.	• Anticipation of the placebo effect: a phenomenon whereby study participants experience improvement in an outcome after receiving 'something' that should in theory not produce an improvement in outcomes. • Prevention of **observer bias** in researchers and analysts.	• It is not always possible or ethical to blind study participants or researchers.	RCT Cohort study
Open-label: an individual is aware of what intervention or exposure they are receiving. Again, this includes the participants, the researchers, and the analysts	• It is not always possible or ethical to blind study participants or research personnel, for example in a study investigating surgery versus no surgery!	• Participants may exaggerate an improvement if they think they are receiving something that is supposed to have an effect • Researchers may exaggerate findings according to their own biases.	RCT Cohort study

Quality assessment: validity, reliability and applicability

So far, this chapter is saturated with theory ... and there is just a little bit more, before the focus turns to 'Doing quality assessment'! To undertake quality assessment, you need to understand the principles underpinning the process. These can be split into three key concepts of **validity**, **reliability**, and **applicability**. Each is considered in turn.

Validity (Are the results of a study true?)

The way in which research is designed and undertaken has a bearing on whether the results can be considered 'true' or 'valid'. Are there any flaws in how the research has been carried out that may invalidate the findings? Simply the act of undertaking research can alter study findings from reality. Imagine if you were informed by one of your tutors that the occupational health department wanted you and your fellow course participants to take part in a study on the frequency of hand washing. Would you be likely to alter your hand-washing practices? Would the findings of the study accurately represent hand-washing practices or would they present a distorted picture?

So in assessing validity, we ask, 'How much have the methods used to obtain the results thrown into question the findings themselves?'(Booth and Brice, 2004). The rigour of the research refers to the degree to which the design of the study and its conduct minimises the risk of **bias** and takes into account **confounding**; the two key flaws that can affect all studies. Bias is 'anything that erroneously influences the conclusions about groups and distorts comparisons' (Rose and Barker, 1994). Systematic errors in the conduct of a study include how subjects are selected to take part, how outcomes are measured, or how data is analysed. All of these can lead to inaccurate results (College of Emergency Medicine, 2010, w046). **Confounding** is where you cannot ascertain whether an effect is caused by the variable you are interested in or by another variable. For example, a study may demonstrate a link between alcohol consumption and lung cancer. However, alcohol consumption is commonly associated with smoking, and thus smoking is a potential confounder for your study. Studies can be designed to take account of confounding by taking potential confounders into account in the analysis, or by ensuring groups within the study are stratified to allow equal distribution of participants with the confounding factor (in this example smoking). Whichever method is chosen, the researcher should demonstrate that they have identified potential confounders at the beginning of the study. Common confounding variables are age, sex, and ethnicity.

To illustrate **sources of bias** and **confounding**, read the accompanying study scenario (Exercise 6.1), and try to answer the questions that have been set.

Study scenario

Can an ICT intervention improve primary schoolchildren's performance in solving maths problems?

A group of 20 primary schoolchildren are selected by their teacher to take part in this study as a reward for good behaviour. At the start of the study, each child completes a maths problems test consisting of 10 questions. Each child then completes a one-hour online workbook on the class computer, in which they complete a series of maths problems in the form of fun games and exercises. The children then complete another maths problems test of 10 questions, and the number answered correctly is recorded. The teacher asks each child to recall how many they got correct in the maths test before the study started.

1 What sources of bias can you see?

Hint 1 – might the children selected to take part in the study differ in any way from those who did not take part?

Hint 2 – do you think the children could accurately (and truthfully!) recall their score for the test they took at the beginning of the study?

2 Aside from the sources of bias in this study, what other factors might limit the credibility of the study findings?

Reliability (What are the results?)

All research results are subject to the possible effects of chance. Reliability refers to the trustworthiness of the results, i.e. 'What is the likelihood that this study reports something that is reproducible as opposed to being a "fluke" or chance result' (Booth and Brice, 2004)? Statistical tests can be undertaken to determine the likelihood that results are due to chance. Techniques exist to provide a range of plausible values for the repeated measurement of the effect. This allows you to judge whether you would make the same decision based on the very best and the very worst estimate of the effect. However, statisticians choose arbitrary thresholds for determining chance, typically 5 per cent or 1 in 20, i.e. if something occurs more frequently than this, it is considered unlikely to be due to the play of chance (Booth and Brice, 2004) and is labelled **statistically significant**. It is also important to determine whether results are meaningful, i.e. is the effect large enough to be **practically significant?** For example, a study might demonstrate a change in five points on a scale measuring improvement in computer skills. This change of five points might be **statistically significant** but it might take a change of 10 points or more before a teacher considers this to be **practically significant**.

Applicability (Can we generalise the results?)

Once you have assessed the validity and reliability of a study, you need to determine whether the results actually are useful. Validity and reliability are concerned with estimating the strength of the evidence, whereas applicability is concerned with the strength of recommendations for practice (based on the study results).

Continuing with our study scenario, imagine you are the headteacher of a primary school and you are reading the results of a systematic literature review investigating whether an ICT intervention improves primary school-children's performance in solving maths problems. The review found seven studies designed to test this research question; however the results are conflicting between the studies. Five studies found that ICT did improve students' performance in a weekly maths test, whilst two showed no evidence of such an effect. By examining the studies in more detail, you realise that the five supportive studies were undertaken in a group of children aged eight to nine years old, whereas the two studies that did not find a positive effect were undertaken in children of a younger age group (four to five years old). Thus, it might be reasonable for you as headteacher to suggest that the ICT-based maths computer program should be taken up only by classes of older children at the school. Note this is not a flaw of the individual studies included in the review, but simply reflects a difference in age of study participants and thus relates to how applicable the findings are to your situation.

Doing quality assessment

Now that the theory has been covered, how do you tackle assessing the quality of studies? Whilst every article is different, assessment of quality can be split into four stages (LoBiondo-Wood et al., 2002) (Box 6.1).

Box 6.1   Four stages of quality assessment

Preliminary understanding – skimming or quickly reading to gain familiarity with the content and layout of the paper.

Comprehensive understanding – increasing understanding of concepts and research terms.

Analysis understanding – breaking the study into parts and seeking to understand each part.

Synthesis understanding – pulling the above steps together to make a (new) whole, making sense of it and explaining relationships.

Even if you do not undertake full quality assessment for your review, you will always need to follow the first two steps in Box 6.1. In developing a preliminary and then comprehensive understanding of each study, you will arrive at an overall understanding of the individual contribution of that study. Most literature reviews involve some form of analysis understanding. The depth to which you break down the study into parts depends on which data are most important for your review. For example, in a systematic mapping review you may be concerned with a few items of information such as the type of studies, country, and key themes. In contrast, in a systematic review, the details of study design are required in great depth, and so this will involve you 'drilling down' into the study for much of the necessary detail.

A useful place to start is by reading the abstract. The format of the abstract varies between disciplines. Increasingly within the medical literature, structured abstracts (i.e. with headings) are being adopted. These help the reader quickly assess the study design, participants and key results. Abstracts in other disciplines may be less structured but give a flavour of what the study is about. After reading the abstract, to gain a deeper understanding of the study, you should start to read the paper in full. Whilst the introduction, discussion, and conclusion can help in understanding the paper, it is the Methods section that allows you to determine the quality of the paper. The Results section, too, provides some indication of the significance of the individual study. Remember that practical relevance may not feature in the results section but may be considered in the Discussion section.

Using checklists

For experienced and novice reviewers alike, checklists can be particularly helpful in guiding the process of quality and relevance assessment. For the novice reviewer, checklists provide a comprehensive list of everything to consider in terms of quality assessment, and may help when considering study relevance, which is typically considered by the last three questions on Critical Appraisal Skills Programme checklists (CASP, 2010, w054). However, as you become more experienced at quality assessment, checklists act as a prompt to help you consider all relevant points. The Tools section in this chapter points to a range of multi-disciplinary sources of checklists for a range of study designs. However, be sure to investigate articles within your discipline as they may give pointers as to how quality assessment is undertaken within your research area. For example, checklists in social work and social care have been discussed (Wells and Littell, 2009) and developed (Taylor et al., 2007).

Do not be put off by the first few occasions you undertake quality assessment. It takes some time – from our experience quality assessment of a complicated study can take anything up to a couple of hours. However, you will soon get more proficient and consequently, quicker. You will find that the more quality assessment you undertake, the more adept you become at spotting the key strengths or weaknesses of a study – the same flaws in published studies will occur again and again!

Box 6.2   Some tips on checklists

- Remember quality and relevance assessment may vary by discipline. Take a look at reviews in your discipline and examine how the authors have undertaken quality and relevance assessment, and also which checklist they have used. See Table 6.8 in the Tools section of this chapter for some examples and key features of reviews in different disciplines.
- Stick to checklists that have been validated or are widely accepted in your discipline. Again, examining reviews in your discipline will help to identify the accepted checklists.
- Avoid checklists that employ scoring systems. It is dangerous to label studies with scores, and not particularly helpful in understanding how the study strengths and weaknesses contribute to the validity of the study findings. In fact, the Cochrane methods guide for systematic reviews actively discourages the use of those checklists that assess quality using a scoring system (Higgins and Green, 2008, w043).
- Remember what you are trying to achieve through quality and relevance assessment – checklists are only a guide. You may spot study features that are not picked up by your checklist and these can still be reported.
- Lastly, you can get creative with checklists, and may want to select criteria from different checklists and devise your own super checklist. (However, do remember to justify why you have done so and to reference the contributing checklists.)

Quality assessment of qualitative research

There is considerable debate around the quality assessment of qualitative research as to whether it can, or indeed should, be done. There is little consensus on how quality assessment should be undertaken within qualitative research with over a hundred sets of proposals on quality in qualitative research (Dixon-Woods et al., 2004) and widely opposing views on the matter. Popay and colleagues (1998) describe two camps: those who believe that the concepts used in quantitative research apply equally to qualitative research, without further interpretation (i.e. reliability, validity), and those who believe that there are no quality criteria by which qualitative research can be assessed. There is further contention about how best to approach quality assessment given evidence that it cannot be performed reliably; Dixon-Woods and colleagues demonstrated widely different results from quality assessment using three appraisal approaches and six different reviewers (Dixon-Woods et al., 2007).

The Cochrane Qualitative Methods Group has drafted a chapter discussing quality assessment within qualitative reviews. This affirms that **critical appraisal** is an essential component of qualitative Cochrane Reviews (Cochrane Qualitative Research Methods Group, 2010, w045). The chapter adapts the broad principles of **quality assessment** in quantitative reviews, and refers to the concepts being assessed as *credibility, transferability, dependability* and *confirmability.* To find out more about quality assessment of qualitative research, read the chapter which is freely available online (Cochrane Qualitative Research Methods Group, 2010, w045).

If you decide to undertake quality assessment, you need to consider which checklist to use or whether to consider devising your own. There are examples within the literature where researchers have devised their own criteria, basing them on existing quality criteria (Thomas and Harden, 2008, w191), and papers which discuss the methods more generally (Barnett-Page and Thomas, 2009, w011). There are also instances where briefer prompts of criteria for qualitative quality assessment have been suggested (Dixon-Woods et al., 2004; Popay et al., 1998). Dixon-Woods and colleagues developed a brief set of prompts to investigate the quality of studies on access to healthcare by vulnerable groups (Dixon-Woods et al., 2006, w063). The prompts they used can be seen in Box 6.3.

Box 6.3   Quality assessment prompts

- Are the aims and objectives of the research clearly stated?
- Is the research design clearly specified and appropriate for the aims and objectives of the research?
- Do the researchers provide a clear account of the process by which their findings were reproduced?
- Do the researchers display enough data to support their interpretations and conclusions?
- Is the method of analysis appropriate and adequately explicated?

(Dixon-Woods et al., 2006, w063)

Secondly, it is important to bear in mind the purpose of undertaking quality assessment of qualitative research. Examples exist in the literature where studies are excluded on the basis of quality (Brunton et al., 2006, w025), however as in quantitative reviews the majority of qualitative reviews do not exclude studies on the basis of quality. Sandelowski and colleagues (1997) advise caution in using checklists to exclude studies from a review arguing that any exclusions must be supported by an explicit account of the researcher's view of 'good' and 'bad' studies, and reason for exclusions.

Lastly, it is important to remember that quality assessment of qualitative research is a developing area, and further work is being done in this field. Recent research suggests that there may be little value in quality assessing qualitative studies in systematic literature reviews because the appraisal activity has little impact on the overall review findings, i.e. the exclusion of weaker studies shows no effect (Carroll et al., 2010; Thomas and Harden, 2008, w191).

Applying quality assessment

Quality assessment of studies generates large quantities of information. Typically, in systematic reviews where quality assessment is standard, the Results section will present a few paragraphs that attempt to synthesise this information, focusing on its impact on individual study findings. The information can also be tabulated by drawing out the key points of the checklist. Generally the Discussion focuses on the key flaws, but you should not forget to include what has been done well! As mentioned previously, it is critical that you have an awareness of those study flaws that are 'fatal' and those that are not – remember that it is the *impact* on the study findings that is crucial.

Reviews do not generally exclude studies on the basis of quality. However, sometimes a **subgroup analysis** is performed to examine the results of the quality assessment. This involves splitting the studies into subgroups according to a particular study design feature that might impact on study findings, for example the country in which the study was undertaken, and exploring how this might impact on the findings of the review. For example, smaller studies are known to overestimate study findings (Higgins and Green, 2008, w043) and subgroup analysis can demonstrate this.

Finally, be cautious about labelling studies according to a level of quality (for example high, medium, and low). Whilst in principle this might appear useful, you need to be explicit about the criteria by which studies are categorised, so that ultimately the classification of studies could be reliably reproduced. Given this may be a highly subjective exercise, there is the potential to mislead the reader since their concept of a high-quality study may differ from your own.

Problems or challenges in quality assessment

Assessing the quality of research is time-consuming, particularly when you are new to the process. With experience, it does become quicker the more familiar you become with the study designs and their inherent and anticipated weaknesses. Choosing a checklist may also be difficult given the number from which to choose. As discussed earlier, you will find it helpful to examine examples of reviews to identify the more common and well-used checklists in your subject area.

Quality assessment is a subjective process. For systematic reviews, methods guides suggest that quality assessment should be carried out by more than one person and the results compared (Centre for Reviews and Dissemination, 2009, w036; Higgins and Green, 2008, w043). However, this is not always practical or necessary. Having a second reviewer check a sample of quality assessments might be a more reasonable alternative, particularly for those elements of which you are unsure (with a supervisor or mentor perhaps). Use of checklists typically makes it easier to achieve consensus. As previously stated, fundamental issues concerning the subjectivity of quality assessment of qualitative research remain to be resolved.

Lastly, remember quality assessment examines what is reported within a study, and thus studies can only be as good as their reporting. Often studies do not report enough details of the methods of a study and thus the quality assessment measures only the quality of reporting. Whilst it is possible to track authors down to elicit missing details, a good paper should include enough detail to allow you to assess its quality. The quality of reporting of research has been subject to recent attention, with several standards being published regarding the quality of research reporting for specific study designs; the PRISMA statement in systematic reviews (w158) (Moher et al., 2009, w137); the CONSORT statement in RCTs (CONSORT Group, 2010, w048), and the STROBE statement for observational studies in epidemiology (STROBE Group, 2010, w181). Over time, as more studies adopt such standards in their reporting, the task of quality assessment will become, at least in theory, much easier – assuming that standardised reporting does not make it more difficult to identify the poorer studies!

▬▬▬▬▬▬▬▬▬▬ APPLY WHAT YOU HAVE LEARNT 6.3 ▬▬▬▬▬▬▬▬▬▬

Quality assessment

In Table 6.7, three articles from the British Medical Journal (BMJ) are presented for you to test out your quality assessment skills. Each of the three articles is accompanied by a commentary from the *Student BMJ*, which summarises the key issues relating to quality.

Although these examples are from the BMJ, the selected articles are of different study designs and are not exclusively health-focused. The skills that you acquire from undertaking this exercise are transferable when appraising studies from other disciplines.

First, read the full article (freely available online at the BMJ website). Then try undertaking a quality assessment using an appropriate checklist (suggested checklists are provided in Table 6.7). Then take a look at the accompanying reference provided for each of the three articles at the *Student BMJ* (w182), which provides a **critical appraisal** summary of the article, drawing out the key issues. Try the **quality assessment** yourself (do not look at the corresponding *Student BMJ* article until you have completed it) and then take a look to see if you've identified the key points.

Table 6.7   Quality assessment of an article

Study reference	Student BMJ summary	Checklist
Effect of antibiotic prescribing on antibiotic resistance in individual children in primary care: prospective cohort study (Chung et al., 2007, w039)	Student BMJ (2007) **15**, 337–82 (w185)	CASP Cohort study checklist (w055)
Experiences of belittlement and harassment and their correlates among medical students in the United States: longitudinal survey (Frank et al., 2006, w082)	Student BMJ (2006) **14**, 353–96 (w184)	BestBETS Survey worksheet (w017)
Relation between a career and family life for English hospital consultants: qualitative, semi-structured interview study (Dumelow et al., 2000; w065)	Student BMJ (2000) **8**, 236–40 (w183)	CASP Qualitative checklist (w056)

Summary

All literature reviews involve some assessment of the evidence base. The first step is to systematically select those studies identified by the literature search that are relevant to your research question. The type of review that you are undertaking and its purpose will determine the accompanying tasks related to assessing the included studies in your literature review. For some reviews, this may entail a brief characterisation of the key features of the evidence base. In other reviews, you need to conduct a more in-depth assessment of study quality to help answer the review question. Using checklists will help you in this process, and they are particularly useful if you are a novice reviewer. Many useful resources exist to support the process. Quality assessment is a difficult and time-consuming process to begin with. However, do persevere as it does become easier with experience and practice.

Key learning points

1 Use the inclusion and exclusion criteria devised in Chapter 4 to help you select studies for your review in a transparent manner.
2 Consider the extent to which you need to assess the evidence based for your review by thinking about the aim of your review.
3 Consider how the design features of studies included in your review can impact upon the research findings.
4 Three core components of quality assessment and to consider when reading a study are:

- Are the results of a study true? (validity)
- What are the results? (reliability)
- Can I generalise the results? (generalisability)

5 Quality assessment checklists are helpful in guiding the process of quality and relevance assessment.

6 Look at research within your discipline, particularly existing reviews to see how quality assessment is undertaken in your area.

Suggestions for further reading

Find reviews within your topic area/area of research from the following sources:

1 EPPI Centre (w072)
2 The Campbell Library (w030)
3 The Cochrane Library (w044).

Tools for quality assessment

This Tools section focuses on the many tools that are freely available to support you in the quality assessment of studies. The best starting point is to look at examples of existing reviews in your discipline (Table 6.8). You will then want to move on to the relevant checklists for your chosen type of study before considering how these have been applied in available summaries of research articles.

Existing reviews in your area

You can start to understand the process of quality assessment in your discipline by investigating the methods used in existing reviews in your topic area. This enables you to gain a good understanding of the general approach taken including justification for the approaches used, which checklists (or combinations of checklists) are widely used, and how the authors present the information. Finally, such a review may provide you with an indication of the key study flaws and strengths most likely to occur in your topic area.

Some examples of systematic reviews in a variety of disciplines are presented in Table 6.8, each demonstrating a different approach to quality and relevance assessment. Similar variation will be apparent if you look at other types of literature reviews such as mapping and scoping reviews (examine the reviews we listed in Table 6.1). There are also examples of several different types of reviews throughout this book which may be useful. Further examples can be found at resources such as the EPPI Centre (w072), the Campbell Library (w030, and the Cochrane Library (w044).

Table 6.8 Examples of systematic reviews in different disciplines

Topic area	Reference	Quality assessment strategy
Health	Structured telephone support or telemonitoring programmes for patients with chronic heart failure (Inglis et al., 2010, w109)	As per the Cochrane Handbook criteria of assessment of risk of bias (Higgins and Green, 2008, w043).
Social welfare	Kinship Care for the Safety, Permanency, and Well-Being of Children Removed from the Home for Maltreatment (Winokur et al., 2009, w205)	Studies were assessed according to the following criteria from the Cochrane Handbook: selection bias, performance bias, detection bias, report bias, and attrition bias (Higgins and Green, 2008, w043). The authors state that 'the methodological criteria' were operationalised as follows: • Selection bias: was group assignment determined randomly or might it have been related to outcomes or the interventions received? • Performance bias: could the services provided have been influenced by something other than the interventions being compared? • Detection bias: were outcomes influenced by anything other than the constructs of interest, including biased assessment or the influence of exposure on detection? • Report bias: were the outcomes, measures, and analyses selected a priori and reported completely? Were participants biased in their recall or response? • Attrition bias: could deviations from protocol, including missing data and dropout, have influenced the results?
Psychology	Individual and group-based parenting for improving psychosocial outcomes for teenage parents and their children (Coren and Barlow, 2003, w050).	Quality assessment was based on assessing the following criteria: • Blinding • Allocation concealment • Numbers of participants in each group • The method of dealing with attrition/drop-outs • Whether there was any assessment of the distribution of confounders. The authors did not refer to how or why these criteria were selected, for example to a published text.

(Continued)

Table 6.8 (Continued)

Topic area	Reference	Quality assessment strategy
Education	Impacts of After-School Programs on Student Outcomes (Goerlich Zief et al., 2006, w090)	The study reviewers met and listed 39 qualities that they felt should be included in the reporting of a rigorous experimental study. These were adapted from the What Works Clearinghouse Study Review Standards (w202). From these, four specific standards were selected that the reviewers believed needed to be met in order for a study to be included in this review: (a) no specific evidence of control group contamination, (b) neither overall study attrition nor differential attrition would bias the impact estimates, (c) appropriate statistical measures were used for the analyses, and (d) the primary impact analyses were conducted on all available sample members at follow-up (i.e. intention to treat and not 'treatment on treated'). Two reviewers independently read each full study, applied the study quality criteria, and recommended whether the study should be included in the final review.
Library and information science	Effective methods for teaching information literacy skills to undergraduate students: a systematic review and meta-analysis (Koufogiannakis, and Wiebe, 2006, w122).	Used a previously published checklist (Morrison et al., 1999) with nine questions focusing on the validity and applicability of the study to be appraised. A methodological quality filter was also applied to all included studies. Fifty-five studies with a comparative study design, comparing two different teaching methods, and whose outcomes were based on tests of statistical significance 'passed the quality filter' and were analysed to determine the results of effectiveness for different teaching methods.
Computer sciences	Dyba, T. and Dingsoyr, T. (2008) Empirical studies of Agile software development: a systematic review. Information and Software Technology, 50, 9–10, 833–59.	Eleven criteria devised from CASP checklist and by the principle of good practice for conducting empirical research in software engineering proposed by Kitchenham et al. (2002)

Table 6.9   Key checklists resources

Study design checklists	
Resource	Details
Critical Appraisal Skills Programme (CASP, w054)	Checklists for the following study designs: • Systematic reviews • Randomised controlled trials (RCTs) • Qualitative research • Economic evaluation studies • Cohort studies • Case control studies • Diagnostic test studies
STrengthening the Reporting of OBservational studies in Epidemiology (STROBE) (w181)	Checklists for the following study designs: • Cohort, case-control, and cross-sectional studies (combined) • Cohort studies • Case-control studies • Cross-sectional studies
BestBETS (w015)	Checklists for the following study designs: • Case-control checklist (including harm) • Cohort • Decision rule • Diagnosis • Economic • Guideline • Prognosis • Qualitative • Randomised control trial • Review or meta-analysis • Screening • Survey (including pre-test probabilities
Case studies (Atkins and Sampson, 2002, w007)	Case studies
Qualitative research (Dixon-Woods et al., 2006, w063)	Prompts for qualitative research
Topic-specific checklists	
Evidence-based library and Information science (Glynn, 2006, w088)	
Education (Koufogiannakis et al., 2008, w123)	
Educational Intervention (BestBETS, w016)	
Generic checklists	
Standard quality assessment criteria for evaluating primary research papers from a variety of fields (Kmet et al., 2004. w121)	

Checklists

With many freely available checklists the task of choosing one has, perversely, become more challenging! It is useful to start with checklists that are widely accepted and used. If necessary, you could devise your own checklist by selecting criteria from different checklists. Remember that the aim is to see how the study design may impact upon the findings and checklists remain only a guide. Table 6.9 lists a few key checklist resources by study design or topic.

Pre-existing summaries

Lastly, it can be helpful to identify published examples where someone has performed a quality assessment of a published study, so investigate the journals in your discipline (particularly student versions of journals) to see if they do. And if they do not, why not suggest that they do?
Examples include:

- *Student BMJ* (w182)
- TERSE reports at the Centre for Evaluation and Monitoring (w188)
- Evidence Based Library and Information Practice (EBLIP) (w081)

References

Barnett-Page, E. and Thomas, J. (2009) Methods for the synthesis of qualitative research: a critical review. *BMC Medical Research Methodology*, **9**, 59. (w011)

Booth, A. (2007) Who will appraise the appraisers? – the paper, the instrument and the user. *Health Information and Libraries Journal*, **24**, 1, 72–6.

Booth, A. and Brice, A. (2004) Appraising the evidence, In: Booth, A. and Brice, A. (eds) *Evidence Based Practice for Information Professionals: A Handbook*. London: Facet Publishing.

Brunton, G., Oliver, S., Oliver, K., and Lorenc, T. (2006) A synthesis of research addressing children's, young people's and parents' views of walking and cycling for transport London, EPPI-Centre, Social Science Research Unit, Institute of Education, University of London. (w025)

Carroll, C., Booth, A., and Lloyd-Jones, M. (2010) Should we exclude poorly reported qualitative studies from systematic reviews? An evaluation of three reviews of qualitative data. In: Joint Colloquium of the Cochrane and Campbell Collaborations, *Bringing Evidence-Based Decision-Making to New Heights*. Keystone Resort, Colorado, USA 18–22 October 2010.

Centre for Evidence Based Medicine (2009) Study designs. (w033)

Centre for Reviews and Dissemination (2009) CRD's guidance for undertaking reviews in healthcare, 3rd edn. York, Centre for Reviews and Dissemination. (w036)

Chalmers, I., Glasziou, P., Greenhalgh, T., Heneghan, C., Howick, J., Liberati, A., Moschetti, I., Phillips, B., and Thornton, H. (2009) Steps in finding evidence ('Levels') for different types of question (w034).

Anon (no date). Critical appraisal of qualitative research (in draft). (Chapter 6). Cochrane Qualitative Research Methods Group Handbook. Adelaide: Cochrane Qualitative Research Methods Group (w045)

College of Emergency Medicine (2010) Bias and Confounding. (w046).

Schulz, K.F., Altman, D.G., Moher, D., CONSORT Group (2010) CONSORT 2010 Statement: Updated Guidelines for Reporting Parallel Group Randomised Trials. PLoS Medicine 7(3): e1000251. doi:10.1371/journal.pmed.1000251 (w048)

Critical Appraisal Skills Programme (2010) *Critical Appraisal Skills Programme Tools*. (w054).

Dixon-Woods, M., Shaw, R., Agarwal, S., and Smith, J. (2004) The problem of appraising qualitative research. *Quality and Safety in Health Care*, **13**, 223–5.

Dixon-Woods, M., Sutton, A., Shaw, R., Miller, T., Smith, J., Young, B., Bonas, S., Booth, A., and Jones, D. (2007) Appraising qualitative research for inclusion in systematic reviews: a quantitative and qualitative comparison of three methods. *Journal of Health Services Research and Policy*, **12**, 42–7.

Dixon-Woods, M., Cavers, D., Agarwal, S., Annandale, E., Arthur, A., Harvey, J., Hsu, R., Katbamna, S., Olsen, R., Smith, L., Riley, R., and Sutton, A.J. (2006) Conducting a critical interpretive synthesis of the literature on access to healthcare by vulnerable groups. *BMC Medical Research Methodology*, **6**, 35. (w063)

EPPI Centre (2010). Quality and relevance appraisal. (w075)

Grant, M.J. and Booth, A. (2009) A typology of reviews: an analysis of 14 review types and associated methodologies. *Health Information and Libraries Journal*, **26**, 2, 91–108. (w095)

Hammersley, M. (2001) On 'systematic' reviews of research literatures: a 'narrative' response to Evans and Benefield. *British Educational Research Journal*, **27**, 5, 543–54.

Higgins, J.P.T. and Green, S. (2008) *Cochrane Handbook for Systematic Reviews of Interventions*, Version 5.0.1. Oxford: Cochrane Collaboration. (w043)

Kitchenham, B.A., Pfleeger, S.L., Pickard, L.M., Jones, P.W., Hoaglin, D.C., El Emam, K., and Rosenberg, J. (2002) Preliminary guidelines for empirical research in software engineering. *IEE Transactions on Software Engineering*, **28**, 8, 721–34. (w118)

LoBiondo-Wood, G., Haber, J., and Krainovich-Miller, B. (2002) Critical reading strategies: overview of the research process. In: LoBiondo-Wood, G. and Haber, J. (eds) *Nursing Research: Methods, Critical Appraisal, and Utilization*. 5th edn. St Louis, MI: Mosby.

Moher, D., Liberati, A., Tetzlaff, J., Altman, D.G., and PRISMA Group (2009) Preferred reporting items for systematic reviews and meta-analyses: the PRISMA statement. *PLoS Medicine*, **6**,7, e1000097. (w137)

Morrison, J.M., Sullivan, F., Murray, E., and Jolly, B. (1999) Evidence-based education: development of an instrument to critically appraise reports of educational interventions. *Medical Education*, **33**, 890–3.

Parkes, J., Hyde, C., Deeks, J., and Milne, R. (2001) Teaching critical appraisal skills in health care settings. Cochrane Database of Systematic Reviews, Issue 3, (Art. No.: CD001270. DOI: 10.1002/14651858.CD001270). (w149)

Petticrew, M. and Roberts, H. (2006) *Systematic Reviews in the Social Sciences: A Practical Guide*. Malden, MA: Blackwell Publishing.

Popay, J., Rogers, A., and Williams, G. (1998) Rationale and standards for the systematic review of qualitative literature in health services research. *Qualitative Health Research*, **8**, 3, 341–51.

Rose, G. and Barker, D.J.P. (1994) *Epidemiology for the Uninitiated*, 3rd edn. London: BMJ Publishing Group.

Sackett, D.L., Richardson, S., Rosenberg, W., and Haynes, R.B. (1997) *Evidence-Based Medicine: How to Practise and Teach EBM*. London: Churchill Livingstone.

Sandelowski, M., Docherty, S., and Emden, C. (1997) Qualitative metasynthesis: Issues and Techniques. *Research in Nursing and Health*, **20**, 1, 365–71.

STROBE Group (2010) STROBE Statement (w181).

Taylor, B.J., Dempster, M., and Donnelly, M. (2007) Grading gems: appraising the quality of research for social work and social care. *British Journal of Social Work*, **37**, 335-54.

Thomas, J. and Harden, A. (2008) Methods for the thematic synthesis of qualitative research in systematic reviews. *BMC Medical Research Methodology*, **8**, 45. (w191)

Wells, K. and Littell, J.H. (2009) Study quality assessment in systematic reviews of research on intervention effects. *Research on Social Work Practice*, **19**, 1, 52-62.

What Works Clearing House US Department for Education (2005) Evidence Standards for Reviewing Studies. (w202)

SEVEN

Synthesising included studies

| Learning Objectives |

After reading this chapter, you should be able to:

- Describe the defining characteristics of synthesis and the value that this phase will add to your review.
- Identify the contribution of data extraction to the subsequent process of synthesis.
- Select an appropriate strategy for synthesis to meet the particular requirements of your data.
- Conduct synthesis within the context of a variety of different types of data presentation including textual, graphical, numerical and tabular.

Introduction

The value of any review does not lie in merely identifying and bringing together related studies. Synthesis is the stage of a review in which evidence extracted from different sources is *juxtaposed* to identify patterns and direction in the findings, or *integrated* to produce an overarching, new explanation or theory which attempts to account for the range of findings (Mays et al., 2005a). As you examine the composite **evidence base** for similarities, whether related to the **homogeneity** ('sameness') of study characteristics (i.e. how they were carried out) or relatedness of findings (i.e. what they found) you can contribute significant added value to your review process.

As Mulrow (1994) comments:

> The hundreds of hours spent conducting a scientific study ultimately contribute only a piece of an enormous puzzle. The value of any single study is derived from how it fits with and expands previous work, as well as from the study's intrinsic properties.

Explicit to this idea of synthesis is the principle that the reviewer is 'making a new whole out of the parts' (Pope et al., 2007). This manufactured 'new whole' may be in the form of a new line of argument, in construction of a new theory or in advocating a new conclusion. The frequently used analogy of building blocks is particularly relevant here – existing 'bricks' (articles) can be rearranged within an existing fabrication, they can be integrated with new bricks or they can be used to produce an entirely new construction.

Synthesis-analysis, analysis-synthesis?

Some authors may take issue with our SALSA framework in separating synthesis from analysis. Others may contend with our suggestion that synthesis precedes analysis. Such a distinction can be illustrated with reference to the specific technique of meta-analysis (interestingly the initial 'meta-' element of this term suggests synthesis while the following 'analysis' aligns with our own usage of the term). For meta-analysis the specific steps are as follows:

1 Tabulate summary data (data extraction)
2 Graph data (synthesis)
3 Check for heterogeneity (synthesis)
4 Perform a meta-analysis if heterogeneity is not a major concern (synthesis)
5 If heterogeneity is found, identify factors that can explain it (analysis)
6 Evaluate the impact of study quality on results (analysis)
7 Explore the potential for **publication bias** [analysis]

Thus we can see that, following data extraction, three steps associated with synthesis culminate in production of the well-recognised **meta-analysis** display of data. However, rather than being an endpoint, this **meta-analysis** is actually a starting point for further investigation and inquiry. Three steps of analysis include trying to identify factors associated with variation, examining study quality as a possible explanation for variation and investigating the likelihood that important studies have been overlooked or omitted.

It should be noted that in many methods of qualitative evidence, synthesis, the processes of synthesis and analysis are iterative rather than linear. A hypothesis or finding may be generated by the process of synthesis and then the reviewer will seek to confirm its presence in the existing data through some analytical technique. Indeed many analytical techniques are common to multiple types of synthesis. The distinction between synthesis and analysis is therefore most useful in defining the tools available for each process from which the reviewer is encouraged to select judiciously.

Overview of approaches to synthesis

Synthesis relies heavily on pattern recognition. This is why Hart places an emphasis on such techniques as *analogy* (looking for similarities between different phenomena), *metaphor* (thinking about one thing as if it were the same as another), and *homology* (looking for direct and corresponding relationships between natural and synthetic structures e.g. between nature and human society) (Hart, 1998).

Furthermore Hart and other authors emphasise how important it is to use the basic critical and analytical components of *comparison* and *contrast* (Hart, 1998; Cresswell, 2003; Gray and Malins, 2004).

> [Some] references may be organized chronologically in parts of your review where you may be evaluating developments over time; some may be arranged thematically, demonstrating similarities and allowing you to make creative connections (cross-currents) between previously unrelated research; and some arranged to demonstrate *comparison and contrast* perhaps using a common set of criteria as an 'anchor'. (Gray and Malins, 2004)

Comparison and contrast may therefore be used within a literature review to compare study by study (usually only possible where there are a limited number of items for inclusion) or by findings (i.e. similarities and differences across studies). Within a larger literature review, as carried out for a dissertation or thesis, it may be desirable to combine elements of both approaches.

Approaches to synthesis can be characterised in three main forms; quantitative, qualitative and integrative (i.e. bringing together both quantitative and qualitative). Once you have identified which type of data you shall be using, you need to decide how best to synthesise and analyse your data. Of course the most readily apparent options are to use quantitative approaches for handling quantitative data and qualitative approaches for processing qualitative data. However your synthesis toolkit also includes using quantitative approaches to qualitative data (i.e. where the occurrence of themes or words is quantified such as in **content analysis**) or qualitative approaches to quantitative data (i.e. where different types of quantitative study are described narratively) (Mays et al., 2005b).

Quantitative approaches can be best exemplified by the technique of meta-analysis which has certainly been in the ascendancy over the last couple of decades. Alongside such *quantitative* techniques as meta-analysis, Dixon-Woods and colleagues (2004) have identified no fewer than 12 *qualitative* approaches to research synthesis (Box 7.1).

Box 7.1 Twelve qualitative approaches to synthesis

1 Narrative synthesis
2 Grounded theory – constant comparison
3 Meta-ethnography
4 Meta-synthesis
5 Meta-study
6 Logical analysis
7 Data analysis techniques
8 Metaphorical analysis
9 Domain analysis
10 Hermeneutical analysis
11 Discourse analysis, and
12 Analytic induction

A synthesis may be **aggregative** (focused on bringing evidence together and looking for generalisable lessons), comparative or **replicative** (focused on the extent to which different sources of evidence reinforce or agree with one another), or focused on the development of theory or explanations (Mays et al., 2005a; Hammersley, 2002, w102).

Use of three approaches in particular, **narrative synthesis**, **meta-ethnography**, and **realist synthesis**, has increased rapidly across different disciplines (Denyer and Tranfield, 2006; Armitage and Keeble-Allen, 2008). Before looking at specific techniques of synthesis we will look at a key step on the path to synthesis, namely data extraction.

Extracting data for your review

Data extraction is a key element in demonstrating that a systematic approach has been followed as it seeks to approach different studies in a consistent manner. Pawson and colleagues (2004) characterise data extraction in terms of its centrality to the systematic review process and in terms of the intensive effort it requires:

> The next stage in systematic review is often considered its core, and a time consuming, uphill slog to boot.

This process allows the reviewer to examine which elements of data are present in each individual study report. However, at a practical level, data extraction is also valuable for other types of review. Studies are reported differently according to the requirements of the particular journal within which they have been published. They vary in completeness, in level of detail, and in degree of contextual richness, occasionally referred to as 'thickness' (Popay et al., 1998). Extracting data from this disparate set of studies facilitates comparisons in relation both to what is reported and, indeed, what is missing. It is difficult for the human brain to assimilate variables from more than a handful of studies at the same time so converting these study reports into a common format, a lowest common denominator if you like, helps the interpretation of the body of evidence and aids the subsequent process of pattern recognition (Petticrew and Roberts, 2006). While Pawson and colleagues do not pretend to be publicists for the process they do manage to summarise succinctly its overall intent:

> The conventional systematic reviewer proceeds by lining up primary studies that have made it through the quality filter, fine-tuning the set of characteristics through which to compare them, combing through each source to extract precisely the same nugget of information from each, and recording these data onto a standard grid (often reproduced as an appendix to the review). (Pawson et al., 2004)

As Light and Pillemer (1984) conclude:

> A reviewer unarmed with formal tools to extract and summarize findings must rely on an extraordinary ability to mentally juggle relationships among many variables. Systematic ways of exploring such relationships would make it far easier both to detect and understand them. (p.4)

For systematic reviews it is common to use a data extraction form for this process (Box 7.2). Such forms can either be designed from scratch or, more commonly, adapted from a similar type of review. Extended reports of systematic reviews frequently include a data extraction form as an Appendix. The form provides a link between your original review question and the data from included studies. It also provides an audit trail for the extraction and synthesis process. Finally, it provides the raw material from which the subsequent synthesis and analysis will emerge (Evans, 2007).

Typically the data extraction template is created as a word processor document although some authors use spreadsheet or database facilities for form design. Your final choice will be determined by the type of data that you will be extracting. If data will be in a consistent format, using pre-specified codes and categories and thus suited to retrieval by database queries, and the analysis will be primarily aggregative then a database will be of value. If however the data synthesis and analysis is to be more interpretive with considerable variation in the content and format of the data then separate word-processed forms may be appropriate. Even though the data is machine-readable you may find it helpful to print out the data extraction forms so that you can compare data across forms and instantly follow up possible lines of inquiry.

Box 7.2 Possible elements for inclusion in a data extraction form

1 Eligibility: explicit statement of inclusion and exclusion criteria with the opportunity to indicate whether study is to be included in the review or not.
2 Descriptive data: information about study characteristics including setting, population.
3 Quality assessment data: information about the quality of the study. A formal checklist may be incorporated within the documentation.
4 Results: information about the results of the study in the form of data to be used in your review. Data may be in 'raw' format as taken directly from the paper and/or in a uniform format. Ideally it will be in both forms to indicate variation in methods but also to allow checking for accuracy.

Data extraction may be undertaken at the same time as quality assessment (see Chapter 6) or it may be performed separately, either before or after the overall judgement of quality. Authors argue the merits and disadvantages of both approaches. Obviously it may be considered more efficient to examine the detail of reporting *and* the quality of the study from a single pass through the literature as both require an in-depth reading of a study. Others argue that the two processes are dissimilar in that data extraction encourages you to focus on the minutiae of the report while quality assessment involves an overall holistic judgement of a study. For these reasons some prefer to arrive at an overall assessment of quality to temper or moderate their subsequent examination of findings. Others prefer to immerse themselves in the detail of the study report before stepping back to view the whole that emerges from the sum of its parts (Barnett-Page and Thomas, 2009, w011).

The level of detail for data extraction, and the corresponding time spent upon the activity, varies according to the type of review being undertaken. At its simplest level, the traditional review method of writing a full reference and judiciously selected quotations from a paper on a 5-by-3-inch index card is a form of data extraction. However, this does assume that you can anticipate what the most significant contribution of a paper will be in advance of reading the entire body of the literature. For a scoping or mapping review you may simply be extracting key features of study characteristics such as the setting, the study design, number of participants, etc. (Budgen et al., 2008; Ryan et al., 2009). As Petticrew and Roberts (2006) observe, such a study will attempt:

> to determine what sorts of studies addressing the systematic review question have been carried out, where they are published, in what databases they have been indexed, what sorts of outcomes they have assessed, and in which populations.

The time constraints associated with rapid reviews may require that you extract data directly into tables rather than go through the additional intermediate stage of designing a data extraction form and then extracting data from each individual study (Watt et al., 2008; Ganann et al., 2010). However, for most other review contexts the time you spend in extracting data is rewarded with the ease with which you will subsequently be able to produce data displays, to identify shared characteristics and patterns across studies and to spot particular discrepancies or inconsistencies that benefit from subsequent analysis. You can display such data in the form of matrices, graphs, charts, or networks (Whittemore and Knafl, 2005). Such displays help you to visualise patterns and relationships within and across the constituent studies. This provides you with a good starting point for interpretation and subsequent analysis (Knafl and Webster, 1988; Sandelowski, 1995). An example of a data display that can be used to look at correlations between study characteristics and study setting is given in Table 7.1. This can be simply produced once data extraction has been completed.

Table 7.1   Matrix for examining possible correlations

Country of origin	Canada	United States	Singapore	South Africa	Australia	France	Germany	India	Poland	Japan	Netherlands	Sweden	Spain	United Kingdom	Italy	Romania
Roosevelt et al. (2009)		X														
Cosmo et al. (2007)		X			X	X	X	X	X	X	X	X	X	X		
Washington et al. (2005)		X														
Bull (2004)														X		
Ceauşescu et al. (2001)																X

In Table 7.1 the reader can see at a glance by looking down the columns that three of the studies (by Roosevelt et al., 2009; Cosmo et al., 2007 and Washington et al., 2005) contain data from the United States. Conversely, by looking across the rows they can see that only one study (Cosmo et al., 2007) is a multi-country study while all the others report data from a single country.

Pawson and colleagues (2004) observe that qualitative reviews are increasingly subjected to a similar process.

> Qualitative reviews increasingly conform to this expectation about completing comprehensive and uniform extraction sheets. A crucial difference on this variant, however, is that grid entries can take the form of free text and usually consist of short verbal descriptions of key features of interventions and studies.

The value of data extraction for qualitative research depends upon whether the overall intent is **aggregative** (where bringing multiple studies together in a common format will assist in the subsequent process of assimilation and summing up) or **interpretive** (where data extraction may help in managing the evidence base but needs to be enhanced by more creative techniques if the reviewer is to maximise the explanatory value of the data). The units of extraction in this case will be specific findings and illustrative excerpts from the text that demonstrate the origins of such findings.

Table 7.2   Sample data extraction form for journal article

Title of review		
Publication details		
		Reference number
Author(s)		Year
Title of article		
Title of journal		
Volume	Issue	Pages
Study details		
Study type		
Study design		
Study aims		
Any further research questions addressed		
Country in which study was done		
User/carer stakeholder involvement in design/conduct of study		
Setting (e.g. rural/urban), context and key characteristics (e.g. of organisation)		

(Continued)

Table 7.2   (Continued)

Target population	Number of participants
(e.g. primary school children, secondary school children, etc.)	
Sampling/how recruited	
(any info re: age, ethnicity, gender)	
Details of any theory/conceptual models used	
Characteristics of participants	
(e.g. practitioners, types of job roles, age, sex, gender, ethnicity, type of policy makers)	

Nature of the study

Study date and duration	
Methods of data collection and who collected by	
(e.g. researcher/practitioner)	
Any research tools used	
Analysis used	
Aim of intervention	
Country	Location/setting
Target population	
(age, ethnicity, gender, etc.)	

Intervention

Who provided the intervention (e.g. teacher, volunteer, etc.)?	
Description of intervention	
How was intervention/service delivered	
(e.g. groupwork, home visits, teaching module)?	
Duration	Intensity
How and why was intervention developed	
(e.g. reasons for development, any 'needs assessment' or involvement of target population)	
Any theoretical framework used to develop the intervention	

Results

Outcome measures used
Details of outcomes/findings
Strengths/limitations of the study (including diversity of sample)

Authors' conclusions:

Reviewer's notes or comments

Planning your synthesis strategy

A key early stage in the process of synthesis is planning your initial **synthesis strategy** – how you will approach the literature once it has been assembled (Kitchenham, 2007). You have several choices as to how you will accomplish this task; your approach will be governed by the nature of your review and its objectives.

You may in fact need to switch from your initial strategy (Box 7.3) to a more appropriate alternative as patterns from the literature become clearer.

Box 7.3   Planning your synthesis strategy

1   Decide whether to read swiftly through all papers OR to work through papers in detail one by one.
2   Decide upon the method of documentation (memos, notes, structured form).
3   Select starting paper (e.g. index paper – according to age, conceptual richness, number of citations, source discipline, etc.).
4   Decide on approach for subsequent papers (chronological, purposive sampling, maximum variation sampling, etc.).
5   Construct cross case comparisons (e.g. tabulation, etc.).

Some reviewers prefer to start with a holistic approach that involves reading through the body of literature, with very little hesitation or interruption, perhaps occasionally **memo-ing** or annotating with brief points to which they will return later (Finfgeld-Connett, 2009). Other reviewers start with an **index paper** against which all subsequent papers are to be compared. Considerable variation exists in how this index paper is identified or defined and this reflects genuine variety in what each review is trying to achieve; it may be the earliest paper, the most cited paper, the richest in terms of either data or conceptual development, etc. Garside and colleagues (2008) justify their selection of the index paper for their review of the experience of heavy menstrual bleeding as follows:

> In the event, [Paper X] was chosen as an index paper against which the other papers were compared, as this was the only one with a strong conceptual framework. Other papers, while organising data under emergent themes, showed little attempt to provide explanatory concepts.

In this instance, the interpretive nature of their review (a **meta-ethnography**), with its endpoint of creating explanatory models, justified an approach targeted at conceptual richness.

Alternatively your topic may be more suited to a sampling approach. The literature may fall within individual cognate disciplines from which you wish to sample. In their review on the diffusion of innovations Greenhalgh and colleagues (2005) drew on the thinking of Kuhn (1962) and purposively attempted to capture the development of concepts within different disciplines and they sampled accordingly.

Table 7.3 Approaches to synthesis in different types of reviews

Type of review	Approaches used to synthesis	Application	Review example
Scoping review	Coding Narrative synthesis Tabular presentation	Descriptive coding was applied to include study features such as design, country of origin, type of behaviour targeted, characteristics of population and type of incentive used. Outcome studies were coded in greater depth. Paragraphs described the features of studies for each variable (e.g. types of intervention and incentive). Tables complemented narrative synthesis with frequencies and percentages of each type.	A scoping review of the evidence for incentive schemes to encourage positive health and other social behaviours in young people (Kavanagh et al., 2005, w117).
Mapping review	Keywording Mapping studies not synthesised because they were 'disparate in their focus'	EPPI-Centre core keywording strategy (w073) used to classify studies according to a range of criteria, including bibliographic details (how the study was identified and whether it has been published), and contextual details (the language in which the study was written/published and the country where the study was conducted). Key aspects of the study also coded, such as topic focus of study, and information about the subjects of the study Mapping stage of review describes studies found to be relevant, gives overview of the field of study, and enables reviewers to focus on particular areas of map. Brief commentary given on each study with emphasis on conclusions not methods.	A systematic map into approaches to making initial teacher training flexible and responsive to the needs of trainee teachers (Graham-Matheson et al., 2005, w094).
Systematic review	Categorisation Data extraction Quality assessment Narrative synthesis Tabular presentation Meta-analysis not possible because of variability of studies.	Articles categorised by type of publication. Data from intervention studies included study design, sample and intervention characteristics, and data collection methods and measures. Studies assessed using checklist. Narrative description and tabulation of study features and of methodological adequacy.	A systematic review of work-place interventions for alcohol-related problems (Webb, et al., 2009).
Qualitative systematic review	Meta-ethnography Conceptual model Graphical display Narrative description	Extraction of key concepts, translation of these concepts, construction of conceptual model of factors influencing effective dissemination. Conceptual model portrayed graphically. Graphical display of how concepts link together in Boolean relationship. Narrative description of each theme.	Constructing a model of effective information dissemination in a crisis (Duggan and Banwell, 2004, w064).

Table 7.4   Strategies for conducting an evidence synthesis

Which type of data have I got?									
Quantitative				Qualitative			Quantitative and qualitative		
Are outcomes reported in a comparable format?				Is the objective validation or generation of a theory?			Is the objective validation or generation of a theory?		
No	Yes			Generation	Validation	No/not sure	Generation	Validation	No/not sure
Use narrative synthesis and tabular presentation	Consider using meta-analysis			Consider meta-ethnography or grounded theory approaches	Consider framework synthesis	Consider narrative synthesis or thematic synthesis	Consider critical interpretive synthesis, meta-narrative or use of logic models	Consider realist synthesis or Bayesian meta-synthesis	Consider narrative synthesis or thematic synthesis
	Are the studies heterogeneous?								
	No	Yes	Not sure						
	Use fixed effects method	Use random effects method	Use random effects method						

While we are writing here about your *initial* synthesis strategy, and this is open to subsequent refinement and change, you nevertheless need to have a reasonably clear picture of your direction of travel. Clearly if your final intention is to read and review an entire body of literature, albeit centred on a very focused question, decisions on the order in which you will handle the papers are less critical. Each paper is given the same opportunity to contribute equally to the final map or the pooled result (quantitative) or will be compared with all previous papers, perhaps using the **constant comparative method** (qualitative). If, however, your final intention is to sample judiciously from the literature, perhaps until a point of **informational redundancy** and/or **theoretical saturation** (Combs et al., 2010) then you need to have confidence that your sampling frame has been constructed appropriately. However, as Atkins and colleagues (2008) observe:

> Key difficulties with this approach include how to establish the population of studies from which to sample without first identifying all relevant studies. It is also unclear how data saturation is determined in a synthesis, where access to the original data is limited, and little guidance on this is available.

Cognitive research indicates that the human brain often finds it inordinately easier to identify overall patterns or similarities in data ahead of being able to spot inconsistencies or exceptions to the rule (Petticrew and Roberts, 2006). This trait holds several dangers to the objectivity of the review process. The reviewer is likely to be subconsciously influenced to impose explanatory patterns over data that is either not present or non-apparent. As Bergman and Coxon (2005) state:

> Of course, skilled authors are able to selectively make authority arguments that bolster a particular line of argument, so this strategic verification of knowledge, although effective and widespread, is the most threatening to the integrity of a study and its results.

Furthermore, we are more likely to accept data that support our underlying opinion and to reject or explain away data that are uncomfortable or that do not fit easily. While 'line of argument' is dealt with first for these reasons, it is very important that equal time and attention is paid to the more nuanced findings from inconsistencies or contradictions. Indeed, we maintain that we should consciously construct mechanisms that maximise opportunities to 'challenge' a persuasive or seductive line of argument. Where a proposed review has an experienced researcher who 'holds all the cards' in terms of being more senior, being more familiar with the review methodology, and being more familiar with the subject area for the review, when compared with an associate partner-reviewer, there are many warning signs concerning the validity of the subsequent process of synthesis. While such an unequal alliance is less likely given the distributed expertise of a larger review team it is important to make sure that those closest

Table 7.5   Elements of data analysis

Elements	Application within synthesis methods
Noting patterns and themes	Meta-ethnography, thematic synthesis
Seeing plausibility (ensuring conclusions make good sense)	Meta-ethnography
Clustering	Content analysis, framework synthesis, meta-ethnography, thematic synthesis
Making metaphors	Meta-ethnography, meta-narrative review
Counting	Cross-case analysis, meta-analysis, meta-summary
Making contrasts/comparisons	Meta-ethnography, meta-narrative review
Partitioning variables	Framework synthesis, meta-ethnography, meta-analysis
Subsuming particulars into the general	Meta-analysis, meta-ethnography
Noting relations between variables	Logic models, realist synthesis
Finding intervening variables	Logic models, realist synthesis
Building a logical chain of evidence	Logic models, realist synthesis
Making conceptual/theoretical coherence	Concept maps, logic models, meta-ethnography, meta-narrative review, realist synthesis

Based on Miles and Huberman (1994)

to the data, especially if junior members of the team, are given the opportunity to challenge and resist interpretations within which data is inappropriately 'shoehorned'.

While distinctions between different methodologies are conceptually useful, it is helpful to concentrate pragmatically on three components of a synthesis (Suri and Clarke, 2009):

- Pursuing a line of argument
- Examining consistencies
- Identifying the disconfirming case

These three techniques have received particular prominence within the domain of evidence synthesis, partly due to their emphasis within meta-ethnography (Noblit and Hare, 1988). However as Whittemore and Knafl (2005) make clear (Table 7.5) many more techniques are available to populate our repertoire, during the iterative phases of synthesis and analysis.

After considering techniques for handling data, we will look at how such activities may be undertaken within the context of different types of data presentation, namely textual, graphical, numerical and tabular.

Pursuing a line of argument

Thinking around the **line of argument** with regard to synthesis is most developed within the type of review known as **meta-ethnography**. **Meta-ethnography** is an interpretive approach that seeks to preserve the social and theoretical contexts in which findings emerge (Noblit and Hare, 1988, pp. 5–6). Noblit and Hare state that the aim of a **line of argument** synthesis is to discover a 'whole' among a set of parts'. **Meta-ethnography** involves open coding to identify emergent categories and then **constant comparison** of metaphors across studies. As Pope et al. (2007) observe, this process is essentially based on inference. The reviewer uses published narratives of research within a narrow predefined field to construct an explanatory theory or model. A major weakness is that any interpretation is only one possible reading of the studies (Noblit and Hare, 1988). It is therefore feasible for another investigator to produce an entirely different reading (Noblit and Hare, 1988). Nevertheless, meta-ethnography is the most commonly practised form of qualitative synthesis (Britten et al., 2002; Campbell et al., 2003; Dixon-Woods et al., 2007). Indeed Campbell and colleagues (2003) argue that meta-ethnography is:

> Perhaps the best developed method for synthesising qualitative data and one which clearly had its origins in the interpretivist paradigm, from which most methods of primary qualitative research evolved.

Box 7.4   Meta-ethnography

What is it?

A technique used to translate concepts across individual studies. It involves:

1 Reciprocal translation (establishing where studies share common overarching concepts or themes, even where expressed in different terms).
2 Line of argument synthesis (establishing where studies contribute to a shared line of thought, identified through inference).
3 Refutational synthesis (establishing the extent to which studies contradict or refute each other) (Noblit and Hare, 1988).

What can I use it for?

Typically meta-ethnography may be used to extend existing theory or to develop new theory.

How has it been used?

Siau and Long (2005) synthesised five different stage models of e-government using meta-ethnography. They were able to translate the stages within different models into one another (reciprocal translation) and thus to develop a new e-government stage model. The new e-government stage model had five stages: web presence, interaction, transaction, transformation, and e-democracy.

Meta-ethnography is comparable to a grounded theory approach to the extent that it uses open coding and identifies categories emerging from the data (Tranfield et al., 2003). It draws heavily on the constant comparative method (Beck, 2001). First you would identify and list key metaphors (themes, perspectives, phrases, ideas, and/or concepts) from each individual study (Noblit and Hare, 1988). You then 'put together' these metaphors by linking them across studies. In such a way, you seek to provide a holistic account of the phenomenon (Suri, 1999). Many qualitative researchers consider the results of a study to be specific to one particular context at one point in time (Campbell et al., 2003). Noblit and Hare (1988) argue that all synthesis, quantitative or qualitative, involves interpretation as the reviewer gives meaning to the sets of studies under consideration. Importantly, meta-ethnography enables a reader to translate the studies into their own social understanding (1988, p. 18). However, the reader should always remember that they are seeing the synthesised studies through the worldview of a translator, that is the reviewer (1988, p. 25). As such, advocates of the approach argue that translations are unique forms of synthesis that preserve the interpretive qualities of the original data by:

> carefully peeling away the surface layers of studies to find their hearts and souls in a way that does least damage to them. (Sandelowski et al., 1997, p. 370)

Another approach to pursuing 'lines of argument' involves use of meta-narrative techniques to explore large and heterogeneous literatures by identifying the unfolding 'storyline' of research (Greenhalgh et al., 2005). While the approach can help build an understanding of a field, findings should be seen as 'illuminating the problem and raising areas to consider' rather than 'providing the definitive answers' (Greenhalgh et al., 2005). The literature may possess adversarial characteristics, perhaps with arguments attributed to particular 'schools of thought' – again you will probably wish to sample initially from each of the most prominent stances.

Box 7.5   Meta-narrative review

What is it?

Meta-narrative reviews use a historical and philosophical perspective as a pragmatic way of making sense of a diverse literature. They acknowledge the existence of heterogeneity within the different paradigms. The questioning process starts from Kuhn (1962) by asking:

What research teams have researched this area?
How did they conceptualise the problem?
What theories did they use to link the problem with potential causes and impacts?
What methods did they define as 'rigorous' and 'valid'?
What instruments did they use?

What can I use it for?

To investigate a broad open-ended question in terms of the main research traditions, schools of thought, used to explore that question. This approach fits well with the open-ended exploratory phase that characterises the first year of most PhD work.

(Continued)

(Continued)

How has it been used?

Greenhalgh and colleagues (2009) used the meta-narrative method to examine 'conflicting' findings that illustrate how researchers had differently conceptualised and studied the implementation of the electronic patient record (EPR). They considered 24 previous systematic reviews and 94 further primary studies. The key tensions identified from the literature centred on seven conflicting tensions:

1 the EPR ('container' or 'itinerary');
2 the EPR user ('information-processer' or 'member of socio-technical network');
3 organisational context ('the setting within which the EPR is implemented' or 'the EPR-in-use');
4 clinical work ('decision making' or 'situated practice');
5 the process of change ('the logic of determinism' or 'the logic of opposition');
6 implementation success ('objectively defined' or 'socially negotiated'); and
7 complexity and scale ('the bigger the better' versus 'small is beautiful').

A key finding from their meta-narrative approach was that even though secondary work (audit, research, billing) may be made more efficient by the EPR, this might be at the expense of primary clinical work which may be made less efficient.

Reciprocal translation

An important feature of the **line of argument** component of synthesis is what Noblit and Hare (1988) label **reciprocal translation**. The importance of reciprocal translation is illustrated in Table 7.6.

In Box D, two papers describe the same phenomenon and use the same terms or language to describe this phenomenon. In this case, one assumes a 'direct translation' between the two papers. This is the most straightforward type of translation. It is common where agreed definitions or classifications are used within a single discipline (e.g. stress and coping in the nursing literature). In contrast, in Box A, we have different terms being used by two papers to refer to different phenomena. For different reasons, this is again easy to handle because each of the two papers adds to the conceptual richness of the line of argument. So, for example, the psychological and educational literature may yield completely different facets for an umbrella term of 'Identity'. The fact that a second paper has no

Table 7.6   A conceptual grid for reciprocal translation

	Terms do not match	Terms match
Ideas/concepts do not match	Neither terms nor ideas/concepts match (A)	Terms match but refer to different Ideas/concepts (C)
Ideas/concepts do match	Ideas/concepts match but assigned different terms (B)	Both terms and ideas/concepts match (D)

similarity with the first means that we can be confident that theoretical saturation has not yet been reached. We can also see the value of sampling articles from different disciplines. However it may be subsequently more difficult to establish a relationship between unconnected concepts from the two papers – unless of course we subsequently find a third paper that contains both concepts.

More problematic are translation scenarios where ideas/concepts coincide but terms do not (Box B). These are most typical where different disciplines have explored a phenomenon independently and yet have arrived at a similar conclusion (Curran et al., 2007). Here the reviewer has to decide which of two terms is to be preferred or, indeed whether to settle for a third term that represents a middle ground or that adequately captures the richness of both previous terminologies.

Finally, we encounter translation scenarios where terms coincide but ideas/concepts do not. Clearly it would be confusing to conflate both meanings within a shared terminology where they are intended to convey different meanings. Typically, therefore, a reviewer would assign an independent term to each concept. Alternatively, they might favour one term while making it explicit that this term is not to be used for its subordinate meaning, where an alternative term is to be preferred.

Such a process may seem difficult to follow at an abstract or theoretical level. We shall therefore illustrate these principles with an easy experiment that you could conduct with some of your colleagues (Box 7.6).

Box 7.6   A simple illustration of qualitative synthesis

Ask your colleagues to each provide three phrases to describe their perfect holiday. Some may be very clear and specific e.g. 'good waves for windsurfing'. In this example, there is little possibility for confusion with another concept although further clarification might be needed as to what precisely this requires. What, however, if two or more colleagues use such phrases as 'good weather'? – clearly this will differ between different settings (e.g. temperate versus tropical settings) and different types of holiday (beach versus skiing holiday). Further clarification is required to see if these colleagues have similar or different ideas in mind. Alternatively, colleagues may use different terminology (e.g. 'many places of interest' and 'rich cultural heritage'). In this case, you need to establish whether these two phrases do actually 'translate' into the same concept or idea. If by 'many places of interest' a colleague means restaurants, bars, and discos it is less likely that reciprocal translation between the two phrases is appropriate! Of course the difficulty of this process is compounded in the case of published studies because it is not usually possible to go back to your informants to clarify exactly what was meant.

Notwithstanding this focus on qualitative synthesis, we should emphasise that a similar process takes place albeit for a different purpose, when considering more quantitative review questions. For example, are the *settings* for a particular intervention (e.g. personal counsellors in secondary education) more similar than

different? Are the *interventions* themselves comparable? (For example, if something is described in multiple studies using a common terminology such as a
'policy unit' do these studies refer to the same entity?) Such questions at the
synthesis stage inform subsequent analysis e.g. whether any naturally occurring
subgroups can be identified for more detailed investigation and whether the line
of argument of the synthesis is overly dependent upon particular individual studies or groups of studies. In short, one can decide whether, in fact, it makes sense
to treat all included studies as a group (**lumping**) or whether they make more
sense as a series of separate and distinct groups (**splitting**).

As illustrated by the preceding examples the whole process of constructing a **line
of argument** synthesis is iterative with each additional study used to test or challenge
the robustness and validity of the evolving argument. For this reason, the **constant
comparative method** is often used as the practical means by which such arguments
are developed. An alternative would be to split studies to be included between one
group, to be used to develop the argument or theory, and another group, to be used
to test or validate the emerging theory. Dividing studies in this way could either be
done randomly, to ensure that both groups of studies are similarly representative, or
purposively according to a particular characteristic such as, age group, country, ethnic group, organisation type, etc. So, in this latter example, if you were looking at
models of outreach for underserved groups you might build up a theory or model
based on the literature in general and then examine the extent to which such generalised findings apply to a specific subset of studies relating to refugees or traveller
populations. Such an approach is particularly suited to dissertation or thesis requirements where a generalised theory is explored within the context of a specific population or context to meet the requirement to generate 'new knowledge'.

Examining consistencies

It is not sufficient to simply catalogue all the themes or variables to emerge from
the individual studies and then amalgamate them into a long master list. Following
a pruning or paring down process, by which synonyms are identified and **reciprocal
translation** is effected, you will want to examine possible groupings to the patterns
in your data. This process, which applies to both quantitative and qualitative types
of review, seeks to sensitise the review to major patterns in potential influencing
factors such as, context, intervention type, etc. In a quantitative review these represent **explanatory variables** or **confounding variables** which may be recorded consistently as codes or categories. In a qualitative review, these resemble themes or
constructs, in a variety of forms and formats that emerge from the synthesis process.

A key step in such data analysis is data comparison. This iterative process
involves examining data displays for primary source data in order to identify patterns, themes or relationships. If you identify patterns in the data, you can start to
think about the relationship between these variables or identified themes. Perhaps
the themes exhibit a tension, namely one desirable attribute can only be achieved
at the expense of another competing desirable attribute. For example, in our

review of work-place-based e-learning (Carroll et al., 2009; see Chapter 10) students valued the ability to work at their own pace and yet also valued feedback. For an educator, this produces a tension in that they may need to schedule their availability for feedback but this is not possible if requests for feedback can come at any time from students working at their own pace.

It is difficult to display such tensions in linear form via a list of concepts. It will often be preferable to draw a **conceptual map** to include most of the variables or identified themes (Brown, 1999) and relationships between them (e.g. synergistic or antagonistic). Such a conceptual map would have similar variables grouped in close proximity. If there is a pathway effect i.e. one factor takes place before another in a temporal order this can also be displayed effectively via the conceptual map. As a more complete picture emerges of the relationships between variables or themes you can start to engage with existing theories or even start to develop hypotheses with which to populate an emergent theory.

Although creativity is a very important feature of this stage of pattern seeking and interpretation, it is important that, at all times, you try to ensure that you ground any theories or hypothesis in your data. Conclusion drawing and verification is required if you are to move from the 'particulars into the general'. As new data is accommodated, you need to continually revise any conclusions or conceptual models so that they continue to be inclusive (Miles and Huberman, 1994). You need to verify any patterns, themes, relationships, or conclusions with your primary source data to ensure that they are both accurate and confirmable (Miles and Huberman, 1994). At this stage, you are particularly vulnerable to a **cognitive bias** such as premature analytic closure (being locked into a particular pattern) (Miles and Huberman, 1994) or exclusion of pertinent evidence because it is inconvenient or extraneous to your theorising (Sandelowski, 1995).

To use our earlier example about a holiday, you would probably want to group individual data into overarching constructs, such as weather, location, attractions, companions, food and drink, etc. You may then wish to trace particular responses back to particular respondent characteristics: for example, males may be more likely to mention food and drink or younger respondents may focus on extreme sports or strenuous activities. You may therefore need to re-examine the data in the light of such differences. Furthermore, there may be tensions or conflict between some of the characteristics – if, for example, large numbers of respondents desire 'peace and quiet' and equally large numbers require 'excitement'. Identification of such tensions may lead you to explore in more detail their implications or practical manifestations. In our holiday example, you might ask, 'How does a couple with conflicting expectations of a perfect holiday resolve such a conflict?' You may subsequently come up with such models or constructs as 'taking turns' (strict alternation), 'separate lives' (separate holidays), 'anything for a quiet life' (grudging acquiescence), 'together and then apart' (two holidays/year) or 'your turn now but I'll cash in the goodwill chip when I need it' (delayed trade-off).

In quantitative studies, you are similarly looking for shared characteristics of particular groupings of studies. For example, do particular studies share a certain type of measurement? Are some studies measured using objective measures while others use subjective measurement such as self-reporting? At this point it is helpful to make a distinction between *descriptive* grouping that may contribute to a narrative commentary or synthesis (e.g. 'ten of the fifteen studies were conducted using the Edinburgh Depression Scale while the remainder used self reporting') and analytical grouping (where you may examine such differences to see if they might provide a possible explanation for differences in results) (see Chapter 8).

Clearly examining the data for consistencies requires a greater degree of engagement with the data than identification of an overarching **line of argument**. Typically it moves you from broad questions such as 'what works' towards more nuanced interpretations such as, 'What works under what circumstances?' (Pawson, 2001).

Identifying the disconfirming case

One contrast between systematic approaches to the literature and more traditional narrative reviews is the necessity to expose the emerging review product to deliberate testing of its robustness. As Whittemore and Knafl (2005) state:

> Analytical honesty is a priority; the data analysis process is made transparent with rival explanations and spurious relationships thoughtfully explored.

While such an approach may seem daunting, particularly to the novice researcher, it is essential if the review is to establish itself as a reliable and authoritative contribution to the evidence base.

Identification of the negative or disconfirming case is commonly regarded as the most difficult component of the synthesis process (Whittemore and Knapfl, 2005). It is particularly challenging when conflicting results are equally compelling and derive from high quality reports. Such differences may typically occur across one or more specific variables. It is important at this stage not to attach too much importance to a single preferred variable when a difference may in fact be attributable to many variables working together. For example a review of change management strategies appeared to find that strategies using multiple interventions worked better than those based upon a single strategy (Grimshaw et al., 2004). However, closer examination found this relationship to be more complex. Not only are multiple intervention strategies more difficult to implement in the first place but there may also be a 'scattergun' effect (i.e. if you select multiple interventions you increase the chance of at least one working successfully). In this case it may not be that multiple interventions *work together* more effectively but rather that an individual intervention *works alone* but its specific effect is masked among accompanying interventions.

Of course, individual studies may differ from the main body of studies across a wide range of aspects i.e. they are genuine 'outliers'. In such cases, you may wish to reconsider whether it truly makes sense to include them within an overarching analysis or whether they should be analysed separately. Such considerations of 'sameness' versus 'differentness' are fundamental to the entire process of meta-analysis. Although they may be less readily apparent in qualitative synthesis, they are no less important as you do not want to imply generalisability from an isolated and exceptional case study.

Because of the potential for being led towards a wrong conclusion it is critical that you take steps to document your hunches and other intuitive steps in the process. This will allow you to retrace your steps to a point of divergence and to reconstruct an alternative line of argument. As well as testing the premises for your thinking with a supervisor or mentor, other useful mechanisms may include checking assumptions with stakeholders or user representatives. However, you should not automatically assume that your line of reasoning is wrong just because your perceptions are not confirmed by other parties. After all, by synthesising the literature, you may have access to privileged insights not easily discerned by an individual who is immersed in one particular context. However, if conflicting evidence or conflicting viewpoints persist, you will probably have to recognise that you will not be able to reconcile such perspectives within your own individual review. You may then suggest that further research is needed in order to examine the issue with a design specifically tailored to resolving the conflict.

Approaches to synthesis

Approaches to synthesis may be characterised in many different ways. In keeping with the overview nature of this text, we characterise synthesis according to the type of data that you may be attempting to synthesise.

Narrative and textual approaches

Regardless of the type of review that you are undertaking, it is likely that you will find it necessary to use some form of narrative approach. Here you have a basic choice between the traditional narrative approach and the more formalised development of narrative synthesis. Some researchers promote the benefits of a *traditional narrative approach* (Hammersley, 2001), which has evolved organically as a less formalised method for summarising large quantities of information. This traditional narrative approach largely involves compiling descriptive data and exemplars from individual studies. The output from such a process may well be conceived as a mosaic or map (Hammersley, 2001). Narrative approaches are particularly valuable in the context of qualitative research which attaches great importance to context (Cassell and Symon, 1994). Similarly narrative reviews provide deep and 'rich' information (Light and Pillemer, 1984). They hold the potential to remain faithful to the wholeness or integrity of the studies as a body while also preserving the idiosyncratic nature of individual studies (Pawson, 2001). Unlike meta-analysis, where there must be a 'fit' between the type and quality of the primary sources, a traditional narrative review can accommodate differences between the questions, research designs, and the contexts of each of the individual studies. Indeed it disguises such distinctions by weaving together a common line of argument.

Rumrill and Fitzgerald (2001) argue that there are four potential objectives for this approach:

- to develop or advance theoretical models;
- to identify, explain, and provide perspectives on complicated or controversial issues;
- to provide information that can assist practitioners in advancing 'best' practice;
- to present new perspectives on important and emerging issues.

Furthermore such an approach offers an opportunity for the reviewer to be reflexive and critical (Hart, 1998) (see Chapter 8). However, the flexibility offered by the traditional narrative approach is also its weakness. These limitations are well-rehearsed and include the fact that it is open to bias and misinterpretation. Reviewers may selectively quote only research that supports a particular position and two reviewers reviewing the same question may report contradictory findings (Denyer and Tranfield, 2006). The traditional narrative approach, therefore, falls short of the systematic approaches espoused by this book. A possible middle ground is offered by 'narrative synthesis' which focuses on how studies addressing a different aspect of the same phenomenon can be narratively summarised and built up to provide a bigger picture of that phenomenon.

Narrative synthesis has the benefit of being able to address a wide range of questions, not only those relating to the effectiveness of a particular intervention. It is defined by Popay and colleagues (2006) as:

> An approach to the synthesis of evidence relevant to a wide range of questions including but not restricted to effectiveness [that] relies primarily on the use of words and text to summarise and explain – to "tell the story" – of the findings of multiple studies. Narrative synthesis can involve the manipulation of statistical data.

Despite excellent examples of its application, narrative synthesis was initially criticised within the systematic review community because of its potential bias and lack of both transparency and reproducibility. However Popay and colleagues (2006) have formalised a method of narrative synthesis which involves four steps:

- developing a theoretical model of how the interventions work, why and for whom;
- developing a preliminary synthesis;
- exploring the relationships in the data; and
- assessing the robustness of the synthesised output.

They identify a range of specific tools and techniques for achieving each step. Narrative synthesis is therefore one means of summarising the characteristics and findings of a body of research in a succinct and coherent manner (Evans, 2007). Essentially you are taking a series of slices through your group of included studies according to different study characteristics.

Box 7.7 Narrative synthesis

What is it?

A method of synthesis that primarily uses words and text to summarise the findings of multiple studies. It is therefore a process of synthesising primary studies to explore heterogeneity descriptively rather than statistically.

What can I use it for?

Narrative synthesis is appropriate for use with results from different types of empirical research, including experimental evaluative research and survey research. It may be used to describe the scope of existing research, summarising it into structured narratives or summary tables, and to thus account for the strength of evidence. However, in comparison with thematic approaches it is less good at identifying commonality (Lucas et al., 2007).

How has it been used?

Rodgers and colleagues (2009) describe how they tested narrative synthesis by comparing it against a meta-analysis of the same study data related to implementation of smoke alarms. Although the conclusions of the two syntheses were broadly similar, they detected that that conclusions about the impact of moderators of effect appeared stronger in the meta-analysis. In conclusion, implications for future research appeared more extensive when derived from the narrative synthesis. They emphasise the complementarity of the two approaches and conclude that, despite the risk of overinterpretation of study data, the framework, tools and techniques itemised in their guidance had fulfilled their objective of increasing the transparency and reproducibility of the narrative synthesis process.

Rather than describing each study individually, narrative synthesis attempts to characterise them in terms of multiple groupings. This is a refreshing change from those reviews that spend a paragraph or more of text describing each individual study in turn. It increases the probability that the reader, and indeed the reviewer, will be able to characterise the included studies as a 'body of evidence' (Box 7.8). Most importantly it moves the reader towards starting to identify patterns among included studies. For this reason, narrative synthesis is often used in close conjunction with tabular presentation. Both are essentially methods of **descriptive data synthesis** and it is very common to use tables of data, whether using simple counts or more sophisticated descriptions, to compose the accompanying narrative commentary.

Box 7.8   The inherent advantage of narrative synthesis

You are in an lift with your supervisor or mentor. He/she asks you how your review is going so far. You have reviewed 20 included studies. You start with 'Study 1 is a randomised controlled trial of 150 patients conducted in Sweden ...'. Before you get beyond a description of your fifth included study, the lift arrives and your companion alights with thankful relief. On the way down in the same lift, later that morning, your companion asks another colleague, also involved in a literature review, about their progress.

> Interestingly I found that only two of my 25 included studies target children; the remaining 23 study adult populations. I had thought that the Sheffield Stress Scale was going to be the most common outcome measure but in fact there is a proliferation of researcher-designed instruments. Only five studies used validated outcome measures; three of these used the Sheffield Stress Scale. So I am already starting to plan my own primary study to be targeted at children using a validated outcome scale.

Which review will be the one that the supervisor will remember (for the right reasons) on the way home that evening?

Popay and colleagues (2006) have defined four processes in narrative synthesis. These are helpful reference points although, as we have already seen, they merely formalise processes that should occur naturally through a review:

- *Developing a theory of change:* reviews typically may be used to either generate some explanatory theory or to validate or test some already existing theory.
- *Developing a preliminary synthesis:* this mainly corresponds to the line of argument approach described earlier in the chapter. It involves mobilising findings from the literature and stringing them together in order to tell a plausible 'story'.
- *Exploring relationships in the data:* this embraces the remaining two phases already described in this chapter, that is examining consistencies in the data and actively seeking the disconfirming case.
- *Assessing robustness of the synthesis product;* this corresponds to what we describe as the analysis phase of the SALSA mnemonic (see Chapter 2). This involves using a variety of tools to examine lines of inquiry suggested either *a priori* or as a result of the synthesis process.

Thematic synthesis

Thematic synthesis endeavours to provide a consistent analysis of content across included studies (Box 7.9). It seeks to identify the range of factors that is significant for understanding of a particular phenomenon. It then seeks to organise these factors into the main or most common themes.

Box 7.9 Thematic synthesis

What is it?

Thematic synthesis is based upon **thematic analysis**, a m
analyse data in primary qualitative research. **Thematic synthe
rable type of analysis to bring together and integrate the findings
tive studies within systematic reviews. It includes three principal stages, although
these overlap to some degree: free line-by-line coding of the findings of primary
studies; the organisation of these 'free codes' into related areas to construct 'descriptive' themes; and the development of 'analytical' themes.

What can I use it for?

This method has particularly been used in systematic reviews that address questions
about people's perspectives and experiences (Harden et al., 2004, 2006; Thomas
et al., 2003, 2007). These perspectives may relate to a particular programme or
intervention. Alternatively, they may concern attitudes to a particular condition (e.g.
poor housing) or disease (e.g. stroke). Such literature often involves identification of
barriers or facilitators. **Thematic synthesis** may be used in **mixed methods**
reviews to generate hypotheses to be tested against the findings of quantitative studies.

How has it been used?

Morton and colleagues (2010) describe using **thematic synthesis** to examine
the views of patients and carers in treatment decision making for chronic kidney
disease. This involved line-by-line coding of the findings of the primary studies and
development of descriptive and analytical themes. Their review included 18 studies,
14 focusing on preferences for dialysis, three on transplantation, and one on pallia-
tive management. They identified the centrality of four major themes: confronting
mortality, lack of choice, gaining knowledge of options, and weighing alternatives.
They concluded that a preference to maintain the *status quo* may explain why
patients often stick with their initial treatment choice.

Framework synthesis

Just as **thematic synthesis** draws its origins from **thematic analysis, framework
synthesis** is analogous to **framework analysis**, also used in primary qualitative
research. It stems from recognition that the sheer volume and richness of qualitative research poses a challenge for rigorous analysis. **Framework synthesis** offers
'a highly structured approach to organising and analysing data by utilising an *a
priori* "framework" – informed by background material and team discussions – to
extract and synthesise findings' (Barnett-Page and Thomas, 2009, w011). You can
then express the resulting synthesis in the form of a chart for each key factor or
variable identified. This tabular presentation can subsequently be used to map
the concept under study and to explore consistencies and to identify the disconfirming case.

Box 7.10   Framework synthesis

What is it?

Framework synthesis is based on framework analysis, outlined by Pope and colleagues (2000). It draws upon the work of Ritchie and Spencer (1993) and Miles and Huberman (1994). Its rationale is that qualitative research produces large amounts of textual data in the form of transcripts, observational fieldnotes, etc. **Framework synthesis** offers a highly structured approach to organising and analysing data (e.g. indexing using numerical codes, rearranging data into charts etc.). It is distinct from other methods outlined in this chapter in using an *a priori* 'framework' to extract and synthesise findings. Although it is largely a deductive approach new topics may be developed, added to, and incorporated with those topics already present in the framework as they emerge from the data (Cooper et al., 2010). The synthetic product can be expressed in the form of a chart for each key dimension identified, which may be used to map the nature and range of the concept under study and find associations between themes and exceptions to these (Brunton et al., 2006, w025).

What can I use it for?

This approach is most suitable where a general conceptual model or framework already exists and is well-established and, consequently, where concepts are 'secure'. However it does also hold the potential for new topics to be developed and incorporated as they emerge from the data allowing use of a contingent 'best fit' model that will be enhanced and developed by addition of new data.

How has it been used

Brunton et al. (2006, w025) applied the framework synthesis approach to a review of children's, young people's, and parents' views of walking and cycling. Results of 16 studies of children's young people's, and/or parents' views were synthesised and combined with the results of 15 intervention evaluations to summarise available evidence about the effectiveness and appropriateness of interventions to promote a shift from car travel to more active forms of transport. They identified that children often saw themselves as responsible transport users, that their views might differ from those of their parents and that themes identified from the evidence differed in importance and content depending on the children's age, sex, socioeconomic status, and location.

Tabular presentation

In addition to narrative synthesis, included studies can be described using tabulation. Again as tabulation is being used to describe studies, not to analyse them, it can be used regardless of whether data from studies is quantitative or qualitative. Typical uses for tabulation are to describe characteristics of the population, intervention, comparator and outcome (measures). It may also be used for describing study characteristics (e.g. study design). Some reviewers use tabulation to report how individual studies perform with regard to study

Table 7.7   Other methods used for synthesis of textual data

Method	Description	Application
Grounded theory	**Grounded theory** is a method of analysis used for analysing the primary research literature. Yin (1991) suggested that grounded theory could be used for synthesis of 'multivocal literature'. It provides a methodology for synthesising literature, identifying categories, and generating theories. It utilises such methods as theoretical sampling and the constant comparative method. It therefore has some similarities with meta-ethnography which is a method specifically developed for use in secondary analysis.	Moustaghfir (2008) describes using grounded theory in a review to extend existing theory regarding the 'knowledge-value chain' by integrating the additional concept of dynamic capabilities. Grounded theory was used to synthesise the information, and generate assumptions. The systematic review method was specifically selected as a recognised tool for theory building.
Meta-study	Paterson et al. (2001) coined a multi-faceted approach to synthesis, meta-study. This involves three components undertaken prior to synthesis. These are meta-data-analysis (analysis of findings), meta-method (analysis of methods), and meta-theory (analysis of theory). Collectively, these three elements make up 'meta-study'. These elements can be usefully conducted individually for specific purposes, or conducted concurrently to maximise cross-study insights within a 'new interpretation'. Meta-study allows the impact of methods and theory on findings to be formally explored.	Munro and colleagues (2007) used meta-theory to explore 11 behaviour change theories applicable to long-term medication adherence. They found little research on the effectiveness of these theories but several had the potential to improve adherence to long-term treatments.

quality thereby allowing easy identification of higher-quality studies. In quantitative studies where meta-analysis is not an option, a table may be used to present a summary of results. Cells may indicate whether an effect is positive, negative or neutral and whether a specific effect is statistically significant or not.

Tabulation is therefore particularly valuable within the context of cross-case comparison and for 'eyeballing' patterns across rows or down columns. However it may be criticised, particularly in a qualitative or implementation context because the process of tabulation is necessarily reductive. It can therefore result in a loss of important context or detail that aids interpretation of the studies. More details of tabulation, together with examples, are given in Chapter 9.

Numerical presentation

Where the same effect has been measured by multiple similar studies, it may be possible, and indeed advantageous, to statistically combine their results. Combining studies in this way, known as **meta-analysis**, may help to produce a conclusion about a body of research. For example it, may be that there are insufficient large studies to have proved an effect conclusively. Alternatively, those studies that do exist may show different patterns of effects. In the latter case, using simple vote-counting (i.e. how many studies find in favour of an intervention and how many find against) may be misleading.

Meta-analysis

Statistical meta-analysis involves the aggregation of a weighted average of the results of individual studies in order to calculate an overall effect size for an intervention (Denyer et al., 2008). The logo of the **Cochrane Collaboration** (w042), a stylised plot for a **meta-analysis**, demonstrates an actual scenario where seven small individual studies appeared to show conflicting results but which, when subject to **meta-analysis**, found in favour of a life-saving intervention. Although, mainly through the high profile of the **Cochrane Collaboration** (w042), and its associated **Cochrane Library** (w044) product, it is meta-analyses of **randomised controlled trials** that are best known, meta-analysis may also be used to synthesise other study types such as **observational studies**. **Meta-analysis** can be effective in disciplines where there are suitable and comparable quantitative data available from multiple studies (Denyer et al., 2008).

Meta-analysis as a technique meets a need to demonstrate an 'average effect'. This is at the same time its great strength and its associated weakness. As a strength, if an intervention consistently displays the same effect across a range of situational and contextual variables (e.g. country, population, ethnic group, etc.) we can conclude with increasing confidence that it will apply in our own context. This means that we do not need to replicate these studies with our own population before taking them into account locally. At the same time, it means that if an intervention works differentially in a variety of contexts, being successful in some and unsuccessful in others, we may not be able to conclude about its usefulness in our specific context. Although it may work *on average* we cannot be sure that our context is one where it will realise such benefits. This explains why mere synthesis on its own is not enough. We also need to undertake follow-up analysis to be able to explain differences in findings across multiple studies (see Chapter 8). Where variations exist in study design, the nature of evidence and study context, **meta-analysis** is seen to be problematic (Hammersley, 2001):

> This mixing of diverse studies can make for a strange fruit salad: mixing apples and oranges may seem reasonable enough, but when sprouts, turnips or even an old sock are added, it can cast doubt on the meaning of any aggregate estimates. (Davies and Crombie, 1998)

Box 7.11   Meta-analysis

What is it?

Meta-analysis is a quantitative literature review method used widely as an alternative approach to narrative literature review. It uses a set of statistical procedures to integrate, summarise or organise a set of reported statistical findings of studies that investigate the same research question using the same methods of measurement. Therefore, many reviewers endorse it as a practical and systematic way of drawing review conclusions. A **meta-analysis** follows the five-stage model of the integrative review suggested by Cooper (1982) corresponding to the chapters of this book: (a) problem formulation (Chapter 4), (b) data collection (Chapter 5), (c) data evaluation (Chapter 6), (d) analysis and interpretation (Chapters 7 and 8), and (e) public presentation (Chapter 9).

What can I use it for?

Meta-analysis has several acknowledged advantages. The prescribed procedural methods emphasise the requirement to summarise the findings from studies in a systematic way. Provided that the reviewer makes appropriate assumptions and uses correct methods of analysis, this process reduces the chances of incorrect interpretation of findings and misleading review conclusions. As **meta-analysis** uses systematic data collection and data analysis, it can be effective for reviewing large homogenous bodies of research. It can be useful in highlighting gaps in an extensive literature, although the reader should bear in mind that it is dependent on outcomes that are comparable and quantifiable. The subsequent analysis (see Chapter 8) can also be used to explore the influence of a large number of variables including different contextual factors. Cooper and Dorr (1995) suggest that narrative review (qualitative) and meta-analysis (quantitative) can be used to cross-validate findings from both methods. Therefore, **meta-analysis** can be used to quantify and corroborate review conclusions in preference to using only one of these methods.

How has it been used?

Chua and colleagues (1999) conducted a **meta-analysis** of studies to examine the relationships between computer anxiety and age, gender and computer experience. The **meta-analysis** found that female university undergraduates are generally more anxious than male undergraduates, but the strength of this relationship was not conclusive. The reviewers were also able to make observations about the reliability of instruments measuring computer anxiety and detected a possible inverse relationship between computer anxiety and computer experience that remained to be explored in further research.

It is beyond the scope of this text to provide a full description of methods for meta-analysis. (Cooper and Hedges, 1994; Glass, McGaw, and Smith, 1981; Lipsey and Wilson, 2001; or Rosenthal, 1991, are all excellent guidebooks for conducting meta-analyses). It will suffice to highlight some of the main considerations when using a meta-analysis. First of all, **meta-analysis** is only intended to be undertaken when studies address comparable populations, interventions, comparisons and outcomes using the same study design. Of course the degree of similarity between studies (**homogeneity**) requires what is essentially a subjective judgement – is it meaningful to combine these studies together in pursuit of an average effect? However, such a judgement can be quantified using a **test for heterogeneity**. If studies are considered sufficiently similar (i.e. the test for heterogeneity has a low value) they may be combined using a **fixed effects analysis**. If, however, they are not considered sufficiently similar, they may be combined using a **random effects analysis**. In essence, this distinction means that, where studies that are dissimilar are combined using the random effects method, we produce a more conservative estimate of the intervention effect. This means that we are less likely to conclude that an intervention works where it does not. However, this is at the expense of increasing the likelihood that we conclude that an intervention does not work when it is actually marginally beneficial.

Graphical approaches

Graphical approaches may make an important contribution to synthesis by assisting in the identification of patterns. They have a particular role in helping the reviewer to visualise the relationship of parts to the overall whole. They also may be used for cross-linking across disparate features of a review, e.g. for depicting a link between study characteristics and findings. For example, colour coding might be used to indicate whether qualitative findings from a review are associated with negative (red), neutral (yellow) or positive (green) results. As Whittemore and Knafl (2005) observe:

> Creativity and critical analysis of data and data displays are key elements in data comparison and the identification of important and accurate patterns and themes.

Graphical methods can include techniques for exploring data (Table 7.8) as well as those for actually presenting the data. So **mind maps**, **concept maps** and **idea webs** may be used to map out the main themes or variables in a creative and imaginative way. **Logic models** may be used as an organising structure for logical processes relating to a particular intervention such as inputs, processes, outputs and outcomes. These **logic models**, which can be particularly valuable at the early scoping stage of the review (see Chapter 4), can be revisited as a 'scaffold' from which findings, constructs, or themes may be hung. Graphical approaches have also been developed for specific purposes (such as the harvest plot for 'synthesising evidence about the differential effects of population-level interventions' (Ogilvie et al., 2008)). Nevertheless, it is true to say that, outside the specific requirements of **meta-analysis**, graphical approaches are comparatively underdeveloped and there is much to be learnt from the use of graphics and diagrams for research in general (Wheeldon and Faubert, 2009; Umoquit et al., 2011, w196)

Table 7.8   Graphical methods for exploring data

Method	Description	Application
Concept map	Concept maps can be a useful way of identifying key concepts in a document collection or research area. Concept maps can be used to identify additional search terms during the literature search, clarify thinking about the structure of the review in preparation for writing and understand theory, concepts and the relationships between them (Rowley and Slack, 2004, w165; Alias and Suradi, 2008, w002).	Braithwaite (2010) devised a concept map of key themes in the literature on organisational social spaces, networks, boundaries and holes for his systematic review on between-group behaviour in healthcare.
Idea web	Ideas webbing is a method for conceptualising and exploring connections among findings reported by the studies included in a review. This approach uses spider diagrams to develop a visual picture of possible relationships across study results (Clinkenbeard, 1991).	Arai and colleagues (2007, w006) present an example of idea webbing conducted by one of their reviewers for their review of barriers to smoke alarm implementation.
Logic model	Logic models (also known as impact models) originate from the field of programme evaluation, and are typically diagrams or flow charts that convey relationships between contextual factors, inputs, processes and outcomes. They are considered valuable in providing a 'roadmap' to illustrate influential relationships and components from inputs to outcomes. Such models are used widely in health promotion to identify domains underlying best practice (Baxter et al., 2010), w013)	Dinh-Zarr and colleagues (2001) used a logic model to examine possible mechanisms involved in increased use of safety belts. For example it included the possible effect of penalties for non-use.
Mind map	A mind map is a diagram used to represent words, ideas, tasks, or other concepts linked to, and organised around, a central key word or idea. A mind map is essentially a creative vehicle that operates at a conceptual level rather than representing a logical linear progression (compare logic maps). As such, they may be used at an early stage of a review, before relationships have been identified, and then the exact nature of relationships between concepts can be determined at a later stage following evidence synthesis.	In a review by Atkins and colleagues (2008) on adherence to tuberculosis treatment each author was also asked to develop a mind map of their own model of the synthesis as a basis for subsequent discussion.

One reason for the success of **meta-analysis** as a technique is that it supports the statistical methods that it uses with a fairly intuitive method of graphical presentation known as the **Forest plot** (see tools section in this chapter).

Although graphical methods of presentation are most developed for **meta-analysis** of quantitative studies, they are assuming increasing importance in the presentation of qualitative data. For example, some authors use linked boxes to indicate relationships between included studies with different shading depicting those that contribute to a particular theme. While such graphics conflate methodology and findings (and therefore receive more extensive treatment in Chapter 9) it is worth noting that they have both a **formative** function (as a way for a reviewer or review team to explore patterns within their results) and a **summative** function (to present the ultimate findings from the **qualitative evidence synthesis**).

Helpful graphical display

Briefly reflect on a journal article that you have recently read, not necessarily a systematic review. Which aspects of its use of tabular or graphical display made it easier to read? Were there any aspects that made it more difficult to understand and interpret? If so, why?

Integrating quantitative and qualitative data

To a large degree, the integration of quantitative and qualitative data is the outstanding methodological challenge for systematic approaches to reviewing the literature. Its prominence stems from several factors. Having tackled and overcome many methodological problems from the separate spheres of quantitative and qualitative evidence synthesis, it is now opportune to look at how these two synthetic products might be brought together. Second, there is an increasing awareness of the value of mixed-method approaches for policy makers, including both primary research and secondary synthesis (Pope et al., 2006). Finally, and most importantly, there is recognition that answering questions on effectiveness alone is not enough. Issues of appropriateness, acceptability and equity (Tugwell et al., 2010) are equally important in the success of an intervention.

Several mechanisms are suggested for bringing together quantitative and qualitative data. The high profile methods of the EPPI-Centre at the University of London involve conducting separate reviews of effectiveness and of user views and then bringing the two reviews together to produce a final integrated synthesis (Thomas et al., 2004).

Mays and colleagues (2005a) identify four basic approaches to synthesis involving both qualitative and quantitative data:

1 narrative (including traditional 'literature reviews' and more methodologically explicit approaches such as **thematic synthesis**, 'narrative synthesis', **realist synthesis** and 'meta-narrative mapping');
2 qualitative (which convert all available evidence into qualitative form using techniques such as meta-ethnography and 'qualitative cross-case analysis');
3 quantitative (which convert all evidence into quantitative form using techniques such as 'quantitative case survey' or 'content analysis') and
4 **Bayesian meta-analysis** and decision analysis (which can convert qualitative evidence such as preferences about different outcomes into quantitative form or 'weights' to use in quantitative synthesis).

They conclude that the 'choice of approach will be contingent on the aim of the review and nature of the available evidence, and often more than one approach will be required' (Mays et al., 2005a).

Some attempts have been made to integrate qualitative and quantitative data using **Bayesian meta-analysis** (Roberts et al., 2002). **Bayesian meta-analysis** uses a serial, rather than parallel, approach in eliciting important factors or variables from qualitative data and then attempting to quantify their individual effects within a **meta-analysis**. By favouring quantitative data over qualitative data, such an approach is viewed as an unequal partnership.

Box 7.12   Bayesian meta-analysis

What is it?

A method of synthesis where a summary of qualitative data is used to develop a **probability distribution (prior distribution)**, which can be tested later using a more conventional synthesis of quantitative data. In so doing, the qualitative and quantitative data are combined to produce a posterior distribution. **Bayesian meta-analysis** explicitly acknowledges the importance of subjective judgement within evidence-based decision making. It attempts to identify what it is reasonable for an observer to believe in the light of the available data and therefore explicitly takes account of the perspective of the potential user of the analysis. In doing this, **Bayesian meta-analysis** recognises that perspectives are important in determining the implications of scientific research for decision making.

What can I use it for?

There are few examples of **Bayesian meta-analysis** (Roberts et al., 2002; Voils et al., 2009). However they offer the potential to conduct a synthesis where different forms of evidence need to be brought together. For example they can be used to explore the likelihood of something happening through one type of research evidence and then to establish it more reliably via another type of research (usually qualitative followed by quantitative).

How has it been used?

Voils et al. (2009) examined whether people are less likely to keep taking their medicines if they have a complicated medication schedule as opposed to a more straightforward one. They identified 11 qualitative and six quantitative studies to address this question. They used information from the qualitative studies to arrive at a prior likelihood that the complicatedness of the medication schedule was a factor and then used the reports of quantitative studies to verify this.

Critical interpretive synthesis

The thinking behind **critical interpretive synthesis** resulted from a comprehensive review of existing methods for integrating qualitative and quantitative evidence (Dixon-Woods et al., 2004). The authors had identified deficiencies in existing methods and sought to develop a method that specifically addressed such shortcomings. These included the over-'proceduralisation' of the systematic review at the potential expense of theorising and creativity. The authors also resisted the widespread implication that the product of the review process is necessarily objective, particularly where interpretation is a stated objective of a specific review process. Pragmatically, **critical interpretive synthesis** is an attempt to handle comparatively large bodies of literature addressing wide ranging issues at a level that permitted holistic judgements of quality and coherence rather than deconstructing such issues into units of decontextualised studies that have been individually quality assessed.

Box 7.13   Critical interpretive synthesis

What is it?

Critical interpretive synthesis (CIS) aims to conduct a critique rather than a **critical appraisal**. It therefore treats the 'body of literature' as an object of inquiry, not focusing on isolated articles as units of analysis. It stimulates creative interpretations by questioning 'normal science' conventions and examines what influences the choice of proposed solutions. It is heavily steeped in the context for the literary output. It embraces all types of evidence and is attentive to procedural defects in primary studies without necessarily excluding the contribution that flawed studies might make. It acknowledges the relevance of adjacent literatures as a creative feed, purposively sampling from those literatures in its quest to pursue its explicit orientation towards theory generation. The importance of reflexivity as a constructed part of the process, in recognition of the subjectivity of the review process, is discussed further in Chapter 8.

What can I use it for?

Critical interpretive synthesis has been purposely developed for those situations where a theorisation of the evidence is a specific intended outcome from the review. It can be seen to encourage a critique of literatures and thus to stimulate questioning of taken-for-granted assumptions about concepts and methods (Dixon-Woods et al., 2006).

How has it been used?

Flemming (2010) used **critical interpretive synthesis** (CIS) to synthesise quantitative research, in the form of an effectiveness review and a guideline, with qualitative research, to examine the use of morphine to treat cancer-related pain. CIS had not previously been used specifically to synthesise effectiveness and qualitative literature. The findings of the effectiveness research were used as a framework to guide the translation of findings from qualitative research using an integrative grid (cf. **framework synthesis**). A secondary translation of findings from the qualitative research, not specifically mapped to the effectiveness literature, was guided by the framework. Nineteen qualitative papers were synthesised with the quantitative effectiveness literature, producing 14 synthetic constructs. Four synthesising arguments were subsequently developed drawing on patients', carers', and healthcare professionals' interpretations of the meaning and context of the use of morphine to treat cancer pain.

Realist synthesis

Pawson (2002) argues that the 'primary ambition of research synthesis is explanation building'. To this end, **realist synthesis** attempts to bring together different types of research data, quantitative or qualitative, with other data sources in order to identify an underlying mechanism of effect. Such a mechanism may explain why an intervention works in one context but not in a similar one. Drawing on earlier work on programme evaluation (Pawson and Tilley, 1997), Pawson (2006) contends that research synthesis should be targeted at identifying, and subsequently developing an understanding of, these underlying generative mechanisms. Pawson (2002) proposes **realist synthesis** for analysing the effectiveness of policy programmes through the development and testing of theoretical ideas on intervention–outcome relations. This pragmatic approach has been likened to the use of research synthesis for developing design propositions in management and organisation studies (Denyer et al., 2008). The purpose is to 'articulate underlying programme theories and then interrogate existing evidence to find out whether and where these theories are pertinent and productive' (Pawson, 2006). While programmes are context-specific and not generalisable, intervention–outcome combinations are. Consequently programme reviews aim at discovering context–mechanism–outcome combinations in order to know when, where, and for whom to apply the programme, or elements of it. **Realist synthesis** therefore involves the progressive investigation of the following questions:

- What is the nature and content of the intervention?
- What are the circumstances or context for its use?
- What are the policy intentions or objectives?
- What are the nature and form of its outcomes or impacts?

Realist synthesis, therefore, uses included studies as 'case studies, whose purpose is to test, revise and refine the preliminary theory' (Pawson, 2006). **Realist synthesis** is able to accommodate research evidence from a range of study types.

Box 7.14   Realist synthesis

What is it?

Realist synthesis is used to articulate underlying programme theories and then interrogate existing evidence to find out whether and where these theories are pertinent and productive. It can be seen that the unit of analysis is the **programme theory** with primary data being inspected for what it reveals about the **programme theory**. The explicit purpose of the review is thus to test and refine **programme theory**. **Realist synthesis** therefore examines different types of evidence as they address specific questions or uncertainties within a programme. In some cases,

(Continued)

(Continued)

therefore, these questions can relate to the effectiveness of a particular intervention, particularly as it might apply differentially in different contexts. In other cases, this may examine the acceptability of a programme or the attitudes of stakeholders towards it.

What can I use it for?

Realist synthesis produces 'mid-range theory', lying between minor working hypotheses from day-to-day research and broader systematic efforts to develop a unified theory (Pawson, 2002). It can be used to examine possible theory underlying particular programmes or mechanisms to explain why it works in certain circumstances but not other apparently similar circumstances. Policies or programmes can therefore be examined at a national level or at a local implementation level with variables affecting likely success or failure operating at either or both levels.

How has it been used?

Kane and colleagues (2010) sought a better understanding of the mechanisms by which community health workers (CHWs) might help to reduce the burden of childhood illnesses in low and middle income countries (LMIC). They therefore examined evidence from **randomised control trials (RCT)** from a realist perspective to see if they yielded insight into how such roles worked. This review aimed to use evidence from the RCTs as part of a hypothesis generating exercise. The review identified factors more likely to be associated with the success of programmes as well as negative mechanisms that might compromise CHW performance. This review was successful as a hypothesis-generating exercise but the RCTs did not yield sufficient specificity to go beyond hypotheses that were very general and not well refined. They identified a need to further test and refine these hypotheses in further studies.

More recently the 'logic model' has been seen as a possible vehicle for bringing data from quantitative and qualitative studies together within a conceptual whole (Baxter et al., 2010, w013). Integration of quantitative and qualitative data within a single synthetic product is one way of including diverse forms of evidence and thereby increasing the relevance of reviews for decision makers. Where randomised controlled trials show a high degree of heterogeneity, the inclusion of qualitative research may help to explain that heterogeneity. By eliciting a more complete picture of the research landscape for a particular topic, you can not only identify areas neglected by both paradigms (i.e. research gaps) but you can also locate where promising interventions have not been evaluated for effectiveness or, conversely where effective interventions have not been assessed for acceptability or so-called **social validity**. Furthermore, the multiple questions addressed by a so-called **mixed method review** correspond more closely to the concerns of decision-makers (Pope et al., 2006). Such reviews are also particularly appropriate for the exploratory phase of a dissertation or thesis where an investigator needs to identify what is known together with any research gaps.

Of course by amalgamating quantitative and qualitative approaches to **evidence synthesis**, itself requiring familiarity with both quantitative and qualitative primary research, you are broadening the scale of the review endeavour and increasing its technical complexity. Typically such approaches require a widening of the skills base of the team and may also require formal involvement of stake-holders. Decisions on when and how to bring the two synthetic products together, whether having conducted these in parallel or serially, add further complexity to the already challenging job of project management. On the other hand, it may well be that one of the components has already been undertaken (e.g. a **Cochrane** or **Campbell review**) and you can focus attention on the complementary role of the other review and its ultimate integration.

APPLY WHAT YOU HAVE LEARNT 7.1

Choosing your method of synthesis

Examine the different methods of synthesis outlined in this chapter. Sort them into those of current potential for your review, those that are unlikely to prove useful at present, and those for which you need to obtain further detail. Produce a draft learning plan for further reading/research on data synthesis.

- Bayesian meta-analysis
- Critical interpretive synthesis
- Framework synthesis
- Grounded theory
- Meta-analysis
- Meta-ethnography
- Meta-study
- Narrative synthesis
- Realist synthesis
- Thematic synthesis

Current potential	Further detail required	Not relevant at present

To find out more on data synthesis I am going to read/research:

By __/__/201_

Summary

This chapter illustrates that synthesis is not the mere process of assembling the raw ingredients of the review (i.e. the individual studies) but also includes the more creative elements of seeking patterns, examining for consistency, and identifying the divergent or disconfirming case. In this way, it is a prerequisite to the exploration of reasons for variations, discrepancies, and inconsistencies. This exploration, together with a more general testing of the robustness of findings constitutes the next phase of the review, namely analysis.

Key learning points

- Data extraction is a key step in progress towards synthesis and it is helpful to have a picture of what the final synthesis might look like before selecting the data to be extracted.
- Numerous approaches to synthesis exist and the reviewer will find it informative to look at existing published methods and examples before selecting a methodology that is fit for purpose.
- A reviewer has a large range of types of data presentation to select from including textual, graphical, numerical and tabular approaches.
- Integration of quantitative and qualitative data remains the outstanding methodological challenge for synthesis. Methods do exist for such integration but few published examples are available.

Suggestions for further reading

Barnett-Page, E., and Thomas, J. (2009) Methods for the synthesis of qualitative research: a critical review. *BMC Medical Research Methodology*, **9**, 59. (w011)

Crombie, I.K., and Davies, H.T.O. (2009) *What is Meta-analysis?* 2nd edn. London: Hayward Medical Communications (w057).

Pope, C., Mays, N., and Popay, J. (2007) Methods for evidence synthesis. In Pope, C., Mays, N. and Popay, J. *Synthesizing Qualitative and Quantitative Health Evidence: A Guide to Methods*. Maidenhead: Open University Press, 45–114.

Ring, N., Ritchie, K., Mandava, L., and Jepson, R. (2010) A guide to synthesising qualitative research for researchers undertaking health technology assessments and systematic reviews. (w163)

Tools for study synthesis

With a wealth of specific methods to choose from, this tools section picks out one exemplar of a tool for quantitative synthesis, the **Forest plot** and one example of an approach to cross-study qualitative synthesis, namely qualitative data analysis. However, we would again encourage you to look at the many published examples of synthesis techniques referenced in this chapter in order to identify less common tools that may assist you in your own literature review.

The Forest plot

The **Forest plot** (Figure 7.1) depicts the relationship between the success rate of an intervention of interest and the success rate of its comparator.

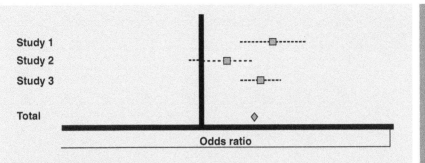

Figure 7.1   Forest plot

This relationship is pictured in relation to a 'line of no effect', that is against the assumption that both intervention and comparator are equally effective/ineffective. The greater the superiority of the intervention (or conversely its comparator), the further away its **point estimate** is plotted from the line of no effect. Multiple studies can thus be plotted on the same graph to provide a pattern of how studies relate both to each other and to the line of no effect. Each **point estimate** is provided with a **confidence interval** to illustrate the amount of variation between a best-case and worst-case scenario for that particular study. Finally, the pooled effect of combining all studies is depicted as a diamond where the centre of the diamond indicates the **point estimate** for all studies combined. The horizontal extremities of the diamond shape indicate the best-and worst-case scenarios for all studies combined. The reader can therefore decide whether he/she wishes to assume a best-case result or a more conservative worst-case estimate and, indeed, whether the difference between these two scenarios is important enough to affect any subsequent action (see Crombie and Davies, 2009, w057).

Qualitative data analysis

Data extraction against themes helps in the identification of patterns. Within the limited number (three studies) of reports included in the thematic matrix (Table 7.9) for a hypothetical review on the attitudes of village communities to peripherally located supermarkets we observe:

Study 1 by Greenwood and Liffey focuses exclusively on economic considerations. Studies 2 and 3 both look at convenience with regard to road traffic. Study 3 by Swathe is overwhelmingly positive whereas Studies 1 and 2 cover positives and negatives. Studies 2 and 3 carry implications for (different) health-related services. Therefore, such a matrix is a useful vehicle for pattern recognition. The themes could have been generated from the data (as with grounded theory, **thematic synthesis**, or **meta-ethnography** approaches) or could have been derived from a published framework or model (as for framework synthesis).

Table 7.9 Hypothetical thematic matrix for review on attitudes to peripheral supermarkets

Theme	Article content		
	Greenwood and Liffey, 2010 (Study 1)	Verdant, 2010 (Study 2)	Swathe, 2011 (Study 3)
Convenience		Good communications via main roads Ample parking	On outskirts of village therefore reduces congestion
Household economy	Reduces price of staple products (e.g. bread, milk)	Reduced petrol prices	Cheap petrol
Focus for community		Location for charitable collections Health education stands	Venue for Blood transfusion service
Threat to local commerce	Challenges bespoke traders (e.g. bakers, dairies)	24-hour competition to petrol stations	
Threat to community identity	Uniform character of hypermarkets – cheap builds	Reduced use of village centre Increased use by non-locals	

References

Alias, M. and Suradi, Z. (2008) Concept mapping: a tool for creating a literature review. In: Cañas, A.J., Reiska, P., Åhlberg, M., and J. D. Novak, J.D. (eds) *Concept Mapping: Connecting Educators Proceedings of the Third International Conference on Concept Mapping*. Tallinn and Helsinki: Tallinn University. (w002)

Arai, L., Britten, N., Popay, J., Roberts, H., Petticrew, M., Rodgers, M., and Sowden, A. (2007) Testing methodological developments in the conduct of narrative synthesis: a demonstration review of research on the implementation of smoke alarm interventions. *Evidence and Policy*, **3**, 3, 361–83. (w006)

Armitage, A. and Keeble-Allen, D. (2008) Undertaking a structured literature review or structuring a literature review: tales from the field. *Electronic Journal of Business Research Methods*, **6**, 2, 141–52.

Atkins, S., Lewin, S., Smith, H., Engel, M., Fretheim, A, and Volmink, J. (2008) Conducting a meta-ethnography of qualitative literature: lessons learnt. *BMC Medical Research Methodology*, **8**, 21. (w008)

Barnett-Page, E. and Thomas, J. (2009) Methods for the synthesis of qualitative research: a critical review. *BMC Medical Research Methodology*, **9**, 59. (w011)

Baxter, S., Killoran, A., Kelly, M.P., and Goyder, E. (2010) Synthesizing diverse evidence: the use of primary qualitative data analysis methods and logic models in public health reviews. *Public Health*, **124**, 2, 99–106. (w013)

Beck, C.T. (2001) Caring with nursing education: A metasynthesis. *Journal of Nursing Education*, **40**, 3, 101–10.

Bergman, M.M. and Coxon, A.P.M. (2005) The quality in qualitative methods. *Forum Qualitative Sozialforschung/Forum: Qualitative Social Research*, **6**, 2, Art. 34. (w014).

Braithwaite, J. (2010) Between-group behaviour in health care: gaps, edges, boundaries, disconnections, weak ties, spaces and holes. A systematic review. *BMC Health Services Research*, **10**, 330. (w022)

Britten, N., Campbell, R., Pope, C., Donovan, J., Morgan, M., and Pill, R. (2002) Using meta-ethnography to synthesise qualitative research: a worked example. *Journal of Health Services Research and Policy,* **7**, 4, 209–15.

Brown, S.J. (1999) *Knowledge for Health Care Practice: A Guide to Using Research Evidence.* Philadelphia: W.B. Saunders Co.

Brunton, G., Oliver, S., Oliver, K., and Lorenc, T. (2006) *A Synthesis of Research Addressing Children's, Young People's and Parents' Views of Walking and Cycling for Transport.* London: EPPI-Centre, Social Science Research Unit, Institute of Education, University of London. (w025)

Budgen, D., Turner, M., Brereton, P., and Kitchenham, B. (2008) Using mapping studies in software engineering. Proceedings of PPIG 2008, Lancaster University, 195–204.

Campbell, R., Pound, P., Pope, C., Britten, N., Pill, R., Morgan, M., and Donovan, J. (2003) Evaluating meta-ethnography: a synthesis of qualitative research on lay experiences of diabetes and diabetes care. *Social Science and Medicine,* **56**, 4, 671–84.

Carroll, C., Booth, A., Papaioannou, D., Sutton, A., and Wong, R. (2009) UK Health-care professionals' experience of on-line learning techniques: a systematic review of qualitative data. *Journal of Continuing Education in the Health Professions,* **29**, 4, 235–41.

Cassell, C. and Symon, G. (1994) *Qualitative Methods In Organizational Research: A Practical Guide.* London: Sage.

Chua, S.L., Chen, D.-T, and Wong, A.F.L. (1999) Computer anxiety and its correlates: a meta-analysis. *Computers in Human Behavior,* **15**, 5, 609–23.

Clinkenbeard, P.R. (1991) Beyond summary: constructing a review of the literature. In: Buchanan, N.K. and Feldhusen, J.F. (eds) *Conducting Research and Evaluation in Gifted Education: A Handbook of Methods and Applications.* New York: Teachers College Press, 33–50.

Combs, J.P., Bustamante, R.M., and Onwuegbuzie, A.J. (2010) An interactive model for facilitating development of literature reviews. *International Journal of Multiple Research Approaches,* **4**, 2, 159–82.

Cooper, K., Squires, H., Carroll, C., Papaioannou, D., Booth, A., Logan, R.F., Maguire, C., Hind, D., and Tappenden, P. (2010) Review of qualitative data on views and attitudes to the taking of agents that may be used for chemoprevention In: Chemoprevention of colorectal cancer: systematic review and economic evaluation. *Health Technology Assessment,* **14**, 32, 79–96.

Cooper, H.M. (1982) Scientific guidelines for conducting integrative research reviews. *Review of Educational Research,* **52**, 2, 291–302.

Cooper, H. and Dorr, N. (1995) Race comparisons on need for achievement: a meta-analytic alternative to Graham's narrative review. *Review of Educational Research,* **65**, 4, 483–8.

Cooper, H. and Hedges, L.V. (eds) (1994) *The Handbook of Research Synthesis.* New York: Sage.

Cresswell, J.W. (2003) *Research Design: Qualitative, Quantitative, and Mixed Method Approaches,* 2nd edn. Thousand Oaks, CA: Sage.

Crombie, I.K. and Davies, H.T.O. (2009) What is meta-analysis? 2nd edn. *What is......?* **1** (8): 1–8. (w057)

Curran, C., Burchardt, T., Knapp, M., McDaid, D., and Li, B. (2007) Challenges in multidisciplinary systematic reviewing: a study on social exclusion and mental health policy. *Social Policy and Administration,* **41**, 3, 289–312.

Davies, H.T.O. and Crombie, I.K. (1998) What is meta-analysis? *What is......?* **1** (8): 1–8.

Denyer, D. and Tranfield, D. (2006) Using qualitative research synthesis to build an actionable knowledge base. *Management Decision,* **44**, 2, 213–27.

Denyer, D., Tranfield, D., and Van Aken, J.E. (2008) Developing design propositions through research synthesis. *Organization Studies,* **29**, 2, 249–69.

Dinh-Zarr, T.B., Sleet, D.A., Shults, R.A., Zaza, S., Elder, R.W., Nichols, J.L., Thompson, R.S., and Sosin, D.M. (2001) Task force on community preventive Services. Reviews of evidence regarding interventions to increase the use of safety belts. *American Journal of Preventive Medicine*, **21**, 4 Suppl, 48–65.

Dixon-Woods, M., Agarwal, S., Young, B., Jones, D., and Sutton, A. (2004) *Integrative Approaches to Qualitative and Quantitative Evidence*, London: Health Development Agency. (w062)

Dixon-Woods, M., Cavers, D., Agarwal, S., Annandale, E., Arthur, A., Harvey, J., Hsu, R., Katbamna, S., Olsen, R., Smith, L., Riley, R., and Sutton, A.J. (2006) Conducting a critical interpretive synthesis of the literature on access to healthcare by vulnerable groups. *BMC Medical Research Methodology,* **6,** 35. (w063)

Dixon-Woods, M., Booth, A., and Sutton, A.J. (2007) Synthesising qualitative research: a review of published reports. *Qualitative Research*, **7**, 375–422.

Evans, D. (2007) Integrative reviews of quantitative and qualitative research: overview of methods. In: Webb, C. and Roe, B. (eds) *Reviewing Research Evidence for Nursing Practice*: Systematic Reviews. Oxford: Blackwell Publishing.

Finfgeld-Connett, D. (2009) Model of therapeutic and non-therapeutic responses to patient aggression. *Issues in Mental Health Nursing*, **30**, 9, 530–7.

Flemming, K. (2010) Synthesis of quantitative and qualitative research: an example using Critical Interpretive Synthesis. *Journal of Advanced Nursing*, **66**, 1, 201–17.

Ganann, R., Ciliska, D., and Thomas, H. (2010) Expediting systematic reviews: methods and implications of rapid reviews. *Implementation Science,* **5**, 56. (w086)

Garside, R., Britten, N., and Stein, K. (2008) The experience of heavy menstrual bleeding: A systematic review and meta-ethnography of qualitative studies. *Journal of Advanced Nursing*, **63**, 6, 550–62.

Glass, G.V., McGaw, B., and Smith, M.L. (1981) *Meta-analysis in Social Research*. Beverly Hills, CA: Sage.

Gray, C. and Malins, J. (2004) *Visualizing Research: A Guide to the Research Process in Art and Design*. Burlington, VT: Ashgate.

Greenhalgh, T., Robert, G., Macfarlane, F., Bate, P., Kyriakidou, O., and Peacock, R. (2005) Storylines of research in diffusion of innovation: a meta-narrative approach to systematic review. *Social Science and Medicine*, **61**, 2, 417–30.

Greenhalgh, T., Potts, H.W., Wong, G., Bark, P., and Swinglehurst, D. (2009) Tensions and paradoxes in electronic patient record research: a systematic literature review using the meta-narrative method. *Milbank Quarterly*, **87**, 4, 729–88.

Grimshaw, J.M., Thomas, R.E., MacLennan, G., Fraser, C., Ramsay, C.R., Vale, L., Whitty, P., Eccles, M.P., Matowe, L., Shirran, L., Wensing, M., Dijkstra, R., and Donaldson, C. (2004) Effectiveness and efficiency of guideline dissemination and implementation strategies. *Health Technology Assessment*, **8**, 6, 1–72. (w100)

Hammersley, M. (2001) On 'systematic' reviews of research literatures: a 'narrative' response to Evans and Benefield. *British Educational Research Journal*, **27**, 543–54.

Hammersley, M. (2002) Systematic or unsystematic, is that the question? Some reflections on the science, art and politics of reviewing research evidence. Talk given to the Public Health Evidence Steering Group of the Health Development Agency. (w102)

Harden, A., Garcia, J., Oliver, S., Rees, R., Shepherd, J., Brunton, G., and Oakley, A. (2004) Applying systematic review methods to studies of people's views: an example from public health. *Journal of Epidemiology and Community Health*, **58**, 794–800.

Harden, A., Brunton, G., Fletcher, A., and Oakley, A. (2006) Young people, pregnancy and social exclusion: A systematic synthesis of research evidence to identify effective, appropriate and promising approaches for prevention and support. London: EPPI-Centre, Social Science Research Unit, Institute of Education, University of London. (w103)

Hart, C. (1998) *Doing a Literature Review: Releasing the Social Science Research Imagination*. London: Sage.

Kane, S.S., Gerretsen, B., Scherpbier, R., Dal Poz, M., and Dieleman, M. (2010) A realist synthesis of randomised control trials involving use of community health workers for delivering child health interventions in low and middle income countries. *BMC Health Services Research*, **10**, 286. (w115)

Kitchenham, B. (2007) Guidelines for performing systematic literature reviews in software engineering, (Version 2.3). EBSE Technical Report: EBSE-2007-01. Software Engineering Group, School of Computer Science and Mathematics, Keele University, Staffordshire. (w119)

Knafl, K.A. and Webster, D.C. (1988) Managing and analyzing qualitative data: a description of tasks, techniques, and materials. *Western Journal of Nursing Research*, **10**, 195–210.

Kuhn, T.S. (1962) *The Structure of Scientific Revolutions*. Chicago: University of Chicago Press.

Light, R.J. and Pillemer, D.B. (1984) *Summing Up: The Science of Reviewing Research*. Cambridge, MA: Harvard University Press.

Lipsey, M.W. and Wilson, D.B. (2001) *Practical Meta-analysis*. Applied Social Research Methods series (Vol. 49). Thousand Oaks, CA: Sage.

Lucas, P.J., Baird, J., Arai, L., Law, C., and Roberts, H.M. (2007) Worked examples of alternative methods for the synthesis of qualitative and quantitative research in systematic reviews. *BMC Medical Research Methodology*, **7**, 4. (w126)

Mays, N., Pope, C., and Popay, J (2005a) Systematically reviewing qualitative and quantitative evidence to inform management and policy-making in the health field. *Journal of Health Services Research and Policy*, **10**, Suppl 1, 6–20.

Mays, N., Pope, C., and Popay, J. (2005b) Details of approaches to synthesis – a methodological appendix to the paper, Systematically reviewing qualitative and quantitative evidence to inform management and policy making in the health field. Report for the National Co-ordinating Centre for NHS Service Delivery and Organisation R and D (NCCSDO), London School of Hygiene and Tropical Medicine. (w129)

Miles, M.B. and Huberman, A.M. (1994) *Qualitative Data Analysis: An Expanded Sourcebook*, 2nd edn. London: Sage.

Morton, R.L., Tong, A., Howard, K., Snelling, P., and Webster, A.C. (2010) The views of patients and carers in treatment decision making for chronic kidney disease: systematic review and thematic synthesis of qualitative studies. *BMJ*, **340**, c112.

Moustaghfir, K. (2008) The dynamics of knowledge assets and their link with firm performance. *Measuring Business Excellence*, **12**, 2, 10–24.

Mulrow, C. (1994) *Rationale for Systematic Reviews*. London: BMJ.

Munro, S., Lewin, S., Swart, T., and Volmink, J. (2007) A review of health behaviour theories: how useful are these for developing interventions to promote long-term medication adherence for TB and HIV/AIDS? *BMC Public Health*, **11**, 7, 104. (w140)

Noblit, G.W. and Hare, R.D. (1988) *Meta-ethnography: Synthesizing Qualitative Studies*. Newbury Park, CA: Sage.

Ogilvie, D., Fayter, D., Petticrew, M., Sowden, A., Thomas, S., Whitehead, M., and Worthy, G. (2008) The harvest plot: a method for synthesising evidence about the differential effects of interventions. *BMC Medical Research Methodology*, **8**, 8. (w145)

Paterson, B., Thorne, S., Canam, C., and Jillings, C. (2001) *Meta-study of Qualitative Health Research*. Thousand Oaks, CA: Sage.

Pawson, R. (2001) *Evidence Based Policy: II. The Promise of 'Realist Synthesis*. ESRC UK Centre for Evidence Based Policy and Practice. London: Queen Mary, University of London. (w150)

Pawson, R. (2002) Evidence based policy: in search of a method. *Evaluation*, **8**, 2, 157–81.

Pawson, R., Greenhalgh, T., Harvey, G., and Walshe, K. (2004) *Realist Synthesis: An Introduction*. Manchester: ESRC Research Methods Programme. (w151)

Pawson, R. (2006) *Evidence-based Policy: A Realist Perspective*. London: Sage.

Pawson, R. and Tilley, N. (1997) *Realistic Evaluation*. London: Sage.

Petticrew, M. and Roberts, H. (2006) *Systematic Reviews in the Social Sciences: A Practical Guide*. Oxford: Blackwell.

Popay, J., Rogers, A., and Williams, G. (1998) Rationale and standards for the systematic review of qualitative literature in health services research. *Qualitative Health Research,* **8**, 341–51.

Popay, J., Roberts, H., Sowden, A., Petticrew, M., Arai, L., Rodgers, M., and Britten, N. (2006) Guidance on the conduct of narrative synthesis in systematic reviews. A Product from the ESRC Methods Programme. (w156)

Pope, C., Mays, N., and Popay, J. (2006) How can we synthesize qualitative and quantitative evidence for healthcare policy-makers and managers? *Healthcare Management Forum,* **19**, 1, 27–31.

Pope, C., Mays, N., and Popay, J. (2007) *Synthesising Qualitative and Quantitative Health Evidence: A Guide to Methods.* Maidenhead: Open University Press.

Pope, C., Ziebland, S., and Mays, N. (2000) Qualitative research in health care: analysing qualitative data. *BMJ,* **320**, 114–16.

Ritchie, J. and Spencer, L. (1993) Qualitative data analysis for applied policy research. In: Bryman, A. and Burgess, R. (eds) *Analysing Qualitative Data.* London: Routledge, 173–94.

Roberts, K.A., Dixon-Woods, M., Fitzpatrick, R., Abrams, K.R., and Jones, D.R. (2002) Factors affecting the uptake of childhood immunisation: a Bayesian synthesis of qualitative and quantitative evidence. *The Lancet,* **360**, 1596–9.

Rodgers, M., Arai, L., Popay, J., Britten, N., Roberts, H., Petticrew, M., and Sowden, A. (2009) Testing methodological guidance on the conduct of narrative synthesis in systematic reviews: effectiveness of interventions to promote smoke alarm ownership and function. *Evaluation,* **15**, 49–73.

Rosenthal, R. (1991) *Meta-analytic Procedures for Social Research,* revised edn. Newbury Park, CA: Sage.

Rowley, J. and Slack, F. (2004) Conducting a literature review. *Management Research News,* **27**, 4, 31–9. (w165)

Rumrill, P.D. and Fitzgerald, S.M. (2001) Using narrative reviews to build a scientific knowledge base. *Work,* **16**, 165–70.

Ryan, R.E., Kaufman, C.A., and Hill, S.J. (2009) Building blocks for meta-synthesis: data integration tables for summarising, mapping, and synthesising evidence on interventions for communicating with health consumers. *BMC Medical Research Methodology,* **9**, 16. (w166)

Sandelowski, M. (1995) Qualitative analysis: what it is and how to begin. *Research in Nursing and Health,* **18**, 371–5.

Sandelowski, M., Docherty, S., and Emden, C. (1997) Qualitative metasynthesis: Issues and techniques, *Research in Nursing and Health,* **20**, 4, 365–71.

Siau, K. and Long, Y. (2005) Synthesizing e-government stage models – a meta-synthesis based on meta-ethnography approach. *Industrial Management and Data Systems,* **105**, 4, 443–58.

Suri, H. (1999) The process of synthesising qualitative research: a case study. Annual Conference of the Association for Qualitative Research, Melbourne. (w186)

Suri, H. and Clarke, D. (2009) Advancements in research synthesis methods: from a methodologically inclusive perspective. *Review of Educational Research,* **79**, 1, 395–430.

Thomas, J., Sutcliffe, K., Harden, A., Oakley, A., Oliver, S., Rees, R., Brunton, G., and Kavanagh, J. (2003) *Children and Healthy Eating: A Systematic Review of Barriers and Facilitators.* London: EPPI-Centre, Social Science Research Unit, Institute of Education, University of London. (w189)

Thomas, J., Harden, A., Oakley, A., Oliver, S., Sutcliffe, K., Rees, R., Brunton, G., and Kavanagh, J. (2004) Integrating qualitative research with trials in systematic reviews. *BMJ,* **328**, 7446, 1010–2.

Thomas, J. and Harden, A. (2007) Methods for the thematic synthesis of qualitative research in systematic reviews. Methods for Research Synthesis Node, Evidence for Policy and Practice Information and Co-ordinating (EPPI-Centre, Social Science Research Unit, London.

ESRC National Centre for Research Methods NCRM Working Paper Series Number (10/07). (w190)

Thomas, J., Kavanagh, J., Tucker, H., Burchett, H., Tripney, J., and Oakley, A. (2007) *Accidental Injury, Risk-taking Behaviour and the Social Circumstances in which Young People Live: A Systematic Review.* London: EPPI-Centre, Social Science Research Unit, Institute of Education, University of London. (w192)

Tranfield, D., Denyer, D., and Smart, P. (2003) Towards a methodology for developing evidence-informed management knowledge by means of systematic Review. *British Journal of Management,* **14**, 207–22

Tugwell, P., Petticrew, M., Kristjansson, E., Welch, V., Ueffing, E., Waters, E., Bonnefoy, J., Morgan, A., Doohan, E., and Kelly, M.P. (2010) Assessing equity in systematic reviews: realising the recommendations of the Commission on Social Determinants of Health. *BMJ,* **341**, c4739.

Umoquit, M.J., Tso, P., Burchett, H.E., and Dobrow, M.J. (2011) A multidisciplinary systematic review of the use of diagrams as a means of collecting data from research subjects: application, benefits and recommendations. *BMC Medical Research Methodology,* **11**, 1, 11. (w196)

Urquhart, C. (2010) Systematic reviewing, meta-analysis and meta-synthesis for evidence-based library and information science. *Information Research,* **15**, 3. (w198)

Voils, C., Hasselblad, V., Crandell, J., Chang, Y., Lee, E., and Sandelowski, M. (2009) A Bayesian method for the synthesis of evidence from qualitative and quantitative reports: the example of antiretroviral medication adherence. *Journal of Health Services Research and Policy,* **14**, 4, 226–33.

Watt, A., Cameron, A., Sturm, L., Lathlean, T., Babidge, W., Blamey, S., Facey, K., Hailey, D., Norderhaug, I., and Maddern, G. (2008) Rapid versus full systematic reviews: validity in clinical practice? *Australian and New Zealand Journal of Surgery,* **78**, 11, 1037–40.

Wheeldon, J. and Faubert, J. (2009) Framing experience: concept maps, mind maps, and data collection in qualitative research. *International Journal of Qualitative Methods,* **8**, 68–83.

Whittemore, R. and Knafl, K. (2005) The integrative review: updated methodology. *Journal of Advanced Nursing,* **52**, 5, 546–53.

Yin, R.K. (1993) Advancing rigorous methodologies: a review of 'towards rigor in reviews of multivocal literatures.' *Review of Educational Research,* **61**, 3, 299.

EIGHT

Analysing the findings

| Learning Objectives |

After reading this chapter, you should be able to:

- Describe the main methods available for analysis of the findings of a review.
- Produce a plan for analysis for your specific review.
- Identify the main uncertainties and likely biases surrounding the findings of a review.
- Consider the implications of your review in terms of its contribution to existing knowledge and recommendations for further research.

Introduction

Once an initial synthesis has been performed, whether using narrative, qualitative or quantitative techniques or a combination of the three, a literature review provides an opportunity to explore both what has been found and what is missing. The synthesis stage aims to tell you what the literature *says*. The subsequent analysis stage focuses on telling you what the literature *means*. If synthesis is analogous to a detective identifying all the clues, the more challenging stage of analysis corresponds to making sense of them.

Analysing what has been found

Essentially analysis provides you with an opportunity to assess the strength of evidence for drawing conclusions about the results of synthesis and their generalisability in your intended context. You have several techniques at your disposal to help you to do this (Box 8.1). These 'tactics' were derived within the context of conducting primary research but may be seen to apply equally within synthesis.

Box 8.1 Tactics for testing or confirming review findings

Elements

Representativeness
Researcher effects
Triangulating
Weighting the evidence
Meaning of outliers
Using extreme cases
Following up surprises
Looking for negative evidence
Make if-then tests
Rule out spurious relations
Replicate a finding
Check out rival explanations
Feedback from informants

Based on Miles and Huberman (1994)

Examining *representativeness* requires that you explore whether the populations being captured by the various study samples (the study populations) match the characteristics of the population being investigated (the target population). As a reviewer you need to examine your component studies and ask yourself, 'Are any particular groups underrepresented? Have any groups been overrepresented? Can I be confident that the characteristics of a particular group have not been misrepresented or misinterpreted?'

A good reviewer will cultivate a healthy scepticism when it comes to the likely presence of *researcher effects*. Such researcher effects may be deliberate as when researchers favour a particular programme or intervention – for example, they may influence the selection of outcomes. Alternatively they may be evidenced as identified inadvertent researcher effects – for example comparison groups may be treated differently aside from the programme being evaluated or data may be misinterpreted.

Triangulating the data may involve the use of different methods to research the same issue with the same unit of analysis. This may involve checking findings within a review across different study designs, different schools of thought, or different methods of data collection. It may involve comparing findings from secondary research with those from your subsequent primary research and bringing the two together in a combined discussion section.

Weighting the evidence asks you to ensure that your conclusions are not simply based on 'vote-counting'. Not all studies are equal – you may need to look initially at the effect of ordering studies from the highest quality to the lowest quality. You can ask yourself 'Are particular directions of effect (e.g. positive or negative) clustered around particular points in this ranking?'

A valuable precaution against over-generalisation is to examine the *meaning of outliers* (i.e. any studies that show particularly extreme results – either very positive or very negative) or, in a qualitative context, those that are a unique source of a particular theme. You may wish to discuss these with colleagues and topical experts, asking them 'Can you identify one or more possible explanations for the difference in the findings?' Such explanations may be explored in the analysis, provided such data is available, or suggested as hypotheses to be explored in future research.

Associated with the exploration of outliers is the tactic of *using extreme cases*. However, whereas the stimulus for looking at outliers relates to the presence of extreme results, extreme cases are stimulated by atypical contexts. Examining the characteristics of the population and the intervention may provide an insight into better than expected or worse than expected (but not necessarily outlying) results.

Following up surprises is one of the most intellectually rewarding tactics for exploring your data. Once you have identified a particular explanation for a pattern of results it can be interesting to identify where one or more studies does not fit its anticipated place in the sequence. Again, this requires a more perceptive analysis than simply looking for outliers. The 'surprise' may lie embedded within the 'pack' of studies but not where predicted. A useful technique is to record such surprises as you encounter them because, within the context of a lengthy literature review project, once a period of time has elapsed, they may lose their initial capacity to surprise you. You should bear in mind that your reader typically starts at a point analogous to where you were before undertaking the synthesis and analysis and so you have a duty as reviewer to treat them as a 'fellow traveller'. Such surprises, once validated, can be usefully highlighted in publications, oral presentations, and, where appropriate, press releases.

Looking for negative evidence is frequently overlooked as a discrete technique, largely because the tendency of any synthesis is to progress towards commonality rather than dissonance. Such a tactic involves actively seeking disconfirmation of what you believe to be true. Within the context of qualitative evidence synthesis it may involve purposively sampling from the literature from fields or disciplines outside the original sampling frame. Indeed this technique is advocated, but infrequently practised (Pope et al., 2007a), as **refutational synthesis**, within the specific methodology of **meta-ethnography**.

Where the intention of a literature review is to make a contribution to **programme theory** it can often be helpful to *make if-then tests*. This would require looking at two seemingly similar programmes to see if specific elements (contextual factors or mechanisms) are either present or absent. This is the approach codified in the methodology of **realist synthesis**. A **truth table**, that is a matrix codifying the presence or absence of particular factors in individual studies, may be a useful practical tool for identifying such relationships (Dixon-Woods et al., 2004; Pope et al., 2007b; Cruzes and Dybå, 2010, w058). This is similar to the thematic matrix demonstrated in Chapter 7 but with binary indicators of presence or absence (e.g. 1 versus 0 or check box versus empty cell) rather than qualitative themes (Table 8.1).

Table 8.1 Hypothetical truth table for review on attitudes to peripheral supermarkets

| | Explanatory variables | | | | | Dependent variable |
| | | | | | | Orchestrated community |
Study	A	B	C	D	E	opposition
Greenwood and Liffey, 2010 (Study 1)	0	1	0	1	1	1
Verdant, 2010 (Study 2)	1	1	1	1	1	0
Swathe, 2011 (Study 3)	1	1	1	0	0	0
Total	2	3	2	2	2	1

A = Convenience; B = Household economy; C = Focus for community; D = Threat to local commerce; E = Threat to community identity.

Note: Findings from this hypothetical truth table appear to show that orchestrated community opposition is less likely to be present if a supermarket emphasises its role as a focus for community activities.

As a follow-up to the if-then testing above you will need to *rule out spurious relations*. To do this you will need to consider whether a third factor or variable may possibly explain away the apparent relationship identified from the data. Ideally, your frame for investigation would include studies reporting the presence of the two conditions, the absence of each and the presence and absence of the third variable. In the example of a truth table (Table 8.1) we may previously have supposed that promoting the benefits of the supermarket for the household economy may help to avoid orchestrated community opposition. However the contribution of the hypothetical Greenwood and Liffey study is to show that such opposition occurred even where this factor was present.

Exploration of the data may also involve reference to external data sources, for example in order to *replicate a finding*. Thus replication of a finding may involve extending a sampling frame to a contiguous area of literature where the underlying explanatory mechanism is still likely to be present. Alternatively, if the original literature review is not based upon a comprehensive sample, you could split your population of studies and use half of the studies to generate the theory or hypothesis and the other half to test and validate it.

A good analyst will keep their mind open to alternative explanations and will therefore *check out rival explanations*. It can be informative to record the theory underpinning each study as you extract the data from each and then to revisit these theories upon completion of your synthesis. Editorial or commentary material may be published in the same issue of a journal as an important original contribution while ensuing correspondence published in subsequent issues may seek to explain findings or reconcile these with prevalent theory.

The use of informants for validation remains controversial, principally because the synthetic product need not necessarily resemble a single contributory study. However this is not an argument against *feedback from informants* (**respondent validation**) *per se* but simply against attaching undue weight to such feedback compared with the synthesis. Clear definition of stakeholder roles and a clear explanation of how feedback will be used can serve as a protection against overturning findings from a well-grounded synthetic product.

It is most helpful to consider the techniques we have itemised as a toolbox from which a reviewer can select according to the robustness of the original synthesis and the underlying purpose of the analysis. For example Slavin (1986) suggests a technique known as 'best evidence synthesis'. This involves a combination of meta-analytic and narrative techniques so that the reviewer can gain insights on effects from the quantitative synthesis combined with contextual data from the accompanying narrative descriptions.

Weight of evidence synthesis

As mentioned in Chapter 6 the categorisation of research studies into strong, moderate, and weak studies allows the reviewer to draw a distinction between those findings which provide a strong basis for confidence (strong weighting), and those which are more speculative, supported only by weak evidence. When writing the conclusions and recommendations (Chapter 9), those studies with a greater strength of evidence should carry more weight than findings based upon less reliable studies. Considerable variation persists between methods for weighting evidence; some examine only the technical performance of studies (i.e. they only factor in rigour) while others conflate rigour and relevance. For example the Social Care Institute for Excellence (SCIE) refers to:

> the synthesis should give greater weight to studies that directly concern the review question (topic relevance) and those people affected by the service in question, and to those studies that give greater confidence in their findings by reporting depth and detail and relevance to wider populations and contexts. Reviewers will rely on some studies more than others because they are assessed as having higher quality, and they will find themselves constantly returning to the quality judgements during qualitative data synthesis. (Coren and Fisher, 2006, w051)

Interestingly, this publication does not prescribe the methods by which studies are weighted. However they do expect a clear description of the weighting scheme. They also specify that it should concern such issues as:

1 centrality of the study to the review topic;
2 strength of design (in relation to answering the review question);
3 generalisability (with respect to context of intervention, sample sizes, and population, etc.), and
4 clarity of reporting of methods.

Use of validity assessment

While the multifactorial approach (Coren and Fisher, 2006, w051) can be seen as fundamentally pragmatic, determined primarily by the practice context in which review findings are intended to be used, there is greater acceptance of the value of the validity assessment as a means for exploring study findings. Indeed a common criticism of reviews, even those performed by the Cochrane Collaboration (w042), is that they may conduct a validity assessment but not use it to discriminate between the findings of high-quality studies and those underpinned by lower-quality studies (de Craen et al., 2005). As previously mentioned, such an assessment can be conducted illustratively by ordering studies by quality and looking for patterns from the findings or, more typically, by dividing studies into the three categories of high, moderate and low quality. This latter approach paves the way for subsequent sensitivity analysis either by removing all studies of low quality or by only including studies of the very highest quality.

Checking with authors of primary studies

Arai and colleagues (2007) report that they consider checking with authors of primary studies as potentially valuable. However they point out that this process depends upon 'the accessibility and generosity' of authors. Although their prior experience of author validation is reported as overwhelmingly positive, this is more likely to be a characteristic of topic areas where researchers provide continuity over many years rather than for the more volatile areas of policy evaluation.

Reviewer effects

It would be naïve to expect that literature reviews, even those that embody systematic approaches, are neutral vehicles for research findings. Naturally, a review reflects the 'perspectives, preferences and propensities' (Sandelowski, 2008) of its reviewers. These may be detected at every stage of the process from the conception of the review and the selection of the principal research question through to study identification, selection and assessment. It can be further identified in the processes of synthesis and analysis. The last of these stages, analysis, is an appropriate juncture for considering the likely effect of researcher effects both in the component studies and in the review itself.

Systematic reviews make much of the virtue of their objectivity, embodied in their methods and in their explicit reporting. However the reality is that the most they can aspire to is what an expert commentator refers to as 'disciplined subjectivity' (Sandelowski, 2008). As an honest reviewer you will seek to conduct an analysis, explicit or otherwise, of the likely challenges posed to objectivity by your own preoccupations and prejudices. You will recognise that the outcomes of your systematic review are 'situated, partial and perspectival' (Lather, 1999, p. 3) and you will seek to communicate these limitations to your reader.

Critical reflection

Critics of systematic approaches to reviewing the literature, including Hammersley (2002, w102), imply that slavish adherence to a review method reduces it to 'essentially an unscholarly or unanalytical pursuit and that it can be conducted by anyone' (Wallace et al., 2003). If such a criticism is to be countered, then a review team, or a single reviewer operating in conjunction with a supervisor or mentor, should actively manufacture opportunities to 'ensure critical reflection on the applicability of the review questions, meaningful data extraction, interpretation and synthesis of the research studies' (Wallace et al., 2003). Indeed Dixon-Woods has embodied the idea of such critical reflection and interpretation within the review process, devising a variant that she and colleagues label 'critical interpretive synthesis'. This method builds upon Sandelowski's previously mentioned concerns regarding the subjectivity of the review process. It moves from the formal **critical appraisal** of individual studies specified by many review methods to a 'critique' of literatures, namely the studies as a body. Such an approach facilitates the development of mid-range theory. More importantly it challenges the assumptions that may underpin individual studies. The review team likens their analysis to that undertaken in primary qualitative research moving from individual papers to themes and then on to the critique. They explicitly state that:

> A key feature of this process that distinguishes it from some other current approaches to interpretive synthesis (and indeed of much primary qualitative research) was its aim of being *critical*: its questioning of the ways in which the literature had constructed [the phenomenon], the nature of the assumptions on which it drew, and what has influenced its choice of proposed solutions. (Dixon-Woods et al., 2006b, w063)

As a consequence of this method the voice of 'the author' is explicit and reflexively accounted for – this method views as untenable the pretence that another review team using similar methods would arrive at the same interpretation. Furthermore, it effectively blurs the distinction made in this book between synthesis and analysis as sequential phases; in truth an oversimplification for all types of review but particularly challenged by this particular method:

> Our critique of the literature was thus dynamic, recursive and reflexive, and, rather than being a stage in which individual papers are excluded or weighted, it formed a key part of the synthesis, informing the sampling and selection of material and playing a key role in theory generation. (Dixon-Woods et al., 2006b, w063)

Such a creative approach may provide a useful mechanism for critiquing the significant bodies of literature from different disciplines and schools of thought associated with the early stages of a dissertation or thesis. At the same time it provides challenges in the lack of a formal documented method, the difficulties of establishing a formal audit trail and issues relating to how it should be reported. As Dixon-Woods and colleagues acknowledge:

However, it is important to note that, as with any qualitative analysis, full transparency is not possible because of the creative, interpretive processes involved. Nonetheless, the large multidisciplinary team involved in the review, and the continual dialogue made necessary by this, helped to introduce 'checks and balances' that guarded against framing of the analysis according to a single perspective. (Dixon-Woods et al., 2006b, w063)

Subgroup analysis

Whether one is examining a quantitative or qualitative body of research it is instructive to move iteratively between an examination of the whole and scrutiny of the component parts. Data extraction and coding will have revealed different groups or 'families' of studies, perhaps sharing population characteristics (e.g. small firms versus large firms, streamed classes versus mixed ability classes, acute hospitals versus primary care settings) or characteristics around the intensity or exact nature of a programme or intervention. The important question is whether such a subgroup, defined by its study characteristics, indeed conforms to the average effect or finding or in fact provides an exception to the rule. As an example of this, Thomas and colleagues (2004) examined interventions to promote healthy eating among children. After establishing overall effect estimates, they started to unpack the different components of the included programmes. After removing studies that contained a physical activity component, identified as qualitatively different, they further divided the studies into those that emphasised health messages and those that did not. They found that the studies that achieved the most significant gains in vegetable consumption were those with little or no emphasis on health messages. This subgroup analysis achieved two main purposes – it helped to explain significant heterogeneity between the different studies and led to generation of a hypothesis to inform and possibly direct the development of future programmes or interventions.

Of course even a relatively homogenous group of studies will include numerous areas of possible variation, dependent in part on how extensive the reporting of studies has been and how thorough the extraction of data. It is therefore particularly helpful, and a more robust approach methodologically, to identify possible subgroup analyses before examining any of the results. Indeed the review protocol should specify the main areas of likely variation and the principal subgroup analyses that will be used in exploring such variation. However Thomas and colleagues (2004) state that this was not possible in their case as the key components of each programme were not identified until the qualitative component of their review had been completed. Mills and colleagues (2005) describe how they explored the findings of their review on parental attitudes to childhood vaccination by analysing by variations in study methods (e.g. semi-structured interview versus focus group) and by publication date.

Sensitivity analysis

Greenhalgh (2010) neatly characterises the process of **sensitivity analysis** by describing it as the formal 'exploration of "what ifs"'. Throughout the review process, you will have made several arbitrary decisions of what to do where methods or data are missing, unclear or obviously incorrect. Depending upon the purpose of your review, and indeed the amount of data you have had to choose from, you will have decided whether to interpret such limitations strictly or generously. Of course, the most extreme position is to actively exclude studies on the basis of such omissions. More typically you will include such studies, perhaps flagged with a question mark and then, once you have combined studies to look for an overall pattern, revisit such question marks to examine their implications for your review. In a **meta-analysis**, for example, a single effect size will typically be accompanied by a confidence interval. The simplest type of **sensitivity analysis** would be to ask: 'Would I make the same decision based upon this review if I assume that the actual result is located at the less favourable end of the confidence interval compared with assuming that the actual result is at the most favourable end?' The most typical indications for performing some type of **sensitivity analysis** are given in Box 8.2.

Box 8.2 Reasons for considering a sensitivity analysis (quantitative)

You might consider conducting a **sensitivity analysis** where:

- you have had significant and persistent doubts about whether a study is eligible for inclusion within a review; you could look at the effect of including and then excluding the result of that study from your review.
- you have identified significant differences in the quality of included studies; you could calculate results using all studies and then excluding poorer quality studies.
- you are uncertain about whether included studies are heterogeneous or homogeneous; you might perform calculations using the two alternative methods of meta-analysis (fixed and random effects) to assess the robustness of the results to the method used.
- you observe that one study has results very different from the rest of the studies (i.e. it is an obvious outlier); you might investigate what might happen were you to exclude it.
- you have made some assumption about a missing value (for example you have carried forward the last available measurement or, alternatively, you have assumed a least favourable outcome); you may seek to explore what happens when you change the basis for your estimate.
- you consider the overall result to be particularly influenced by one particular study (e.g. the largest, the earliest, etc.); you might look at the pattern of results were this study to be excluded.

Although **sensitivity analysis** is most frequently associated with examining the results of quantitative research studies, it is increasingly being recognised within the context of systematic approaches to qualitative research. The methods of investigation and analysis are comparable (Box 8.3). What is less clear, however, is the action to be taken once such sensitivities have been identified.

Box 8.3   Reasons for considering a sensitivity analysis (qualitative)

You might consider conducting a **sensitivity analysis** where:

- you have had persistent doubts about whether a study is eligible for inclusion within a review; would exclusion of this study result in the disappearance of one or more themes from your synthesis?
- you have identified significant differences in the quality of included studies; are particular themes only present in poorer-quality studies or are they distributed across both good and poor-quality studies?
- you are uncertain about whether included studies are heterogeneous or homogeneous; qualitatively do studies have more in common than they have dissimilarity and how important are such similarities or differences likely to be in explaining the overall phenomenon?
- you observe that one study has results very different from the rest of the studies (i.e. it is an obvious outlier); qualitatively does that study have important differences from all other studies or does it simply reflect a similar number and type of differences as are present in other studies?
- you have assumed equivalence between apparently related themes; how open is your assumption to an alternative interpretation or nuance?
- you consider the overall framework or itemisation of themes to be particularly influenced by one individual study (e.g. the most content rich, the earliest, etc.); can you still find evidence of all the themes were you to exclude this study? (Bear in mind too that later authors may have a vested interest in emphasising additional or alternative themes – do they acknowledge the conceptual legacy of the earlier paper in their citations or were such themes simply not identified?)

Several commentators, including Pawson (2006) and Dixon-Woods (2006a), point out that excluding an entire study on the basis of an appraisal of study quality may not be appropriate. Pawson, for example, argues that:

> the 'study' is not the appropriate unit of analysis for quality appraisal in research synthesis. There are often nuggets of wisdom in methodologically weak studies and systematic review disregards them at its peril. (Pawson, 2006)

Identifying gaps

A key concern for all reviewers at the analysis stage relates to the adequacy of their literature sample; whether they have identified *all* studies (comprehensive sampling), whether they have enough studies (purposive sampling), or whether they have identified the right studies (theoretical sampling). Combs and colleagues (2010) describe the potential ambiguities for reviewers at this point in their review:

> The student might note feelings of optimism and relief, particularly as he/she begins to experience information saturation. At the same time, the student might experience anxiety related to the uncertainty of whether every possible key source has been located.

As acknowledged by the requirement of the **Cochrane Collaboration** (w042) to update reviews every two years, preparation of a review is an ongoing and continuous process. New studies are appearing continuously; chasing cited references may repeatedly extend the review task and reading in adjacent literatures may imperceptibly cause **scope creep** (see Chapter 4). For these reasons, it is important for the reviewer, perhaps in conjunction with a supervisor or mentor, to agree mechanisms by which closure of the study identification process might be achieved. Models of conducting systematic reviews and meta-analysis, fuelled by what we have termed the 'big bang approach' to literature searching (i.e. all the literature identified *a priori* before the synthesis and analysis commences) might suggest that agreement of when to stop should appear at the search stage of the SALSA model. However we have deliberately chosen to discuss this in connection with the analysis stage in recognition that some reviews are more iterative with some analytical processes suggesting further lines for inquiry.

For an **aggregative** review, such as a **meta-analysis**, the decision on when to stop is relatively simple and involves one of three choices. The reviewer can either elect to conduct a single phase of study identification or to nominate one or more search update intervals during the life of the review project (when the full **search strategy** is repeated) or to put in place regular updating mechanisms so that new studies are identified up to the point when the final report is produced. This latter approach opens up the possibility of bias in the identification of studies but may be appropriate for a literature review in a policy context (e.g. a **rapid evidence assessment**) where policymakers will not want to be 'caught out' by the appearance of an important new study.

For a more interpretative review you will want to evaluate, with a colleague, supervisor or mentor, whether theoretical saturation is likely to have been achieved. This will typically require that you produce a **formative** presentation of evidence:

> This evidence might include literature review maps/diagrams, matrices, or outlines that indicate main themes, subthemes, categories, subcategories, patterns and sequencing of ideas. (Combs et al., 2010)

Such decisions as to whether the sample of literature is adequate are able to demonstrate, at least to some degree, that they have followed systematic approaches. This contrasts with the typical advice given in the context of a traditional narrative review:

> Of course, it is likely that new articles will come to light after the data collection period has concluded. However, unless the new article is critically important, I suggest leaving it out. Otherwise, the reviewer may have to open the floodgates and start anew the data collection process. (Randolph, 2009, w160)

Table 8.2 Examining methods of analysis used in reviews

Type of review	Methods of analysis used	Application of methods	Review example
Scoping review	Identifying gaps Checking with authors of primary studies (i.e. projects in progress)	Identifies absence of systematic reviews on use of incentives in young people. Identifies existence of significant work in progress to inform future reviews. Following discussion with funders identified need for systematic review on effectiveness and implementation aspects.	A scoping review of the evidence for incentive schemes to encourage positive health and other social behaviours in young people (Kavanagh et al., 2005, w117).
Mapping review	Identifying gaps Subgroup analysis	Failed to find research that explicitly considers how to make initial training responsive to individual needs of trainee teachers. Reports most common aspects of training. Concludes further research is needed in this area.	A systematic map into approaches to making initial teacher training flexible and responsive to the needs of trainee teachers (Graham-Matheson et al., 2005, w094).
Systematic review	Use of validity assessment Sensitivity analysis Identifying gaps	Identified considerable methodological problems that limit internal validity and generalisability of results. Emphasises implications for future research. Suggests possible avenue of future research.	A systematic review of work-place interventions for alcohol-related problems. (Webb et al., 2009).
Qualitative systematic review	Identifying gaps	Proposes model of dissemination. Identifies role for opinion leaders and need for training and education.	Constructing a model of effective information dissemination in a crisis (Duggan and Banwell, 2004, w064).

Now we have considered the variety of techniques that comprise the analysis section of the reviewer's toolkit, we shall briefly revisit the sample reviews we have used throughout this book to see how they have utilised such techniques according to their purpose (Table 8.2).

Revisiting the review question(s)

While you should expect to have to return to your review protocol and question throughout the review project, for example for arbitration of scope or for planning of your synthesis strategy, it is especially important that you do this at the analysis stage. We could say that your intensive and extensive engagement with the literature holds the inherent danger that your project will now become literature-driven, rather than question-driven as previously. You will need to check that the questions you are answering are the ones identified by the original finalised review question(s). You will also need to establish that you have identified literature that maps to each question, perhaps needing to conduct purposive supplementary search strategies to populate any gaps. For a mapping review, it will be sufficient to identify where gaps exist, provided you can be reasonably confident that you have looked in the right places. For a policy review, you may have to settle for a less rigorous study design than for the overall review benchmark, drilling down to lower forms of evidence such as case series, case study, or even expert opinion. Such decisions will have implications for your description of methods, your discussion of uncertainties surrounding the evidence base and for your recommendations for action and for future research. If a **logic model** featured in your original mapping of your review questions it will be helpful to map the literature against each node to gain a picture of which questions are well-covered and which are data poor. Finally, revisiting your review question will not only be a mechanism for checking the alignment of your review but also may suggest lines of inquiry that your analysis might take. For example, a reference in your objectives to 'evaluating the quantity and quality of the retrieved literature' may prompt use of tabulation and mapping to reflect the quantity of the literature and of sensitivity analysis to investigate its corresponding quality.

Discussing the limitations of the evidence

Recognising the limitations of the evidence is important if we are going to place review findings in context (Ionniadis, 2008). A reviewer should clearly highlight how each article, and the review as a whole, has performed with regard to its **validity**, its closeness to the truth. In this way a reviewer can help the reader by ascribing a level of credibility to a review's conclusions.

Where a discussion of limitations is done well, it will go beyond a mere listing of the magnitude and direction of random and systematic errors and any associated problems with validity. This would be rather like a plumber who meets any problems, regardless of severity, with a sharp intake of breath! Instead the reviewer should act as an interpreter of the meaning of any errors and their likely influence. The reader will therefore take away from the discussion section a clear picture of the influence of any validity problems on the published findings of the review.

Recognising the likelihood of bias

In theory, systematic reviews should evaluate and take into account the **internal validity** (i.e. the extent to which systematic errors or bias are avoided) of each included study but also the **applicability** and **generalisability** or **external validity** (i.e. whether the results of a study can be reasonably applied to a definable population in a particular setting in day-to-day practice) (Dekkers et al., 2009).

Recently, the **Cochrane Collaboration** (w042) has developed the **risk of bias tool** to appraise the **internal validity** of trial results included in systematic reviews (Lundh and Goetzche, 2008) (see the tools section in this chapter). Such an approach is still experimental with some evidence to suggest that those items that require more judgement achieve lower rates of consensus (Hartling et al., 2009). Comparison with established methods of quality assessment suggests little agreement indicating that the two approaches may, in fact, be capturing different study features. However, the overall assessment of the **risk of bias** did demonstrate some potential usefulness in identifying low-quality studies that may be exaggerating likely treatment effects.

Just as it is important to take steps to avoid being misled by biases and the play of chance in planning, conducting, analysing and interpreting individual primary studies, similar steps must be taken in planning, conducting, analysing and interpreting evidence syntheses. When you are conducting your overall evaluation of your review and its limitations you need to ask such questions as specified in Box 8.4.

Box 8.4   Questions to ask when assessing the likelihood of bias in your review

1 Have I clearly specified the question to be examined by my review, how included studies address this question and the extent to which my conclusions resolve this question?
2 Have I defined explicit and objective eligibility criteria for studies to be included?
3 To what extent am I confident that I have identified all potentially eligible studies?
4 Have I ensured that the eligibility criteria have been applied in ways that limit bias (possibly resulting from inappropriate acceptance or rejection)?
5 Have I assembled as high a proportion as possible of the relevant information from the included studies (guarding against a bias in outcome selection)?
6 Have I used a variety of analyses to explore any uncertainties associated with my review findings?
7 Have I presented my findings and conclusions in a structured report with clear links between what is observed and what is concluded?

Your answers to the questions in Box 8.4 will, to a large extent, both determine what you cover in your discussion of review limitations and mediate the strength of any recommendations made on the basis of the evidence you have found. In particular questions 3 and 5 from Box 8.4 highlight two aspects that may be largely beyond your control as you are in the hands of the study authors. These points target **publication bias** and **selective reporting bias** respectively and are briefly expanded upon below.

APPLY WHAT YOU HAVE LEARNT 8.1

Identifying bias in your review

Using the template provided identify the main threats to validity (likely **sources of bias**) for your particular review. What steps might you take to minimise the potential threats posed by each source of bias? (You may wish to revisit this exercise once you have read through the following section.)

Threat	How it might prove a threat to my review?	How I could counter this threat?
Change of scope		
Publication bias		
Selection bias		
Inclusion of poor-quality primary studies		
Selective outcome reporting		
Misinterpretation of findings		
Researcher bias in presentation		

Publication bias

Criticisms of the systematic review method, and **meta-analysis** in particular, include that it is subject to **publication bias** (i.e. that **statistically significant** results tend to be published more than non-statistically significant results). Chan and Altman (2005) conclude a milestone paper by stating that 'the [medical] literature represents a selective and biased subset of study outcomes'.

There is every reason to believe that this observation extends to other less investigated literatures. While typically perceived as a problem for quantitative studies Petticrew and colleagues (2008) examined publication rates of qualitative conference presentations, finding an overall publication rate of 44.2 per cent, directly comparable to that for quantitative research. However likelihood of publication for qualitative research was positively related to the quality of reporting of study methods and findings in the abstract as opposed to the direction and significance of results.

In fact, **publication bias** refers to an entire family of biases that include **language bias, location bias**, and **database bias** , etc. These have more recently been grouped as 'Dissemination- and publication-related biases' (Song et al., 2010, w176).

What steps can you as a reviewer take in your analysis to try to identify whether your review is a likely victim of dissemination- or publication-related biases? Some suggestions are given in Box 8.5.

Box 8.5   Suggested ways of exploring dissemination or publication biases

1 Look at the list of databases and other sources that you have chosen to search. How likely is it that non-English studies/unpublished studies will be retrieved by each of these routes?
2 Look at your final list of included studies. How high a proportion of these are published in languages other than English?

3 Look at your final list of included studies. How high a proportion of these are published in the grey literature/fugitive literature?
4 If you only intend to examine English-language studies examine abstracts of non-English studies that would otherwise be included. Is the direction of effect comparable to that for your included English language studies?
5 Map sample size versus effect size on a graph as a funnel plot. Are small negative studies and small positive studies similarly represented?

Table 8.3 Types of reporting bias with definitions

Type of bias	How does it happen?	What is its effect?
Citation bias	When chance of study being cited by others is associated with its result (Song et al., 2010, w176).	Use of reference lists may be more likely to locate supportive studies, which could bias the findings of the review (Egger and Davey Smith, 1998).
Database bias	When there is biased indexing of published studies in literature databases (Song et al., 2010, w176).	Journals indexed in databases are more established, in the language favoured by database producer and include larger studies. Journals from developing countries are less likely to be represented in databases produced in the developed world (Egger and Davey Smith, 1998).
Funding bias	When design, outcome, and reporting of industry-sponsored research may result in sponsor's product showing favourable outcome (Lexchin, 2003).	Positive studies supporting a product are more likely to be published. Negative studies may be delayed or even suppressed.
Grey literature bias	When results reported in journal articles are systematically different from those in reports, working papers, dissertations, or conference abstracts (Song et al., 2010, w176).	Studies may contain interim findings, may not have been subjected to peer review, or may include selective reporting of outcomes.
Language bias (including English- language bias)	When reviews are more likely to include studies published in the language of that review.	Problem for English-language reviews with non-English authors more likely to publish significant results in English rather than in their own language (Egger and Davey Smith, 1998).
Multiple publication bias (duplicate publication bias)	When multiple/duplicate publications are produced from single studies.	Studies with significant results are more likely to lead to multiple publications and presentations, making them more likely to be located and included in reviews. The inclusion of duplicated data may lead to overestimation of the effect size (Egger and Davey Smith, 1998).
Outcome reporting bias	When study in which multiple outcomes were measured reports only those that are significant, rather than insignificant or unfavourable (Song et al., 2010, w176).	Important clinical outcomes are present in some studies but not in others.
Publication bias (also known as positive results bias)	Selective submission of papers (by authors) or selective acceptance of papers (by editors).	Authors may anticipate rejection (Egger and Davey Smith, 1998) and decide not to submit their paper.
Study quality bias	Studies of (typically) lower quality are associated with positive or favourable results.	Studies of lower quality less likely to be published (Song et al., 2010, w176).

While Box 8.5 applies mainly to quantitative studies similar questions can be asked to examine likely publication bias with regard to qualitative studies or theoretical/conceptual studies. For qualitative studies you might use a matrix approach to examine whether any populations, age groups, or countries where the phenomenon of interest is common are comparatively under-represented. For theoretical/conceptual studies you might brainstorm, either singly or with colleagues or a mentor, those disciplines that are likely to have studied the phenomenon of interest. Compare your list with the corresponding characteristics of your included studies. Again are any disciplines comparatively under-represented?

Selective outcome reporting bias

Selective outcome reporting bias has assumed recent prominence. It is a specific instance of a more generic problem, **selective reporting bias**, defined as the 'selection of a subset of analyses to be reported'. Whereas publication bias refers to a problem relating to missing studies, selective reporting bias is very much a problem of missing data within a study. Consequently it may prove more difficult to detect and requires a greater degree of familiarity with the topic area under consideration. Selective outcome reporting is the principal concern because it relates to biased selection of outcomes and so may present a particular programme or intervention in a more favourable light and thus lead to erroneous conclusions as to whether such an intervention should be introduced into practice (Williamson and Gamble, 2005). At its most innocuous, but nevertheless still potentially harmful, it may involve a researcher having measured the same outcome in multiple ways and then selecting which of these ways contributes best to an understanding of the data. The researcher then only provides results using the chosen method. Obviously such an approach has particular limitations in connection with **meta-analysis** where such an analysis is only usually possible where the same methods of outcome measurement have been used by multiple studies. More serious, however, would be where a study has measured important and meaningful outcomes but suppresses the results because they are unfavourable to the overall verdict.

Expert knowledge of a particular topic may help you to identify a more problematic variant of selective outcome reporting, namely the use of surrogate outcomes. Such outcomes may have the virtue of being comparatively easy to measure, but bear little relation to what is most important when judging success or achievement of an 'effect'. Consider, for example, where a government agency might record the number of new small businesses to which it has pro-vided 'start up' funds where the public is more interested in how many of such businesses return an operating profit after x years. Similarly, a drug may be reported to have an effect on lowering blood pressure by a certain number of units but the doctor and patient are much more interested in whether it reduces the occurrence of health-threatening events (such as strokes or heart attacks).

How can you as a reviewer analyse your included studies for the presence of any of these variants of selective outcome reporting? Some suggested questions to ask of your data are provided in Box 8.6.

Box 8.6   Questions to detect possible outcomes reporting bias

1 To what extent does the list of outcomes identified from the literature match the outcomes that stakeholders in your topic area would consider important and meaningful?
2 Examine the full list of outcomes compiled across all studies. Are there any studies that seem to have neglected important outcomes from this list? Do any studies report demonstrably fewer outcomes than their counterparts?
3 Try to identify study protocols for your included studies. How does the list of proposed measurements compare with the list of actual measurements reported in the published papers?
4 Try to identify abstracts from conference proceedings for your included studies. Are any particular measurements reported in interim results but not reported in final published papers?
5 Contact authors of published papers and ask for any additional data, either on specific outcomes or on all non-reported outcomes. Can they point you towards any supplementary publications that you have not previously identified?

What steps can you as a reviewer take in your analysis to try to identify whether your own review is a likely victim of selective outcome reporting bias? Some suggestions are given in Box 8.7.

Box 8.7   Questions to detect possible reporting bias in your own review

1 In your initial reading of a paper, look at which outcome measures have been reported. Are all the outcome measures that have been reported associated with statistically significant results? If so, they are more likely to reflect selective reporting.
2 Again in your initial reading of a paper, count how many separate outcomes are reported. If there are fewer than five different outcomes there is a very high likelihood, between 5 and 10 a high likelihood, and between 11 and 20 a moderate likelihood of selective reporting bias
3 In your initial reading, look at the outcome measure being used for calculating the sample size. Is this identifiable as the primary outcome from the Results and Conclusions? Has its role as primary outcome been 'hijacked' by a less important outcome?
4 Finally, in your initial reading of the paper, look for evidence of **data dredging** i.e. where potentially significant associations are stumbled upon during data analysis and an outcome is being attributed with greater importance than a practitioner would invest it with.
5 In following up includable papers, try to obtain relevant study protocols and compare the list of intended outcomes with the list of those actually reported in the final paper. Are they identical? Are there any missing? Have any been promoted in terms of prominence?
6 In following up includable papers via protocols are sample size and statistical methods in published trials clearly discrepant with respect to the pre-specified protocols?

(Continued)

(Continued)

7 In synthesising your data across studies, construct a matrix of all reported outcomes against all studies. Are any common outcomes missing from individual studies? Are any important outcomes comparatively under-reported?
8 In analysing your data from included studies, is the performance of any outcomes particularly dependent on presentations at meetings or appearance in conference abstracts? Is this performance confirmed by subsequent publication?

(Chan et al., 2008)

While Box 8.7 is primarily intended for use with quantitative studies, similar questions may be asked with regard to likely reporting bias in qualitative studies or in theoretical/conceptual studies. If you have used a framework approach for examining qualitative studies, you might look to see whether any themes, concerns or issues are missing or under-represented. You might also consider qualitatively whether any specific themes or concerns might not be reported because of stigma, peer pressure, the influence of the researcher, limitations of the methodology or concerns about confidentiality or possible reprisals. If you are conducting a review of barriers and facilitators you can examine whether (a) positive and negative expressions of the same barrier are equally present in the literature (e.g. time pressures and lack of time) albeit in different papers, and (b) whether barriers may be paired with corresponding facilitators. Of course, your subsequent analytical task is to examine whether any gaps are a feature of the data collection process, of incomplete reporting or of being genuinely unrecognised. At the same time you should take care to recognise that the frequency of reporting of particular themes is not necessarily related to their importance for, as Dixon-Woods and colleagues (2006a) observe:

> it has to be acknowledged that sampling research papers is fundamentally not like sampling people. Unlike people, research papers have a vested interest in being different from one another, and are (in theory at least) only published if they are saying something new. Missing out some papers may therefore risk missing out potentially important insights.

For theoretical/conceptual studies you may wish to construct diagrams that examine citation patterns. Areas where authors have neglected to cite a particular author or school of thought working within the same field may prove particularly fruitful. These may indicate ignorance of particular arguments or connections, possible conflicts, or tensions, or intentional omission. It may also be informative to look for patterns of cross-fertilisation or alternatively existence of a 'silo mentality' between disciplines. All such observations may help to guide your analysis and subsequent presentation.

Triangulation

The technique of **triangulation**, a navigational metaphor, may include using multiple data sources (e.g. members of the public, those delivering a service or programme and other stakeholders), multiple data collection methods (e.g. use of in-depth interviews and focus groups), multiple disciplinary perspectives (e.g. education, management science, and psychology), and comparison with existing theory (Cook et al., 2001).

Identifying recommendations for action

One possible outcome of your review will be to identify methods or interventions that can be utilised in practice. However, it is not automatic that review results will be able to be used in this way. Many factors will have a bearing on whether research may be applied within a specific context (Dekkers et al., 2009). If you are going to be able to apply the results of your review to the outside world, you need to have a good picture of the context in which they would be implemented. You may have the inherent advantage of being a practitioner-researcher or you may need to engage with a steering group that can advise on the implications of your findings.

Other mechanisms for tailoring your recommendations may include consultation documents, interim presentation of results to review commissioners, stakeholder conferences and presentations at professional meetings. This iterative process, when your findings are fresh and their interpretation still fluid, can be seen as part of the analysis phase rather than the subsequent presentation and dissemination. Other factors involved in judging how you may apply your review findings to the external world may be more technical. For a quantitative review they will include statistical considerations, such as the degree of statistical significance and the accompanying uncertainty that surrounds the pooled results. For results from both quantitative and qualitative studies, they will include your detailed knowledge of the eligibility criteria for your review (Dekkers et al., 2009). If you decide to focus your review for practical and logistic reasons this may have had the effect of limiting its applicability to populations outside your main focus. For example, a qualitative review of breastfeeding limited to studies with similar cultural characteristics to the United Kingdom (e.g. the United States, Australia, Canada, New Zealand, Australia) was found to have much more limited applicability than its quantitative equivalent which included all randomised controlled trials.

A further constraint on your recommendations for practice may be the extent of reporting of the included studies. There may simply not be sufficient information in the original reports for you to judge the external validity and applicability of the results of included studies. For example, Glasziou and colleagues examined reports of non-drug treatments that had been shown to be promising and found deficiencies in the description of interventions that made it impossible to replicate these in practice. Even where the characteristics of the intervention itself are clearly described there may be correspondingly little detail on *how* it has been implemented. Work on **implementation fidelity** identified at least six factors that may have a bearing on how well an intervention actually works in practice when compared with its evaluation in empirical studies (Carroll et al., 2007, w032).

Highlighting recommendations for future research

Any review has the potential to identify research gaps. However, the familiar semi-serious injunction for all researchers to start writing up with the statement 'Further research is needed' is rightly treated with caution. Given that one of the objectives of the review is to consolidate a body of evidence, the reviewer should seek to be as specific as possible about what is lacking in research conducted to date. Does a theoretical framework already exist for the review area? If so, does it require further exploration or validation? If not, are we any further in identifying what its essential features might be? Have any population groups that might benefit from an inter-vention been under-researched or completely neglected? Has the potential effec-tiveness of an intervention been mooted or already explored in small-scale studies? How large will a rigorous randomised controlled trial need to be to establish such effectiveness conclusively? Are any adjustments to an intervention, suggested by stakeholders or by qualitative synthesis, yet to be investigated for effectiveness? Are the right outcomes being measured and reported (Moher et al., 2007)? Is there a need for the development or utilisation of rigorous outcome measurement tools?

The American Educational Research Association (2006) explains how new research can contribute to existing research. These purposes apply equally well to the main contributions of evidence synthesis (Box 8.8).

Box 8.8   The contribution of evidence synthesis to existing research

Theory testing or validation: if a review is a contribution to an established line of the-ory and empirical research, it should make clear what the contributions are and how the study contributes to testing, elaborating or enriching that theoretical perspective.

Theory generation: if a review is intended to establish a new line of theory, it should make clear what that new theory is, how it relates to existing theories and evidence, why the new theory is needed, and the intended scope of its application.

Problem solving: if a review is motivated by practical concerns, it should make clear what those concerns are, why they are important, and how this investigation can address those concerns.

Fact finding: if a review is motivated by a lack of information about a problem or issue, the problem formation should make clear what information is lacking, why it is important, and how this investigation will address the need for information.

REFLECTION POINT 8.1

The contribution of new research

Look at the four contributions that new research can make to existing research (Box 8.8). Which seem particularly relevant to your own review? Are there any other contributions that your review might make that are not covered by these four generic headings?

Summary

Analysis is a high-order research skill required when undertaking any systematic approach to reviewing the literature. In contrast to synthesis, which has received considerable attention, analysis is very often presented as a naturally occurring sequel requiring little in the way of formal procedures. Nevertheless such procedures do exist and may be adapted to the specific area of literature review from the research domains of qualitative and quantitative analysis. Essentially, analysis involves identifying patterns to data and included studies, investigating conflicting or outlying cases and exploring relationships between particular variables.

In addition particular techniques have been developed within the science of systematic review and evidence synthesis. These include use of **funnel plots** (for the investigation of publication bias), **subgroup analysis** (for exploring commonalities that exist at a level beneath that of the complete population of studies) and **sensitivity analysis** (for testing the robustness of results to particular assumptions). Once these analytical techniques have been used to explore the internal validity of the review, attention may proceed to the corresponding concern of external validity. Concerns about applicability, generalisability, replicability and implementation fidelity will combine to shape the likely recommendations for research and for practice. Once such recommendations have been drafted and exist in a fluid or malleable state, attention can turn to how best to present the report, the focus for Chapter 9.

Key learning points

- The analysis stage focuses on interpreting what the results of the review mean. Multiple techniques exist for testing or confirming findings.
- Analysis initially involves testing the robustness of your synthesis in the light of what you know about the quality of included studies.
- Particular concerns will relate to the presence of dissemination- and publication-related biases.
- Once an assessment of the overall robustness has been achieved, your attention will focus on the extent to which the findings may be applied within the specific context of your review.

Suggestions for further reading

Deeks, J.J., Higgins, J.P.T., and Altman, D.G. (eds) (2008) Analysing data and undertaking meta-analyses. In: Higgins, J.P.T. and Green, S. (eds) *Cochrane Handbook for Systematic Reviews of Interventions*, Version 5.0.1 (updated September 2008), The Cochrane Collaboration. Bognor Regis: Wiley-Blackwell. (w043)

Egger, M. and Davey Smith, G. (1998) Meta-analysis: bias in location and selection of studies. *British Medical Journal*, **316**, 61–6.

Greenhalgh, T. (2010) *How to Read a Paper: The Basics of Evidence-based Medicine*, 4th edn. London: BMJ Books.

Higgins, J.P.T and Altman, D.G. (eds) (2008) Assessing risk of bias in included studies. In: Higgins, J.P.T. and Green, S. (eds) *Cochrane Handbook for Systematic Reviews of Interventions*, Version 5.0.1 (updated September 2008), The Cochrane Collaboration. Bognor Regis: Wiley-Blackwell. (w043).

Sterne, J.A.C., Egger, M., and Moher, D. (eds) (2008) Addressing reporting biases. In: Higgins, J.P.T. and Green, S. (eds) *Cochrane Handbook for Systematic Reviews of Interventions*, Version 5.0.1 (updated September 2008), The Cochrane Collaboration. Bognor Regis: Wiley-Blackwell (w043)

Tools for data analysis

The key to the robustness of the results from a review is some consideration of the presence or absence of bias. The Tools section selects probably the best developed instrument for this purpose, the **risk of bias tool** from the **Cochrane Collaboration** working through the three stages of this process. It then concludes with a brief example of the usefulness of a funnel plot for examining **publication bias**.

The risk of bias tool

The **Cochrane Collaboration** (w042) has developed an innovative tool to help in the assessment of the risk of bias in individual studies and then to examine systematic bias within a number of component studies within a review. The process begins with the quality assessment of an individual study (see Chapter 6). An example of such a structured assessment is seen in Table 8.6.

Table 8.4   Example of a 'risk of bias' table for a single study (fictional)

Entry	Judgement	Description
Adequate sequence generation	No	**Quote:** 'patients were allocated according to alternate days presenting at the clinic'
		Comment: this opens up possibility of systematic bias
Allocation concealment	No	**Quote:** 'allocation was performed from a printed schedule'
		Comment: opportunity to break allocation via alternation
Blinding (for each outcome)	Yes	**Quote:** 'biochemical tests used to corroborate abstinence at three months'
		Comment: objective measure ascertained by laboratory
Incomplete outcome data addressed (for each outcome)	No	15 smokers missing from intervention group only five from control group.
Free of selective reporting?	No	No reporting of independently confirmed smoking cessation at one year
Free of other bias?	No	Trial supported financially by nicotine patch company

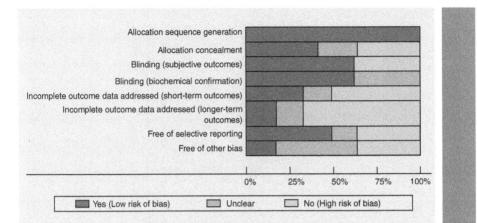

Allocation sequence generation
Allocation concealment
Blinding (subjective outcomes)
Blinding (biochemical confirmation)
Incomplete outcome data addressed (short-term outcomes)
Incomplete outcome data addressed (longer-term outcomes)
Free of selective reporting
Free of other bias

0%   25%   50%   75%   100%

Yes (Low risk of bias)   Unclear   No (High risk of bias)

Figure 8.1   Example of a risk of bias graph

Once the tabular assessment has been completed, the qualitative data on
risk of bias can be 'translated' into a quantitative form. Each threat of bias
is quantified and a graphical display is produced (Figure 8.1). This graphic
display uses a red-amber-green colour scheme to aid in the identification of
patterns across the individual study.

Finally, the risk of bias instrument comes into its own as a tool for synthesis. Each component study in the review (six studies in our hypothetical
example) is colour-coded, again using the red-amber-green notation, against
each of the eight quality domains (Figure 8.2). At a glance, the reviewer can
identify systematic patterns of bias across studies. Such patterns can be
explored in more detail and linked to an overall assessment of the robustness of the review's conclusions and the strength of its recommendations.

The funnel plot

A **funnel plot** is a graphical device for helping you to explore the likelihood of **publication bias**. It plots a measure of study size (e.g. standard
error) against a measure of effect size (e.g. log odds ratio or relative risk)
and looks for the systematic absence of certain groups or populations of
studies (e.g. small studies with negative effects). If **publication bias** is not
present, you would expect your funnel plot to be roughly symmetrical,
the shape of an inverted funnel (Figure 8.3). Where publication bias is
possibly present, there will be a missing 'chunk' of data (Figure 8.4). For
a funnel plot to be valuable requires there to be more than a mere handful of studies. A funnel plot is only an indication, not a guarantor of bias,
so it must be seen as a starting point for further investigation, not an end
in itself.

Study	Adequate sequence generation	Allocation concealment	Blinding (subjective outcomes)	Blinding (biochemical confirmation)	Incomplete outcome data (short-term outcomes)	Incomplete outcome data (long-term outcomes)	Free of selective reporting	Free of other bias
Bamboozle (1982)	+	+	+	+	−	+	−	−
Barr and Humbug (1991)	+	+	+	−	+	+	−	+
Bunkum and Hornswoggle (2001)	+	−	?	+	?	+	+	+
Hook (2002)	+	+	+	+	?	?	?	?
Line (1999)	+	+	+	+	+	+	?	+
Sinker (2011)	+	−	−	?	+	−	−	−

Figure 8.2   Example of a risk of bias summary

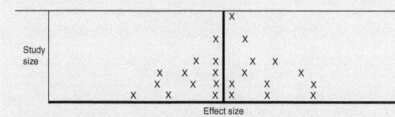

Figure 8.3   Funnel plot with no evidence of publication bias

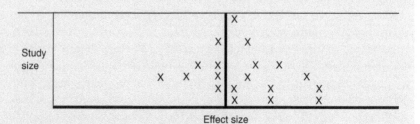

Figure 8.4   Funnel plot with possible publication bias

NB: In Figure 8.4 a possible population of studies (those at the bottom of the left-hand side of the funnel) appears not to have been detected by the meta-analysis.

References

American Educational Research Association (2006) Standards for reporting on empirical social science research in AERA publications. *Educational Researcher*, **35**, 6, 33–40.

Arai, L., Britten, N., Popay, J., Roberts, H., Petticrew, M., Rodgers, M., and Sowden, A. (2007) Testing methodological developments in the conduct of narrative synthesis: a demonstration review of research on the implementation of smoke alarm interventions. *Evidence and Policy*, **3**, 361–83. (w006)

Carroll, C., Patterson, M., Wood, S., Booth, A., Rick, J., and Balain, S. (2007) A conceptual framework for implementation fidelity. *Implementation Science*, **2**, 40. (w032)

Chan, A.W. and Altman, D.G. (2005) Identifying outcome reporting bias in randomised trials on PubMed: review of publications and survey of authors. *BMJ*, **330**, 7494, 753.

Combs, J.P., Bustamante, R.M., and Onwuegbuzie, A.J. (2010) An interactive model for facilitating development of literature reviews. *International Journal of Multiple Research Approaches*, **4**, 2, 159–82

Cook, D.J., Meade, M.O., and Perry, A.G. (2001) Qualitative studies on the patient's experience of weaning from mechanical ventilation. *Chest*, **120**, 6, Suppl, 469S-73S.

Coren, E. and Fisher, M. (2006) *The Conduct of Systematic Research Reviews for SCIE Knowledge Reviews*. Using Knowledge in Social Care Research Resource 1. London: Social Care Institute of Excellence. (w051)

Cruzes, D.S. and Dybå, T. (2010) Synthesizing evidence in software engineering research. ESEM 10, Proceedings of the 2010 ACM-IEEE International Symposium on Empirical Software Engineering and Measurement. Association for Computing Machinery, New York. (w058)

de Craen, A.J., van Vliet, H.A., and Helmerhorst, F.M. (2005) An analysis of systematic reviews indicated low incorpororation of results from clinical trial quality assessment. *Journal of Clinical Epidemiology*, **58**, 3, 311–13.

Dekkers, O.M., von Elm, E., Algra, A., Romijn, J.A., and Vandenbroucke, J.P. (2009) How to assess the external validity of therapeutic trials: a conceptual approach. *International Journal of Epidemiology*, **39**, 1, 89–94.

Dixon-Woods, M., Agarwal, S., Young, B., Jones, D., and Sutton, A. (2004) *Integrative Approaches to Qualitative and Quantitative Evidence*. London: NHS Health Development Agency. (w062)

Dixon-Woods, M., Bonas, S., Booth, A., Jones, D.R., Miller, T., Shaw, R.L., Smith, J., Sutton, A., and Young, B. (2006a) How can systematic reviews incorporate qualitative research? A critical perspective. *Qualitative Research*, **6**, 1, 27–44.

Dixon-Woods, M., Cavers, D., Agarwal, S., Annandale, E., Arthur, A., Harvey, J., Hsu, R., Katbamna, S., Olsen, R., Smith, L.K., Riley, R., and Sutton, A.J. (2006b) Conducting a critical interpretive review of the literature on access to healthcare by vulnerable groups. *BMC Medical Research Methodology*, **6**, 35. (w063)

Egger, M. and Davey Smith, G. (1998) Meta-analysis: bias in location and selection of studies. *BMJ*, **316**, 61–6.

Greenhalgh, T. (2010) *How to Read a Paper: The Basics of Evidence-based Medicine*, 4th edn. London: BMJ Books.

Hammersley, M. (2002) Systematic or Unsystematic, is that the question? Some reflections on the science, art and politics of reviewing research evidence. London, Health Development Agency text of talk to Public Health Evidence Steering Group. (w102)

Hartling, L., Ospina, M., Liang, Y., Dryden, D.M., Hooton, N., Krebs Seida, J., and Klassen, T.P. (2009) Risk of bias versus quality assessment of randomised controlled trials: cross sectional study. *BMJ*, **339**, b4012

Ioannidis, J.P.A. (2007) Limitations are not properly acknowledged in the scientific literature. *Journal of Clinical Epidemiology*, **60**, 4, 324–9.

Lather, P. (1999) To be of use: the work of reviewing. *Review of Educational Research*, **69**, 2–7.

Lundh, A. and Gotzsche, P.C. (2008) Recommendations by Cochrane Review Groups for assessment of the risk of bias in studies. *BMC Medical Research Methodology*, **8**, 22. (w127).

Macura, A., Abraha, I., Kirkham, J., Gensini, G.F., Moja, L. and Dorio, A. (2010) Selective outcome reporting: telling and detecting true lies. The state of the science. *International Emergency Medicine*, **5**, 151–5.

Mills, E., Jadad, A.R., Ross, C., and Wilson, K. (2005) Systematic review of qualitative studies exploring parental beliefs and attitudes toward childhood vaccination identifies common barriers to vaccination. *Journal of Clinical Epidemiology*, **58**, 1081–8.

Moher, D., Tetzlaff, J., Tricco, A.C., Sampson, M., and Altman, D.G. (2007) Epidemiology and reporting characteristics of systematic reviews. *PLoS Med*, **4**, 3, e78. (w136)

Pawson, R. (2006) Digging for nuggets: how 'bad' research can yield 'good' evidence. *International Journal of Social Research Methodology*, **9**, 2, 127–42.

Petticrew, M., Egan, M., Thomson, H., Hamilton, V., Kunkler, R., and Roberts, H. (2008) Publication bias in qualitative research: what becomes of qualitative research presented at conferences? *Journal of Epidemiology and Community Health*, **62**, 552–4.

Pope, C., Mays, N., and Popay, J (2007a) Interpretive approaches to evidence synthesis. In Pope, C., Mays, N. and Popay, J., *Synthesising Qualitative and Quantitative Health Evidence: A Guide to Methods*. Maidenhead: McGraw Hill, 82.

Pope, C., Mays, N., and Popay, J. (2007b) Quantitative approaches to evidence synthesis. In Pope, C., Mays, N. and Popay, J., *Synthesising Qualitative and Quantitative Health Evidence: A Guide to Methods*. Maidenhead: McGraw Hill, 67–70.

Randolph, J.J. (2009) A guide to writing the dissertation literature review. *Practical Assessment, Research and Evaluation*, **14**, 1–13. (w160)

Sandelowski, M. (2008) Reading, writing and systematic review. *Journal of Advanced Nursing*, **64**, 1, 104–10.

Slavin, R.E. (1986) Best-evidence synthesis: an alternative to meta-analysis and traditional reviews. *Educational Researcher*, **15**, 9, 5–11.

Song, F., Parekh, S., Hooper, L., Loke, Y.K., Ryder, J., Sutton, A.J., Hing, C., Kwok, C.S., Pang, C., and Harvey, I. (2010) Dissemination and publication of research findings: an updated review of related biases. *Health Technology Assessment*, **14**, 8, 1–193. (w176)

Thomas, J., Harden, A., Oakley, A., Oliver, S., Sutcliffe, K., Rees, R., Brunton, G., and Kavanagh, J. (2004) Integrating qualitative research with trials in systematic reviews. *BMJ*, **328**, 1010–12.

Wallace, A., Croucher, K., Quilgars, D. and Baldwin, S. (2003) Meeting the challenge: developing systematic reviewing in social policy. Paper presented to Social Policy Association Conference, University of Teeside, 16 July 2003.

Williamson, P.R. and Gamble, C. (2005) Identification and impact of outcome selection bias in meta-analysis. *Statistics in Medicine*, **24**, 1547–61.

NINE

Writing up and presenting data

Learning Objectives

After reading this chapter, you should be able to:

- Describe the main elements required when writing up and presenting data from a systematic approach to the literature.
- Produce a draft literature review appropriate to the topic and objective of your review question.
- Identify reporting standards that relate to your chosen approach to reviewing the literature.
- Conduct a range of methods for data presentation to illustrate key messages from your review.

Introduction

As mentioned throughout this book, many inherent advantages of systematic approaches to reviewing the literature relate to the transparency and auditability of the review product. While a subject expert may be tempted to present minimal detail on the methods of the review, preferring to concentrate on the findings, it is the methods that contribute to the credibility and objectivity of the final review. As a review author, you must not only consider the nature of your topic and the methods of your chosen type of review. You must also give detailed consideration to your audience. As Major and Savin-Baden (2010) emphasise:

> in presenting the synthesis, it is critical for synthesists to speak directly to a specific intended audience. Further we suggest that the selection of an intended audience is likely to drive decisions about how the synthesis is presented.

Considering your audience

Many reasons explain why a particular review may fail to capitalise on the inherent advantages embodied in the structured methods of review presentation. Concerns with technical detail or methodological niceties may interfere with the intended message. The measured, cautious tone of a review with its acknowledgement of nuances may mask the potential usefulness of the review findings. In particular, the comprehensive identification of similar evidence in multiple contexts and circumstances may appear to offer contradictory advice. The poverty of detail in the source reports may make it impossible to replicate an intervention or programme, even when demonstrated to be effective. The specific question being asked may be deliberately narrow to facilitate conduct of the review but this may limit its usefulness and applicability. Particular sectors of the community may be excluded, either from the evidence base or from the review conclusions. Finally, the timeframe within which the review has been conducted may result in its being out of step with areas of current concern or importance. Clearly many of these potential dangers should have been anticipated much earlier in the review process, particularly at the commissioning and scoping stages (see Chapter 4). This chapter therefore focuses on those aspects that may yet be determined at the point of writing up the review.

There is never a *single* target audience for a review product (Hammersley, 2002, w102). However it should always be possible to identify the *primary* audience:

> whenever we address a particular audience we have to take account of what we can assume they already know, what they would and would not be interested in, and perhaps also what they might misinterpret. (Hammersley, 2002, w102).

In this way you will be able to prioritise those aspects of presentation that relate to the primary audience without compromising too much on the needs of other, secondary, audiences. However, the all-too-important ingredient of political context should be added to this technical requirement :

> We need to take account of the politics of how reviews are received and read by audiences. The reception of reviews is often driven by audiences' current preoccupations, and guided by relatively fixed preconceptions. (Hammersley, 2002, w102)

Such concerns may appear less important if the intended output is an academic piece of work, particularly for a dissertation or doctorate. However the tone of the accompanying narrative will be determined by the prior state of belief of the audience and where the author intends them to be upon completion of the review. Will the intention be to exhort, reason, cajole or even berate? To a certain degree, the prevailing tone will depend upon whether the reviewer is trying to encourage adoption of some new method or technique, dispense with an ineffective practice, or simply to open an audience's minds to some tentative future possibility.

APPLY WHAT YOU HAVE LEARNT 9.1

Consumers of your review

In marketing terms, we think about a synthesis product in terms of its primary audience (the main consumers of your review) and its secondary audiences (others who may be interested in your review. For example, the primary audience of a review included in your thesis might be the external examiner and secondary audiences might be your supervisor, other academics in your discipline and, possibly, practitioners in your chosen field.

For your own review complete the following grid

Primary audience(s)	What I already know about their reading preferences. How could I find out more about their reading preferences?
Secondary audience(s)	What I already know about their reading preferences. How could I find out more about their reading preferences?

Writing for research funders

Research funders wish to be assured that they have made a wise investment of the money entrusted to their care. They are particularly interested in incremental knowledge gains made as a result of the review. They will also be interested in the added value offered by a systematically conducted review over and above other possible research approaches, whether these involve primary research or other types of synthesis. Finally, they will want to know if you have identified any other areas for research; either follow-up questions identified in the course of your review or proximate areas that you have not covered in your own work. Your research funders will find it particularly helpful if you identify first, what is already known about the topic and second, what this review adds. You will find it helpful to summarise your own review as two boxes of bulletpoints and then to use this structure for constructing your own conclusions.

A further feature of interest is *recommendations for future research*. The ubiquitous conclusion 'More research is needed' is justifiably viewed with disdain (Phillips, 2007). If you have spent many person-hours immersing yourself in the literature covered by the review, you will quite rightly be expected to be able to identify specifically what has or has not been researched or where considerable uncertainty remains. It is also helpful to give a clear idea of the specific question and the type of research that will be required to provide an answer (see EPICOT+ in the tools section of this chapter). Rather than generate a seemingly endless list of areas for future research, it will be useful if you can think in terms of a finite amount of funds and prioritise research that is both feasible and important. You should continue in your review author role as honest broker and not write as a potential beneficiary of future research commissioned in the area; if you subsequently happen to benefit from a gap that you have highlighted, then this should be an unexpected bonus.

Writing for policy makers

Although policymakers will wish to know that the conclusions of your review are based on high-quality research studies wherever possible, a particular concern will be the external validity (or generalisability) of your review (Ahmad et al., 2010). In other words, they will want to know the extent to which the results of your review can be reasonably applied or generalised to a definable population/populations in a particular context. If studies have not been conducted within the setting of interest, they will want to know any limitations or reservations they might have in applying results across contexts. They will also want to have an idea of the limitations of the evidence in terms of any unresolved areas of uncertainty.

You should particularly bear in mind that policymakers need reviews for decision support (i.e. to provide answers or direction) rather than for knowledge support. Reviews that plumb lower-level study types, provided that the consequences of doing so are clearly stated, are preferable to general conclusions that 'robust studies are unable to provide answers'. Similarly, policymakers will generally appreciate a more holistic picture of all issues to inform their decision (i.e. they should 'address the full range of questions asked by managers and policymakers') rather than a simple lens offering an answer to a very tightly focused question. Increasingly, we are seeing models of iterative interaction that involve decision-makers in the entire review process, from asking the research questions to providing context for the question under study (Lavis et al., 2006; Pope et al., 2006).

As well as a focus on pragmatic answers, policymakers have a particular interest in how reviews are presented. In particular it is helpful if they can be:

> more easily scanned for relevance, decision-relevant information, and factors that would influence assessments for local applicability. (Lavis et al., 2006)

In some cases, this need has provided impetus to the presentation of reviews in the 1:3:25 format (involving corresponding numbers of pages for take-home messages (1), the executive summary (3), and the full systematic review (25) (Lavis et al., 2005, 2006)).

Writing for practitioners

A well-conducted systematic review is invaluable for practitioners. Many of us feel overwhelmed by the volume of literature in our discipline and, as a result, often prefer summaries of information to publications of original investigations (Williamson, 1989). Thus, review articles can help us keep up-to-date. High-quality systematic reviews can define the boundaries of what is known and what is not known and can help us avoid knowing less than has been proven. It is unusual for single studies to provide definitive answers, but systematic reviews can help practitioners solve specific problems. By critically examining primary studies, systematic reviews can also improve our understanding of inconsistencies among diverse pieces of research evidence. By quantitatively combining the results of several small studies, **meta-analyses** can create more precise, powerful, and convincing conclusions. In addition, **systematic reviews** of several studies may better inform us about whether findings can be applied to specific subgroups of the population.

Concern has been expressed at the limitations of systematic reviews where evidence is limited, for example in so-called **empty reviews** or where there is only a single study (Pagliaro et al., 2010). It seems that practitioners favour having some evidence, albeit of low quality, over no evidence, even where this may reflect a higher-quality threshold. The value of consultation with current practitioners is emphasised by the fact that it is very easy to apply a rigorous technical process to studies of an intervention that no longer reflects standard practice, thus producing an outdated review (Pagliaro et al., 2010). Similar reservations relate to the length of reviews (typically 40 pages or more) and the unhelpfulness of their recommendations for practice (Pagliaro et al., 2010). Clearly, such concerns have implications for the writing up of reviews; many relate back to the scoping of the review (Chapter 4).

Writing for the research community

The research community is particularly interested in well-conducted reviews because they help to identify gaps in the evidence base and provide a quantitative basis for informing new research initiatives. Typically, a researcher responding to a funding call will seek to find a systematic review or overview around which they can build their argument for a research proposal. In particular contexts, a systematic review may be of significant value in designing new studies (Cooper et al., 2005). However it is still true to say that reviews are not as heavily used in the design of studies as we might expect. Within medicine, there has been a recent and welcome trend to require that study authors identify related studies when presenting their own primary research. This imperative seeks to reduce the numbers of 'islands without continents' that is primary studies that fail to make a connection with their own evidence base (Clarke and Chalmers, 1998). Increasingly funders provide vignettes as part of the tender documentation that refer to findings from relevant systematic reviews. Certainly, the inclusion of encouragement in guidelines for publication or for funding applications to consider and cite review results is a trend to be welcomed.

Writing for the media

It is frequently observed that the interests of the review author and the journalist fail to correspond. At best, the interaction between these two parties may seem a short-lived marriage of convenience. Certainly the 'discovery value' of research synthesis pales alongside the dramatic laboratory experiment or the miracle cure. Nevertheless a review author can place great store by the fact that findings from a review carry more accumulated weight than a single study.

In 1996 Smith bemoaned the absence of systematic approaches to reviewing the evidence base:

> We are, through the media, as ordinary citizens, confronted daily with controversy and debate across a whole spectrum of public policy issues. But typically, we have no access to any form of a systematic "evidence base" – and therefore no means of participating in the debate in a mature and informed manner. (Smith, 1996)

Fortunately this situation has been undergoing gradual change over the last 15 years. Reviewers are starting to emphasise that the methodology of synthesis may result in the first occasion when one has been able to see the whole picture from otherwise conflicting research. Another selling point is the cumulative number of subjects, patients, studies or events that the review considers when compared with a single paper. Table 9.1 illustrates ways in which reviewers have attempted to communicate the features of their approach to journalists and, ultimately, to the public.

Writing for the public

A review author has two particular challenges in communicating the results of their review to the public. The first relates to the specific knowledge associated with the topic. This typically requires simplification of concepts, definition of unfamiliar terms, and the use of more easily accessible terminology. However the second relates to the nature of the review product, its methodology, and its inherent advantages over single studies and over other types of (non-systematic) review.

It is helpful in this context to use a definition of the review that, rather than focusing simply on the technical superiority of the methods used, stresses the relative advantage of the methodology.

What is required

There are many reasons why systematic approaches to the literature are considered of value in the context of the presentation of research findings. We shall consider just four of these under the acronym of CART (*c*larity-*a*uditability-*r*eplicability-*t*ransparency). In seeking to highlight the relative importance of these four criteria (while not necessarily attempting to put the CART before the horse!) we deliberately exclude criteria, such as comprehensiveness (a claimed virtue for quantitative systematic reviews), that may be present in some but not all of such systematic approaches.

Clarity

While clarity has always been a desired characteristic in scientific communication, albeit seen more in the breach than the observance, systematic approaches to the literature frequently seek to take these to a further degree. Clarity should be present in the research question, in the methodology, in the presentation of findings, in discussing the limitations of method and/or evidence and in relating the conclusions back to the original question. Furthermore the structured nature of

Table 9.1 Lay explanations of systematic reviews from media reports

Definition	Source
'Systematic reviews are an important tool for scientists; unlike ordinary reviews, they are seen as original research and help to provide clarity in areas of uncertainty. The basic underpinning of a systematic review is that the process of conducting the review is pre-specified and that the review itself is as comprehensive as possible within these pre-specified limits. Reviews that are not systematic are much more prone to bias, especially with regards to the selection of papers included for review.'	*The Times*: Great minds: attack science at your own risk (7 January 2010)
'the treatment they receive whether alternative or mainstream, is based not simply on single studies but on a systematic review of all the evidence available'	*The Times*: Effective medicine (27 May 2006)
'In its thoroughness, transparency and even-handedness this review is, we believe, the only scientifically defensible assessment of the evidence worldwide.'	*Sunday Times*: Letters to the editor: let us come clean on water fluoridation (18 May 2003)
'One good-quality summary of the research (a systematic review), which included almost 900 people.'	*Guardian*: Heel pain, what treatments work? (2 March 2010)
'A systematic review is a thorough look through published research on a particular topic. Only studies that have been carried out to a high standard are included. A systematic review may or may not include a meta-analysis, which is when the results from individual studies are put together.'	*Guardian*: Heel pain, what treatments work? (2 March 2010)
'Researchers ... pooled together data from 15 studies looking at pain-killer use and Alzheimer's. More than 14,600 participants were involved. Observational studies had previously suggested ... but the results were inconclusive.'	*Daily Mail*: Pill 'cure' for Alzheimer's (18 July 2003)
'the result was not statistically significant. However, this may only have been because the number of studies specifically evaluating the effects of aspirin was small.'	
'The findings come from a review of 25 studies ... the University researchers said: "This systematic review contributes a rigorous and objective synthesis of the evidence for added benefits ...".'	*Daily Mail*: Jogging in the park boosts energy and improves mood more than going to the gym (10 August 2010)

the reporting for many such approaches imposes a further clarity on the review produce as a whole making it easier to navigate and to interpret.

Auditability

Creating an audit trail has always been a requirement of good quality research and it should come as no surprise that it similarly figures in the context of evidence synthesis. The reviewer seeks to carefully document all of the steps that are taken in conducting the review. This audit trail serves as documentation to make clear the evidence that supports each finding, where that evidence can be found, and how that evidence was interpreted (Randolph, 2009, w160). It may be used subsequently to defend a finding or interpretation although typically systematic approaches to the literature seek to anticipate and forestall such potential criticism.

Replicability

The quest for **reproducibility** has long been a major driver in the development of systematic approaches to reviewing the literature. Research indicates that the conclusions of one narrative review can differ completely from another review written by a different author, even when exactly the same articles are reviewed (Light and Pillemer, 1984). In preference to reproducibility, which suggests the repeatability of laboratory experiments, many commentators favour the term **replicability**. This recognises that the intention may well be to create a finished product that closely resembles its predecessor. In a sense we recognise that 'the mould was broken' when a systematically conducted review was completed, but, by careful attention to detail and use of many of the same techniques, we can minimise inconsistencies and produce a product that is essentially similar. Such inconsistencies are still present in more systematic approaches, but at least their influence is more readily identified, more completely understood and appropriate remedial actions attempted. For example Popay and colleagues (2006) demonstrated, in an interpretive context, that *even the same reviewer* may develop a different line of argument on successive days. Furthermore, there is increasing recognition that, even for the **gold standard** systematic review, differences in search methods or the differential application of inclusion criteria can result in different review products. As multiple reviews start to appear on identical, or at least closely related, topics, it becomes clearer that the focus should be more on identifying and explaining such differences rather than eliminating them completely.

In qualitative evidence synthesis, reviewers may decide to reveal their own pre-existing biases and discuss how those biases might have affected the review. This approach, known as **reflexivity**, mirrors that encouraged for primary qualitative research where the investigator reflects on the effect of their own position as researcher. Indeed, one approach to qualitative synthesis, that known as **critical interpretive synthesis**, makes a virtue of such personalised interpretation which acts against **replicability**. Such approaches belong within a research tradition of recognising that there are multiple truths and that by constructing a narrative, in the form of a review, the reviewer is privileging one of many possible interpretations.

In contrast, in quantitative evidence synthesis, the reviewer is encouraged to take a neutral perspective, acting as an honest broker with the data and presenting the review findings as fact. Such reviews belong within a tradition where the reviewer seeks to communicate a single truth but many factors (biases), whether conscious or subconscious, may deflect them from their intention. Mechanisms for handling the dangers of personal interpretation in quantitative reviews are crude by comparison; typically a **conflict of interest statement** identifies areas that relate almost exclusively to financial interest. To equate bias primarily with financial interest is to overlook the fact that researchers will include professionals delivering a service, parents of children receiving an educational intervention, carers of relatives receiving a healthcare or social care provision, taxpayers financing policy interventions, etc. The quest to minimise the effect of bias, or at least to make it easier to identify it where it may likely exist will no doubt lead ultimately to a declaration or statement of prior beliefs. In this way, the reader would be able to identify, for example, where an educator stands with regard to a teaching intervention or a clinician in connection with a new drug or surgical treatment.

Transparency

It is common to see claims of transparency for systematic reviews (The PLoS Medicine Editors, 2007), such as the following statement from the international Campbell Collaboration:

> A systematic review uses transparent procedures to find, evaluate and synthesize the results of relevant research. Procedures are explicitly defined in advance, in order to ensure that the exercise is transparent and can be replicated. (w029)

While the quality of transparency is linked to replicability, it is typically attributed to the availability of supporting documentation such as procedure manuals. To date, little attention has been paid to the fidelity with which such procedures have been followed – the implication, albeit a suspect premise, is that the manual acts as a guarantor for all review products associated with that documentation. This is, perhaps, one step too close to the 'eminence based' practice of the past which judged published outputs according to their author or the journal in which they were published. The emphasis should be on the ability of the reader to make their own judgements on review quality. The redeeming feature of transparency is that it makes such judgements more practicable.

A sample review structure

Once you have completed the data extraction, quality assessment, synthesis, and analysis of the literature, you will need to consider how your review will be structured and written. The key to a good academic paper is the ability to present the findings in such a way that it demonstrates your mastery of the review topic. To some extent, the structure of your review will depend upon its purpose. For example, systematic reviews have a clear structure that must be followed and that will dictate for the most part how the writing should be undertaken. However, many readers will be conducting their review as part of a coursework assignment, research proposal, or research dissertation. As such you will need an overall direction of travel and a few major signposts but you will be able to maintain some freedom in how your writing is structured. The structure of your review report should be immediately apparent to its reader. It is therefore important to be logical, and you will find that some key elements need to be included in *all* literature reviews (Aveyard, 2010) (Box 9.1).

Box 9.1   Key elements in reporting a literature review

1 Title
2 Abstract
3 Introduction
4 Methods
5 Results
6 Discussion
7 Conclusion

This structure is familiar in that it uses the IMRAD (introduction-*methods*-*results-and-d*iscussion) format required when presenting any primary scientific report (Burns and Grove, 2007). This is also the structure largely employed when following the PRISMA Statement (w158) used to report 'full-blown' systematic reviews in peer reviewed journals (see section on reporting standards later in this chapter). The only areas of difference are that the conclusion becomes subsumed under the heading of 'Discussion' and the seventh element becomes 'funding'). The PRISMA Statement aims

> to help authors report a wide array of systematic reviews to assess the benefits and harms of a health care intervention. PRISMA focuses on ways in which authors can ensure the transparent and complete reporting of systematic reviews and meta-analyses. (Moher et al., 2009, w137)

However, as already demonstrated, the similarities between PRISMA and generic approaches to study reporting make it a useful template for reviews using systematic approaches in any discipline. We shall briefly expand on each of these seven areas. However, the reader is referred to the most up-to-date version of the PRISMA Statement (w158).

Title: increasingly, scientific reports not only include a meaningful title indicating the subject but also, following a colon, a subtitle indicating the study type such as, 'The impact of learning on unemployed, low-qualified adults: a systematic review'. Alternatively a **meta-analysis** may have a title such as: 'A systematic review and meta-analysis of set-shifting ability in eating disorders'. The important point is that, by having the study type in the title, you increase the chance of a reader identifying and retrieving the study report from Internet or database searches and of an indexer coding it correctly when adding terms to a database record. The importance of indicating the study type in the title is true for other systematic approaches such as 'a rapid evidence assessment', 'a meta-ethnography', etc.

Abstract: structured abstracts improve the chance that your work will be identified. They also prompt the author to provide essential details concerning the review. Typical headings that can be used for a review abstract include background; objectives; data sources; study eligibility criteria, participants, and interventions;

study appraisal and synthesis methods; results; limitations; conclusions and implications of key findings; systematic review registration number. In essence, the abstract is a review in miniature and a reader should be able to identify immediately how well you searched, how many studies you reviewed and what your main conclusions are. Typically, the abstract should not exceed 250–300 words although you should check individual journals for their specific requirements. The abstract should be sufficiently informative to provide the reader with a brief picture of the overall findings; it should therefore reveal not tantalise (e.g. avoid statements such as 'The review goes on to describe findings of critical importance to all practitioners', but state briefly instead what these findings are). Generally, commentators recommend that the abstract is undertaken last so that it reflects the final emphasis of the review that it summarises (Hendry and Farley, 1998).

Introduction: The Introduction will provide essential details concerning the starting point for the review. These will include a rationale for the review in the context of what is already known and a structured statement of the review question using either **PICOS** (*participants, interventions, comparisons, outcomes, and study design*) or some equivalent such as **SPICE** (*setting, perspective, phenomenon of interest, comparison, evaluation*) or **PICOC** (*population, intervention, comparison, outcomes, context*). Typically we encourage review authors to provide a convincing argument for the importance of the review in terms of how common the problem is, how serious its consequences, how costly it is and its impact both on services and on society more widely. If genuine controversy exists, perhaps seen in significant variations in practice, this should be acknowledged and both sides of the argument characterised as even-handedly as possible.

Methods: the length of literature reviews varies considerably and word limits must be considered when assigning the proportion of the available coverage between the methods and the results, discussion and conclusion. While the extent of the description of methods depends on the type of review you are undertaking and the degree of rigour it requires, it is probably best to start from a complete list of possible items for inclusion and then to pare this down according to your specific requirements. If the review is a formal production for a government agency or an international collaboration, you may wish to indicate where a review protocol exists and how it may be accessed. Some journals will allow you to submit your review protocol as supplementary online material. You might then proceed through such data elements as the eligibility criteria, the information sources accessed, the search strategies, and the process for study selection. Guidelines have been suggested for reporting search strategies (Booth, 2006, w179; Higgins and Green, 2008, w043; Sampson et al., 2008; Sampson et al., 2009) (Table 9.2) although evidence suggests that these have been imperfectly implemented (Yoshii et al., 2009).

You would continue with details of the data collection process and the list of data items or variables of interest. Formal review processes, as used by the **Cochrane Collaboration** (w042), then require details of the risk of bias within individual studies (i.e. a description of methods used for quality assessment) and the risk of bias across studies (see sections in Chapter 8 on **publication bias** and

Table 9.2   Guidelines for reporting search strategies

Cochrane (effectiveness) Reviews (Higgins and Green, 2008, w043).	Qualitative systematic reviews (Booth, 2006, w179) (STARLITE)
Databases searched	**S**: Sampling strategy (e.g. purposive, theoretical, comprehensive)
Name of host	**T**: Type of studies
Date search was run	**A**: Approaches (other than electronic subject searches covered in the electronic sources section) e.g. hand searching; citation snowballing, etc.)
Years covered by search	**R**: Range of years (start date–end date)
Complete search strategy	**L**: Limits
One or two sentence summary of the search strategy	**I**: Inclusion and exclusions
Language restrictions	**T**: Terms used
	E: Electronic sources (reports databases used and, optimally, search platforms, and vendors to assist in replication)

selective reporting). You will also give details of the data being summarised whether by quantitative summary measures (e.g. risk ratio, difference in means), or by qualitative concepts or themes. Finally, once you have described your methods of synthesis (see Chapter 7) you will proceed to your methods of analysis (see Chapter 8). Again, these may be either quantitative (**sensitivity** or **subgroup** analyses, meta-regression) or more qualitative assessments of the robustness of the results and possible explanations for findings.

At this point we have reviewed just over half of the items expanded in more detail in the 27-item PRISMA checklist (w158). Only now have we reached the results. This emphasises that, while you as a reviewer may be most interested in the review question and its findings, the reader first needs convincing that your review product is up to the task.

Results: the Results section starts with a quantitative summary of the number of items identified and then moves on to the detail of the individual studies. A subsection on study selection will give numbers of studies screened, assessed for eligibility, and included in the review, with reasons for exclusions at each stage. Increasingly there is a requirement, as with the PRISMA statement (w158), to produce a flow diagram. Our experience is that this is a useful aid for the reader for any type of review utilising systematic approaches. Tabulation is important in describing the study characteristics (e.g. study size, **PICOS**, follow-up period) and in providing an easy look-up reference point to the individual citations in the reference list. Again you will present results for your assessments of the risk of bias within studies and the risk of bias across studies. These assessments will typically precede the very important sections reporting the results of individual studies and the synthesis of results respectively. Such sections utilise presentation features including tables and Forest plots for each **meta-analysis** and thematic summaries, diagrams, and displays for qualitative data. If using a thematic approach, the account should flow logically from one section or theme to the next, to maintain continuity and consistency (Beyea and Nicholl, 1998). This can be achieved by summarising each theme or section and outlining how it is related to the theme that follows.

Discussion: up to this point you have provided the reader with what might be termed the 'crude' evidence, analogous to oil as it emerges from the ground. You now need to proceed to the *discussion* which corresponds to the 'refined' by-products that allow the findings to be utilised and interpreted by its 'consumer'. You should start with a Summary of evidence giving particular attention to the strength of evidence associated with each finding. Having previously identified the main audiences for your review, you should seek to provide each with the information that they need to answer their particular issues or questions. As Cronin and colleagues (2004) identify, you will also need to spend a significant amount of time discussing limitations of your review both in terms of the characteristics of the included studies, any inconsistencies and contradictions, and what you have or have not been able to do in relation to the review as a whole. They highlight that your role here is to summarise and evaluate evidence about your topic, pointing out similarities and differences and offering possible explanations for any inconsistencies uncovered (Polit and Beck, 2006). If your literature review has been conceived and designed to inform the objectives, design, or conduct of a follow-up primary study, any gaps in knowledge that have been identified should feed into the purpose of the proposed study. In some cases, it may also be possible to use developed themes to construct a conceptual framework or **logic model** to inform the study (Baxter et al., 2010, w013). Finally, you will return to what was previously known, as described in your Introduction, to provide a general interpretation of the results in the context of other evidence, and implications for future practice and/or research (*conclusions*). All reviews will be able to provide some recommendations or implications for practice and for research with the emphasis between each being determined by the extent to which the review question could be answered. If you are following the PRISMA statement (w158) you will conclude with *funding*, describing sources of funding for the systematic review and other support (e.g. supply of data) as well as the role of funders for the systematic review. As previously mentioned, this may be an appropriate juncture to identify other types of *conflict of interest*. It should also act as a prompt to you in providing *acknowledgements* to those who provided substantive support to the review but who do not qualify for authorship.

APPLY WHAT YOU HAVE LEARNT 9.2

Producing a draft report structure

Produce a draft report structure for your review using the sections described above. Try to allocate an appropriate word limit to each section based on the size and scope of your review and its intended focus.

Standards for reporting of reviews

Increasing recognition of the importance of transparency in scientific research, particularly given that much is financed from the public purse, has led in recent years to a veritable industry of publication guidelines and templates for presentation. While few can argue against the benefits of effective communication, opinion is more divided when it comes to such publication conventions. Some argue that attempts to homogenise the presentation of research can make published reports more bland and less informative. In addition, it can introduce a tendency to conceal rather than reveal; for example, encouragement of stock phrases such as 'References were followed up and contact was made with authors' may mask individual differences that are in themselves revealing. Finally, the contents of checklists may focus on the instrumentality of a review, not its overall quality. For example, it is generally agreed that it is good practice to include an appendix with a complete search strategy on a primary bibliographic database (or on all databases according to Cochrane Handbook requirements (Lefebvre et al., 2009)). The same methods section that reports a detailed search process on bibliographic databases may, however, include a statement such as 'Internet searches were conducted using Alta Vista'. This attention to one easily measured aspect at the expense of a less easily measured but equally important alternative may be likened to bolting a gate with a yawning gap in the fence.

From the point of view of you as a reviewer of other people's studies, as opposed to you as a review author, there are considerable benefits to standardisation of the reporting of individual primary studies. It will make the task of creating data extraction forms, using standard quality assessment checklists and tabulating data, much more straightforward. However, as we have implied, this may be at the expense of informative detail of context or revealing slips in the reporting of methods.

Systematic reviews were, after randomised controlled trials, one of the first recipients of reporting standards. The quality of reporting of **meta-analyses** (QUOROM) statement (Moher et al., 1999) has existed for over a decade and has more recently been replaced by the PRISMA statement (w158). Furthermore, separate conventions have been published for systematic reviews of observational studies (MOOSE) and for systematic reviews of diagnostic tests. These statements typically contain standard headings under which specific detail is reported. They may also include a checklist of individual elements to be reported. Finally, a flow diagram of the progress of studies throughout the review process is frequently required, analogous to the flow diagram for patients through a trial required by the CONSORT statement (Schulz et al. and CONSORT Group, 2010, w048).

Notwithstanding the progressive revelation of such standards there is considerable variation in how mechanisms such as the flow diagram are used. Some authors use a strictly *chronological* approach, others superimpose a *logical* structure that may disguise inconsistencies or multiple iterations, yet others re-interpret the diagram as a means of describing *methodological* decision points (Hind and Booth, 2007, w105). While each of these approaches may be useful in different contexts such inconsistencies are potentially confusing.

Table 9.3   Most common standards for reporting studies

CONSORT Statement: Consolidated Standards Of Reporting Trials (w048)	The CONSORT Statement is intended to improve the reporting of a randomised controlled trial (RCT), enabling readers to understand a trial's design, conduct, analysis and interpretation, and to assess the validity of its results. It emphasises that this can only be achieved through complete transparency from authors.
PRISMA Statement (formerly QUOROM): Preferred Reporting Items for Systematic Reviews and Meta-Analyses (w158)	The aim of the PRISMA Statement is to help authors report a wide array of systematic reviews to assess the benefits and harms of a healthcare intervention. PRISMA focuses on ways in which authors can ensure the transparent and complete reporting of systematic reviews and meta-analyses.
STARD Statement: Standards for Reporting Studies of Diagnostic Accuracy (w178)	The objective of the STARD initiative is to improve the accuracy and completeness of reporting of studies of diagnostic accuracy.
MOOSE Statement: proposal for reporting meta- analysis of observational studies in epidemiology (Stroup et al., 2000)	The proposed checklist contains specifications for reporting of meta-analyses of observational studies in epidemiology, including background, search strategy, methods, results, discussion, and conclusion. Use of the checklist should improve the usefulness of meta-analyses for authors, reviewers, editors, readers, and decision makers.
STARLITE Statement: Standards for Reporting Literature Searches (Booth, 2006) (w179)	The mnemonic STARLITE (sampling strategy, type of study, approaches, range of years, limits, inclusion and exclusions, terms used, electronic sources) is used to convey the essential elements for reporting literature searches.
STROBE Statement (and STREGA): STrengthening the Reporting of OBservational studies in Epidemiology (w181), guidelines for the reporting of genetic association studies (STREGA) (w180)	STROBE is an international collaboration of epidemiologists, methodologists, statisticians, researchers and journal editors involved in the conduct and dissemination of observational studies. A subsequent workshop developed guidelines for the reporting of genetic association studies (STREGA).

APPLY WHAT YOU HAVE LEARNT 9.3

Identifying and using reporting guidelines

Many guidelines for reporting, generic and specific, are contained at the useful EQUATOR Network Resource Website (w078). The main standards relating to reviews are given in Table 9.3.

Look through the EQUATOR Network Website (w078). Which guidelines will likely be most informative for your review? Identify the guideline and its source reference in the boxes provided. Once you have found a reporting guideline appropriate to your review, revisit your draft review structure from the previous 'apply what you have learnt' feature and revise it in view of the requirements.

Reporting Guideline	**Reference Citation**

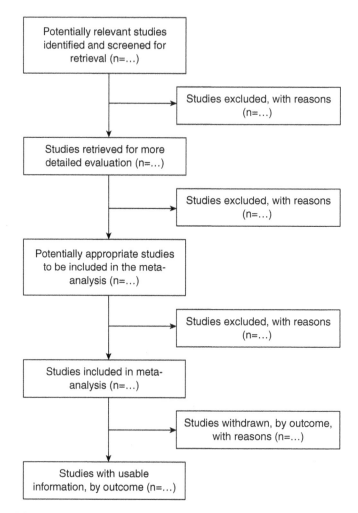

Figure 9.1   PRISMA flow diagram

Flow of included studies

One of the most valuable, and self-evidently useful, features of the PRISMA statement is the flowchart for included studies (w158). Indeed, such a flowchart is of
potential value to other less-structured types of review both in accounting for studies during conduct of the review and in subsequently reporting the review method.
The PRISMA flow diagram depicts the flow of information through the different
phases of a systematic review. It maps out the number of records identified,
included and excluded, and the reasons for exclusions. At each stage, the vertical
'plughole' continuation box and the horizontal 'overflow' box should combine to
total the number of studies in the preceding box ensuring that studies are accounted
for at each point of the process. The main caution in using such a diagram relates
to the difference between references and papers (many duplicate references may
have been identified from multiple databases) and the subsequent difference

between papers and studies (one study may be represented by reports in multiple papers) (Hind and Booth, 2007, w105). Indeed it may be helpful to signal transparently the transition from references to papers and from papers to studies.

Use of tables and figures

Tables and figures can be used to summarise vast quantities of data (as an alternative to an extensive description in the form of narrative text) or as a vehicle for illustrating and supporting what is already present in the narrative. Typically they will be used for a combination of both purposes. In this connection, it will be helpful to draw a distinction between 'summary tables' which are typically to be found within the text and tables of extracted data which are more likely to be included as appendices.

Useful subjects for summary tables will include a:

1 summary of study characteristics (e.g. number of participants, setting, study design, etc.);
2 summary of methodological quality (e.g. whether comparative, which outcome measures have been used, response rates or completeness of follow up, etc.);
3 summary of results (an effect size (or list of themes) for each study; any confidence limits, etc.).

Such summary tables may typically be included within the main body of the text unless the number of included studies exceeds about 20. This is because they are less likely to provide the same disruption to the flow of the text as the more fully reported data extraction tables which may be placed in an appendix to increase the auditability of the review product.

If you have combined studies within a meta-analysis, then your report may include one or more **Forest plots**. While many meta-analysis software packages allow the export of such **Forest plots**, you must be aware that this technical facility may not completely meet the needs of publication (Schrigel et al., 2010). If you need to relabel or even redraw such a display, you must pay careful attention to such details as the orientation of the diagram (is more of an outcome better or worse?), the captioning (What exactly is the outcome of interest?) and the point of no effect (Does the Forest plot present a ratio? – in which case the point of no effect is represented by one – or does it present a difference? – in which case the point of no effect is signified by zero).

Use of appendices and other supporting features

While there is little formal guidance on what should and should not be included within appendices, for a report of a structured literature review, an informal consensus is emerging as evidenced within published reports. Of course a major consideration will be whether the review is being published within a word-limited paper journal or within a larger technical report. The emergence of increasing numbers of online journals as a vehicle for systematic reviews has led to increasing flexibility with regard to published appendices. Typically, the following will be found in Appendices:

1 at least one search strategy (and possibly all available search strategies) used for the review;
2 a sample data extraction form;
3 a list of excluded studies (only for those studies appearing to meet the Inclusion criteria but not included) with a brief reason for exclusion;
4 data extraction tables for included studies;
5 the checklist used (unless commonly available);
6 results of quality assessments.

As awareness of the requirements for rigorous conduct and reporting increases, this list is likely to become even further expanded.

Accurate referencing

The importance of a structured approach to the recording of bibliographic information on included studies has already been emphasised (Chapter 5). Every type of literature review should conclude with a full bibliographical list of all the books, journal articles, reports and other media referred to in the work. Every citation in the text must appear in the bibliography (reference list) and vice versa. Formally structured approaches to the literature such as systematic reviews frequently make a distinction between supporting materials from the background which go into a general reference list and a list of included studies. Indeed, an analysis of the materials that have ended up in the supporting references of the Cochrane Reviews yields one of the Collaboration's more memorable titles: 'Three bibles, three dictionaries, and nearly 25,000 other things' (Clarke and Clarke, 2000)! You will find that it will save you much time at the critical stage towards the end of your review if you compile your list of references as you identify each new item. Although the Internet has made reference checking much easier, it remains a time-consuming procedure and you cannot guarantee that other authors have correctly recorded their own references. Many academic supervisors use the reviews of their supervisees for regular updates in their main topics of interest. You therefore have an added incentive to make every effort to ensure that your reference list is accurate.

Other types of review

It is true to say that the more structured the review, the more likely it is that guidelines will exist for reporting that particular type of review. Some sources seek to apply a structured description of methodology and of presentation of findings to those types of review that lie towards the middle of the structured–unstructured continuum. For example the *Journal of Advanced Nursing* has unilaterally produced guidelines for *concept analysis* reviews. These require 'concept analysis' to appear in the title and the aims to be stated as: 'This paper is a report of an analysis of the concept of X'. The structured abstract will include fields commonly associated with a systematic review such as data sources and review methods. Typically, such an analysis includes a justification of the importance of the concept, details of the concept analysis method used (including quality assessment if present), and results presented according to the accepted terminology of the method (e.g. attributes, definition, antecedents, consequences). The discussion includes an assessment of whether the definition constitutes a middle-range descriptive theory or middle-range explanatory theory.

Arksey and O'Malley (2005) suggest several approaches suitable for presenting a narrative account of findings, specifically from a *scoping review*. It is important to point out that your choice of approaches will depend upon the data you have previously 'charted' from the component studies. The first approach is what we describe as the 'epidemiology' of the literature. Basically, just as a population can be described in terms of its basic characteristics such as the number of males/females, age distribution, ethnic constitution, fertility rate, etc., so, too, a 'population of studies' can similarly be characterised. This involves a 'basic numerical analysis of the extent, nature, and distribution of the studies included in the review'. To achieve this, authors would produce

> tables and charts mapping: the distribution of studies geographically and for the different [population] groups; the range of interventions included in the review; the research methods adopted and the measures of effectiveness used. (Arksey and O'Malley, 2005)

Such an analysis helps to inform the commissioners of the review in that 'it sheds light on the dominant areas of research in terms of intervention type, research methods and geographical location' (Arksey and O'Malley, 2005). It also enables the researchers to 'quickly get a flavour of the main areas of interest, and consequently where the significant gaps were', invaluable when presenting their subsequent recommendations.

An alternative, possibly complementary approach, is to organise the literature thematically, perhaps by a shared characteristic such as intervention type. Arksey and O'Malley (2005) identified 11 such different intervention types. Ideally, categories should be mutually exclusive to minimise duplication and the consequent risk of double-counting but this will not always be possible. As has been previously mentioned, the reviewer will also be constrained by the degree of completeness of reporting of the component studies. Here you will face the choice as to whether to have a minimum dataset of that data that is complete for each study or a more extensive matrix with many empty cells. To a certain extent, this will be determined by whether your focus is on the mapping of the existing evidence base, or the identification of gaps. Furthermore, for a **scoping review** or **mapping review**, where it is not always possible to provide a detailed assessment of component studies you will be heavily dependent upon the classifications and terminology suggested by the authors themselves rather than constructing your own, more specific taxonomy.

These two primary choices were determined by the authors' own priorities for their scoping review and should not be construed as implying the superiority of these two approaches. Indeed, the authors acknowledge that they could have equally organised studies by the 'theoretical or conceptual positions adopted by authors'. This illustrates that the reviewer must preserve some clarity in reporting of data so that readers can determine any potential bias in reporting or recommendations. In order to achieve a consistent approach to reporting the authors developed a 'template' for each of the 11 component groups. This required a template that

> began with a small table summarising basic characteristics of all the studies included in that particular intervention group, and was followed by commentary written under the following nine headings: interventions; sample sizes; participants; research methods; outcomes; evidence relating to effectiveness; economic aspects; UK studies; gaps in the research. (Arksey and O'Malley, 2005)

The value of such a structured approach was apparent in that it allowed reviewers, and indeed readers,

> to make comparisons across intervention types; identify contradictory evidence regarding specific interventions; identify gaps in the evidence gaps about individual interventions and across interventions as well as consider possible "new frontiers" (such as the Internet). (Arksey and O'Malley, 2005)

Other structured approaches to presenting review findings might include an essentially chronological approach, a dialectic approach between competing schools of thought, or something more like the meta-narrative approaches described in Chapter 7 (Greenhalgh et al., 2005) which characterise the literature according to source discipline.

Summary

Clearly, the intense and prolonged effort that goes into production of a literature review that harnesses systematic approaches will only be fully exploited if careful consideration is given to the intended audience for the review. The intended audience will determine the language and the format of the final review. We have seen that secondary products, such as plain language summaries (Santesso et al., 2006; Glenton et al., 2010; Rosenbaum et al., 2011), 1-3-25 reports (see Tools section) and briefings (Carroll et al., 2006) may be needed to target the information preferences of the intended audience. In addition, all reviews have multiple audiences so attention must be given to using multiple channels.

Key learning points

- It is critical when writing a systematic review to base what you write and how you present it on a detailed knowledge of the intended audience.
- In addition to your primary audience your review will have other audiences and you should try, therefore, to factor in their interests.
- Systematic approaches to presenting your methodology and findings will demonstrate clarity-auditability-replicability-transparency (CART).
- Published reporting standards may help in the clear and transparent presentation of your methodology and findings.
- In addition to a structured academic report you may need to consider other methods of presentation for your review including plain language summaries and briefings.

Suggestions for further reading

Aveyard, H. (2010) How do I present my literature review? And other key questions. In Aveyard, H., *Doing a Literature Review in Health and Social Care: A Practical Guide*, 2nd edn. Maidenhead: Open University Press, 147–58.

Major, C.H. and Savin-Baden, M. (2010) 6 – Presenting the synthesis. In: *An Introduction to Qualitative Research Synthesis: Managing the Information Explosion in Social Science Research*. Abingdon: Routledge, 89–104.

Pope, C., Mays, N., and Popay, J. (2007) Organising and presenting evidence synthesis. In: *Synthesizing Qualitative and Quantitative Health Evidence: A Guide to Methods*. Maidenhead: McGraw-Hill, 117–52.

Tools for presenting your findings

A key challenge, once the literature review process has been completed, is to decide upon an appropriate method for presenting your findings to your chosen audience. This Tools section looks firstly at the highly structured 1-3-25 report format increasingly favoured by policymakers. It then turns attention specifically to the reporting of meaningful recommendations for future research using the EPICOT+ structure proposed by representatives of the Cochrane Collaboration and the Centre for Reviews and Dissemination.

1-3-25 report format

The 1-3-25 report format, used by such organisations such as the UK Home Office (w106), Health and Safety Executive (w104), and the Canadian

Health Services Research Foundation (w031), stems from recognition that writing a research summary for decision-makers is not the same as writing an academic journal article. Because the reviewer has a different objective they are required to take a different approach.

Every 1-3-25 report follows the same guidelines: starting with one page of main messages; followed by a three-page executive summary; and concluded with findings presented in no more than 25 pages of writing, in language that is easy for a lay person to understand. Details of these three sections are as follows:

Main messages (the 'one'): one page of main message bullets reporting the lessons decision-makers can take from your review. These go beyond a summary of findings because they have to tell the audience what your findings mean for them. Writing main messages is a challenge for researchers who are typically trained to provide an objective and detached view of the evidence. You will have to strike a balance between having something of interest and practical importance to report without going beyond what is actually present within your review.

Executive summary (the 'three'): These are your findings condensed for consumption by a busy decision-maker. Such an executive summary is problem-focused and therefore uses the journalistic technique of presenting the more meaningful content at the top, followed by the background and context and less important information further down. In this context, you should resist the temptation to labour the meticulous detail of the review methodology – this can be used as a subsequent guarantor of rigour once the findings have been assimilated, understood, and interpreted.

The report (the '25'): the 25-page report of your review allows more detail, but, nevertheless, requires a greater succinctness than typically observed in a final report. not an academic one. Take time to show it to your decision-maker partners. Seven categories of information are recommended for inclusion in the report:

- *Context:* the policy issue or managerial problem with a clear statement of the PICOS review question.
- *Implications:* state what your review findings mean for decision-makers, targeting the implications at your main stakeholders but trying to anticipate other audiences who may be interested in your work.
- *Approach:* outline your review methods, including the type of review undertaken, the database sources and search strategies used, the numbers of studies found and the overall methods of synthesis and presentation. Brief details of limitations of the methods should be given with a fuller explanation provided in a technical appendix.
- *Results:* summarised in a concise and informative way using a full array of graphical and tabular means to highlight key themes and messages. Subsidiary results will be placed in an appendix.
- *Additional resources:* supportive materials (e.g. publications and websites) to help decision-makers follow up issues raised by your review.

- *Further research:* resisting the blanket 'further research is needed' this should frame specific questions that remain to be answered together with suggested research designs to address them.
- *References and bibliography:* typically using the Vancouver numbered reference style with references at the end of the report.

It is typically a challenge to condense the content of a systematic review, or even a rapid evidence assessment, within the 25-page strictures of this format. Nevertheless, creative use of appendices and judicious but rigorous reporting can achieve this aim.

The EPICOT + format for reporting research recommendations

In 2005, representatives of organisations commissioning and summarising research, including the BMJ Publishing Group, the Centre for Reviews and Dissemination, and the UK Cochrane Centre, met to discuss the state of research recommendations and to develop guidelines for improving the presentation of proposals for further research (Brown, 2006). They decided to propose the EPICOT format as the basis for a statement on formulating research recommendations. Subsequently, they identified several optional components of varying levels of relevance and their ensuing discussion resulted in the proposed EPICOT+ format (Box 9.2).

Box 9.2   Suggested format for research recommendations on the effects of treatments (EPICOT+)

Core elements

E Evidence (What is the current state of the evidence?)
P Population (What is the population of interest?)
I Intervention (What are the interventions of interest?)
C Comparison (What are the comparisons of interest?)
O Outcome (What are the outcomes of interest?)
T Time stamp (Date of recommendation)

Optional elements

d Disease burden or relevance
t Time aspect of core elements of EPICOT
s Appropriate study type according to local need

References

Ahmad, N., Boutron, I., Dechartres, A., Durieux, P., and Ravaud, P. (2010) Applicability and generalisability of the results of systematic reviews to public health practice and policy: a systematic review. *Trials*, **11**, 20.

Arksey, H. and O'Malley, L. (2005) Scoping studies: towards a methodological framework. *International Journal of Social Research Methodology*, **8**, 1, 19–32.

Aveyard, H. (2010) How do I present my literature review? And other key questions. In: Aveyard, H., *Doing a Literature Review in Health and Social Care: A Practical Guide*, 2nd edn. Maidenhead: Open University Press, 147–58.

Baxter, S., Killoran, A., Kelly, M.P., and Goyder, E. (2010) Synthesizing diverse evidence: the use of primary qualitative data analysis methods and logic models in public health reviews. *Public Health*, **124**, 2, 99–106. (w013)

Beyea, S. and Nicholl, L. (1998) Writing an integrative review. *AORN Journal*, **67**, 4, 877–80.

Booth, A. (2006) 'Brimful of STARLITE': toward standards for reporting literature searches. *Journal of the Medical Library Association*, **94**, 4, 421–9. (w179)

Brown, P., Brunnhuber, K., Chalkidou, K., Chalmers, I., Clarke, M., Fenton, M., Forbes, C., Glanville, J., Hicks, N.J., Moody, J., Twaddle, S., Timimi, H., and Young, P. (2006) How to formulate research recommendations. *BMJ*, **333**, 7572, 804–6.

Burns, N. and Grove, S.K. (2007) *Understanding Nursing Research – Building an Evidence Based Practice*. 4th edn. St. Louis: Saunders Elsevier.

Carroll, C., Cooke, J., Booth, A., and Beverley, C. (2006) Bridging the gap: the development of knowledge briefings at the health and social care interface. *Health and Social Care in the Community*, **14**, 6, 491–8.

Clarke, M. and Chalmers, I. (1998) Discussion sections in reports of controlled trials published in general medical journals. Islands in search of continents? *JAMA*, **280**, 280–2.

Clarke, M. and Clarke, T. (2000) A study of the references used in Cochrane protocols and reviews. Three bibles, three dictionaries, and nearly 25,000 other things. *International Journal of Technology Assessment in Health Care*, **16**, 3, 907–9.

Cooper, N.J., Jones, D.R., and Sutton, A.J. (2005) The use of systematic reviews when designing studies. *Clinical Trials*, **2**, 3, 260–4.

Cronin, P., Ryan, F., and Coughlan, M. (2008) Undertaking a literature review: a step-by-step approach. *British Journal of Nursing*, **17**, 1, 38–43.

Gall, M.D., Borg, W.R., and Gall, J.P. (1996) *Education Research: An Introduction*, 6th edn. White Plains, NY: Longman.

Glenton, C., Santesso, N., Rosenbaum, S., Nilsen, E.S., Rader, T., Ciapponi, A., and Dilkes, H. (2010) Presenting the results of Cochrane Systematic Reviews to a consumer audience: a qualitative study. *Medical Decision Making*, **30**, 5, 566–77.

Greenhalgh, T., Robert, G., Macfarlane, F., Bate, P., Kyriakidou, O., and Peacock, R. (2005). Storylines of research in diffusion of innovation: a meta-narrative approach to systematic review. *Social Science and Medicine*, **61**, 2, 417–30.

Hammersley, M. (2002) *Systematic or Unsystematic, Is That the Question? Some Reflections on the Science, Art, and Politics of Reviewing Research Evidence*. Text of a talk given to the Public Health Evidence Steering Group of the Health Development Agency, October, 2002. (w102)

Hendry, C. and Farley, A. (1998) Reviewing the literature: a guide for students. *Nursing Standard*, **12**, 44, 46–8.

Hind, D. and Booth, A. (2007) Do health technology assessments comply with QUOROM diagram guidance? An empirical study. *BMC Medical Research Methodology*, **7**, 49. (w105)

Lavis, J., Davies, H., Oxman, A., Denis, J.L., Golden-Biddle, K., and Ferlie, E. (2005) Towards systematic reviews that inform health care management and policy-making. *Journal of Health Services Research and Policy*, **10**, Suppl 1, 35–48.

Lavis, J., Davies, H., Gruen, R., Walshe, K., and Farquhar, C. (2006) Working within and beyond the Cochrane Collaboration to make systematic reviews more useful to healthcare managers and policy makers. *Healthcare Policy*, **1**, 2, 21–33.

Lefebvre, C., Manheimer, E., and Glanville. J (2009) Searching for studies. In: Higgins, J.P.T. and Green, S. (eds) *Cochrane Handbook for Systematic Reviews of Interventions*, Version 5.0.2 (updated September 2009). The Cochrane Collaboration. Bognor Regis: Wiley-Blackwell (w043).

Major, C.H. and Savin-Baden, M. (2010) 6 – Presenting the synthesis In: Major, C.H. and Savin-Baden, M. (eds) *An Introduction to Qualitative Research Synthesis: Managing the Information Explosion in Social Science Research.* Abingdon: Routledge, 89–104

Major, C.H. and Savin-Baden, M. (2010) *An Introduction to Qualitative Research Synthesis: Managing the Information Explosion in Social Science Research.* London: Routledge.

Moher, D., Liberati, A., Tetzlaff, J., Altman, D.G., and The PRISMA Group (2009) Preferred reporting items for systematic reviews and meta-analyses: The PRISMA statement. *PLoS Medicine,* **6**, 7, e1000097. (w137)

Pagliaro, L., Bruzzi, P., and Bobbio, M. (2010) Why are Cochrane hepato-biliary reviews under-valued by physicians as an aid for clinical decision-making? *Digestive and Liver Diseases,* **42**, 1, 1–5.

Phillips, C.V. (2001) The economics of 'more research is needed'. *International Journal of Epidemiology,* **30**, 4, 771–6.

Polit, D. and Beck, C. (2006) *Essentials of Nursing Research: Methods, Appraisal and Utilization,* 6th edn. Philadelphia: Lippincott Williams and Wilkins.

Popay, J., Roberts, H., Sowden, A., Petticrew, M., Arai, L., Rodgers, M., and Britten N. with Roen, K. and Duffy, S. (2006) *Guidance on the Conduct of Narrative Synthesis in Systematic Reviews: A Product from the ESRC Methods Programme.* Version 1. Manchester: Economic and Social Research Council. (w156)

Pope, C., Mays, N., and Popay, J. (2006) Informing policy making and management in health-care: the place for synthesis. *Healthcare Policy,* **1**, 2, 43–8.

Randolph, J.J. (2009) A guide to writing the dissertation literature review. *Practical Assessment, Research and Evaluation,* **14**, 1–13. (w160)

Rosenbaum, S.E., Glenton, C., Wiysonge, C.S., Abalos, E., Mignini, L., Young, T., Althabe, F., Ciapponi, A., Marti, S.C., Meng, Q., Wang, J., De la Hoz Bradford, A.M., Kiwanuka, S.N., Rutebemberwa, E., Pariyo, G.W., Flottorp, S. and Oxman, A.D. (2011) Evidence summaries tailored to health policy-makers in low- and middle-income countries. *Bulletin of the World Health Organisation,* **89**, 54–61.

Sampson, M., McGowan, J., Cogo, E., Grimshaw, J., Moher, D., and Lefebvre, C. (2009) An evidence-based practice guideline for the peer review of electronic search strategies. *Journal of Clinical Epidemiology,* **62**, 9, 944–52.

Sampson, M., McGowan, J., Tetzlaff, J., Cogo, E., and Moher, D. (2008) No consensus exists on search reporting methods for systematic reviews. *Journal of Clinical Epidemiology,* **61**, 8, 748–54.

Santesso, N., Maxwell, L., Tugwell, P.S., Wells, G.A., O'Connor, A.M., Judd, M., and Buchbinder, R. (2006) Knowledge transfer to clinicians and consumers by the Cochrane Musculoskeletal Group. *Journal of Rheumatology,* **33**, 11, 2312–8.

Schriger, D.L., Altman, D.G., Vetter, J.A., Heafner, T., and Moher, D. (2010) Forest plots in reports of systematic reviews: a cross-sectional study reviewing current practice. *International Journal of Epidemiology,* **39**, 2, 421–9.

Schulz, K.F., Altman, D.G., Moher, D., CONSORT Group (2010) CONSORT 2010 Statement: Updated Guidelines for Reporting Parallel Group Randomised Trials. PLoS Medicine 7(3): e1000251. doi:10.1371/journal.pmed.1000251 w048

Smith, A.F.M. (1996) Mad cows and ecstasy: chance and choice in an evidence-based society. *Journal of the Royal Statistical Society,* **159**, 3, 367–83.

Stroup, D.F., Berlin, J.A., Morton, S.C., Olkin, I., Williamson, G.D., Rennie, D., Moher, D., Becker, B.J., Sipe, T.A., and Thacker, S.B. (2000). Meta-analysis of observational studies in epidemiology: a proposal for reporting. Meta-analysis Of Observational Studies in Epidemiology (MOOSE) group. *JAMA,* **283,** 15, 2008–12.

The PLoS Medicine Editors (2007) Many reviews are systematic but some are more transparent and completely reported than others. *PLoS Medicine,* **4**, 3, e147. doi:10.1371/journal.pmed.0040147. (w155)

Williamson, J.W., German, P.S., Weiss, R., Skinner, E.A., and Bowes, F. 3d (1989). Health science information management and continuing education of physicians. A survey of U.S. primary care practitioners and their opinion leaders. *Annals of Internal Medicine* **110**, 151–60.

Yoshii, A., Plaut, D.A., McGraw, K.A., Anderson, M.J., and Wellik, K.E. (2009) Analysis of the reporting of search strategies in Cochrane systematic reviews. *Journal of the Medical Library Association,* **97,** 1, 21–9.

TEN

Managing the literature project

Learning Objectives

After reading this chapter, you should be able to:

- Describe the skills, resources, and time considerations associated with managing a literature project.
- Rehearse pitfalls associated with updating or converting an existing literature review.
- Identify potential software requirements associated with your own literature review.
- Describe the key features of project management for a literature review project.

Introduction

Managing a literature review is similar to managing any research project. You need to identify necessary skills and resources. You also need to consider the major milestones and deliverables throughout the process. This chapter revisits the stages of the typical review process and the specific project management requirements for each stage. Working around an exemplar review it illustrates the different considerations and how they impact upon the final review product. It also examines key problems within the review process and how they might be overcome. A final section examines the different tools available for managing the complex process of the literature review as an exemplar of research project management.

Project management and literature reviews

A study by the Australasian Cochrane Centre found that the most critical barriers to completion of a Cochrane Review were lack of time (80 per cent), lack of financial support (36 per cent), methodological problems (23 per cent), and problems with group dynamics (10 per cent) (Piehl et al., 2002). More recently, another study identified time and author communication as the major barriers hindering the completion of **Cochrane Reviews** (Gillies et al., 2009).

Considerations of time and financial support are particularly marked for **Cochrane Reviews**, which are very vulnerable given that many are subsidised by individuals or organisations and are given neither protected time nor funding. Nevertheless, all these reported barriers are important for all reviews, whether systematic or not. Later in this chapter, we consider some barriers and how they might be tackled. However, as with most research projects, 'an ounce of prevention is worth a pound of cure'. Anticipating likely areas of difficulty and developing strategies to avoid them is by far the preferred course. Project management 'is a discipline of planning, organizing, and managing resources to bring about the successful completion of specific goals' (Cleland and Gareis, 2006).

No review can expect to have an entirely trouble-free progress from initiation to completion. However, most types of difficulty encountered within the relatively controlled environment of a literature-based project can be anticipated. Project management seeks to foresee or predict risks, and to plan, organise, and manage activities so that projects are successfully completed in spite of the risks (Baker et al., 2010). Review methodology provides both a ready-made phased structure for planning and conducting a review. It also supplies a repository of approaches with which to counter the more common types of problem. For this reason, some teams find it helpful to conduct their review using established project management methodologies such as the PRINCE2 methods used by many public sector corporations (Prabhakar, 2009, w157). It is not within the scope of this chapter to rehearse the full configuration of PRINCE2. It is sufficient to say that such ingredients as structures for quality assurance and stakeholder engagement translate well between generic project management and the specific requirements of a review project.

REFLECTION POINT 10.1

Risks to your own review

Think about your own review. What risks are there to you completing a successful literature review? What is the worst thing that could possibly happen? How likely is it? Create a mental picture of the main risks to your project and how likely they are to occur. How would you tackle them?

Two specific project management contexts prove consistently challenging for review authors and teams and merit brief consideration. These are:

1 Updates to existing reviews
2 Conversion of reviews to a different format

In theory, both tasks sound relatively easy when compared with undertaking a full-blown review completely from scratch. Perhaps, for this reason, reviewers and commissioners of reviews commonly underestimate the time and resources required to deliver review updates and conversions.

Updates to existing reviews

Early in the evolution of the systematic review process, our organisation was requested to update an existing systematic review previously conducted by a Spanish organisation. As only a handful of years had elapsed between completion of that review and our planned review update, the commissioners and the review team agreed a cost that represented about one-sixth of our standard price for systematic reviews. After all, it was argued, most of the work had already been conducted – all that was apparently being asked was the identification, addition and synthesis of subsequent included studies. The reality was that, notwithstanding the good quality of the original review, all stages of the review process had to be checked, validated and, essentially, repeated. For example, search strategies had to be updated and inclusion criteria had to be reconceived. These details then had to be operationalised to enable consistency between original and newly added studies. The situation was further complicated by the different languages of the two review teams.

This cautionary tale concluded with this update coming in at least three times over budget, equivalent to half the cost of a standard review, and probably significantly more. These costs were absorbed by our organisation, not the funder, in terms of extra time spent on the project and at a cost of work of the team not being available to work on other projects. This represented a valuable, but costly lesson. We therefore suggest that, when an update to a review is proposed, a review team starts from the standard price of a review and works downwards, discounting only real, not imagined, savings from the pre-existing review. So, for example, if the team can negotiate access to studies originally included in the review, this represents a real saving, otherwise the budget should cost acquisition of both original and newly added studies. In harmony with this, Moher and Tsertsvadze (2006) note that

> updating a systematic review can be as costly and time-consuming as conducting the original review or developing the original guideline. Therefore, it is of paramount importance to know whether or not a systematic review needs to be updated.

When considering whether to sanction a review update as a legitimate academic output, your supervisor/mentor will want to discuss whether such an update is 'worthwhile'. Key to deciding what is worthwhile will be the extent to which your objectives are to gain new skills as opposed to generating new knowledge. Clearly little is to be gained in either case if a reviewer reproduces an exact replica of an existing high-quality review. However, if the objectives are to acquire skills in systematic review and **meta-analysis**, then identifying a few additional studies, extracting data, critically appraising them, and possibly incorporating them in a **Forest plot** will prove valuable. On the other hand, given that the methods of systematic review favour adherence to standards over innovation, even completing such tasks may contribute little if the objective is to create new knowledge. In such a case one is looking for something more; perhaps supplementary analysis, possibly disambiguation or even reversal of a previous pattern of effect (Barrowman et al., 2003).

To make such a decision requires that you or your mentor possess a detailed knowledge of the characteristics of a field and its associated literature. Moher and Tsertsvadze (2006) propose that, when updating a systematic review, the proper timeframe depends 'on the rate of development of a particular ... field'. Frequent updating of systematic reviews in slowly developing areas may waste resources, whereas systematic reviews in rapidly developing areas may quickly become outdated. Arbitrarily choosing fixed updating frequencies (e.g. every two to three years) of systematic reviews or clinical guidelines, as suggested by some authors, may be overly simplistic. Table 10.1 suggests some possible indicators to justify update of a literature review on academic grounds. However, we should emphasise that these are indicators, not rules. Furthermore, they are informed by current evidence on review update characteristics (French et al., 2005; Moher et al., 2008). When applying these indicators it can be borne in mind that an average Cochrane Review (2001 data) included an average of six trials (Mallett and Clarke, 2002).

Box 10.1   Academic justifications for updating an existing review

1 Publication of a single large study (i.e. more participants than all previously included studies combined or larger than the previously largest included study).
2 Publication of multiple small studies (i.e. total number of participants greater than all previously included studies).
3 Interventions likely to have seen measurable improvements in delivery (e.g. progression up learning curve, a volume-outcome relationship, etc.)
4 Appearance and use of validated outcome measures (where previous review relies on subjective or unvalidated measures).
5 Stimulation of both uptake and research by policy initiatives (i.e. more activity and more evaluation).
6 A four-year gap, (or, by exception, two years or even less for volatile topic areas), since completion of previous review.
7 Appearance of new conceptual thinking/theory to supply an alternative framework for analysis.
8 Similar reviews with common included studies that provide conflicting interpretations or results.

If you are considering updating an existing review, you will find it valuable to agree expectations from the update process with your academic supervisor/mentor. Considerations could include those covered in Box 10.2.

Box 10.2 Agreeing expectations for an updated review

1 Will the reviewer extract, appraise, and reanalyse both new and existing studies or simply compare an interim cumulative result from the previous review with a cumulative result from all new studies?
2 Will the reviewer repeat searches for the period covered by the previous review or only search for studies published since that review (allowing for up to two years' overlap in recognition of publication delays)?
3 Will the reviewer extend the search process to cover additional sources, identify additional types of materials, or additional study designs?
4 Will the reviewer enhance the interpretation of the review by including complementary qualitative/quantitative data (e.g. relating to effectiveness or acceptability)?
5 Will the reviewer conduct supplementary analyses looking at specific subgroups, sensitivity to certain study characteristics, or examining likelihood of publication bias?
6 Will the reviewer unpick and isolate factors relating to the implementation of interventions, their fidelity, and their external validity?
7 Will the reviewer enhance the scope and extent of qualitative discussions of review limitations, implications for practice and implications for further research?
8 Will the reviewer re-examine applicability of review findings in the light of a different context, culture or political environment?

Conversion of reviews to a different format

Another task not to be underestimated is conversion of reviews to a different format. The most typical, and most studied, contexts for this are 'importing' or 'exporting' reviews for the **Cochrane Collaboration** (w042). This is seen in existing reviews being converted for adoption by the **Cochrane Collaboration** (w042) (importing) and in **Cochrane Reviews** being suggested as the starting point for more extensive reviews commissioned by other funding agencies (exporting). Recent years have seen increased questioning regarding reviews conducted for the numerous national agencies and whether these are transferable across agencies and countries.

In 2003, the Australasian Cochrane Centre surveyed Australian review authors to find out why they had chosen not to undertake a **Cochrane Review** (Piehl et al., 2003). Most frequently cited reasons were lack of time (78 per cent), the need to undergo specific Cochrane training (46 per cent), unwillingness to update reviews (36 per cent), difficulties with the Cochrane process (26 per cent) and the review topic already registered with the **Cochrane Collaboration** (21 per cent) (w042). These findings illustrate the main considerations when choosing to convert a review. Although much commonality exists between accepted standards for review, many organisations and review initiatives maintain their own procedures and documentation to which a converted review must conform. Becoming familiar with such procedures definitely requires orientation and probably requires training. Review authors or teams will need to read and comprehend documentation for an insight into how the process works. They may also need to revisit operational details or, even more extensively, reanalyse the data.

Nearly half of the respondents stated that they would consider converting their review to Cochrane format. Such conversions require dedicated time, time that typically lies outside the original project, and which may compete with new and existing priorities. Not to be underestimated is the need for assistance when navigating the synthesis organisation's peer review system and procedures and to identify potential assistance with updating and financial support. While some organisations may offer 'conversion grants' these will typically require you to produce a research proposal. There may be further delays in processing the application that may result in a window of opportunity becoming shut. Even though 86 per cent of those surveyed were willing to have their review converted to the Cochrane format by another author, the previous cautions regarding review updates may apply, namely the need to validate the entire process and to re-analyse new and existing data side by side.

A related idea of 'killing two birds with one stone' is to plan to undertake, for example, a systematic review for a master's dissertation or a PhD and, at the same time, to offer the resultant review to synthesis organisations such as the **Cochrane Collaboration** (w042). Such economies of scale are very beguiling, particularly given the challenge faced in keeping up with the demand for coverage by new reviews. Nevertheless, we consistently recommend that students do not pursue such a course. In practice, students undertaking such dual purpose reviews face a tension similar to that for joint supervision, except greatly magnified. The two deliverables typically have different timescales, different peer review processes, and different quality checks. While the starting point may be shared what will the student do, for example, when their supervisor has approved their review protocol and they have started work and then, several weeks later, external review comments from the synthesis organisation recommend modifications and amendments? The dual purpose model works best where the educational process is flexible enough to permit the requirements of the synthesis organisation to be paramount and to take precedence. It is to be hoped that such provisions will increase in the future, perhaps requiring that supervisors or mentors occupy dual roles (as academics and representatives of the synthesis organisation) and that the standards of the synthesis organisation are accredited and thus adopted 'off the shelf' by academic organisations. There will also be a need to make provision for subsequent updating of the review with the supervisor, not the reviewer, offering continuity and a mechanism for 'succession planning'.

Skills and resources

This consideration of project management illustrates that a successful review does not simply require technical skills. If you have no previous experience of managing a review, or you are being advised by someone with limited experience of project management, you will need to put in place a rigorous structure. This will include clear documentation of the methodology, an explicit timetable with frequent deliverables and internal and external deadlines and regular input as regards methodology.

Most reviews are multi-disciplinary in nature, requiring both methodology and subject experts. Consequently, most reviews are conducted and published by collaborative review teams. Ideally, review teams should engage with representatives of stakeholders using one of a number of models of engagement as appropriate to the project management structures. Many reviews have a *steering group* that meets at least monthly. There should also be a secretary, or *secretariat/administration* in larger projects, to support the project on a day-to-day basis arranging meetings, handling correspondence, and perhaps supporting document delivery, database administration, or tabulation of data. The steering group may choose to create small, *ad hoc groups to address specific issues* as they arise; for example in bringing in meta-analysis expertise at the appropriate juncture. A wider *advisory group*, comprising methodology or subject experts and, most importantly, practitioners from the field, may meet quarterly or every six months to provide advice to the steering group or secretariat on clinical, technical or other issues impacting on the review.

Time

'How long does a literature review take?' is the evidence synthesis equivalent to 'how long is a piece of string?' The standard 'it depends' reply is predicated on the type of review and on the phasing of the review process. Chapter 3 presents a range of timescales of between 6 and 12 months for systematic approaches to the literature. Rapid evidence assessments, which do not typically spend as much time on quality assessment and synthesis may be turned around in as little as 8 to 12 weeks. The primary challenge is how to agree and communicate expectations, focusing on constraints and limitations, not the more technical issue of how to complete a systematic review in a telescoped timescale. Gall, Borg, and Gall (1996) estimated that completion of an acceptable dissertation literature review takes between three and six months of effort. However, this estimate predates the era of systematic approaches to the literature which have 'upped the ante' in recent years.

In our workshops on preparing a successful literature review proposal, we emphasise a distinction between those processes that lie within the reviewer's own control (and that may consequently be more flexible) and those that depend on external agencies (which may be conceived as 'fixed'). The latter typically include obtaining interlibrary loans or photocopies from other libraries (see Chapter 3) and subsequent dependencies such as follow-up of citations, quality assessment, and extraction of data. Depending on how review tasks are allocated, external constraints may also include the searching of bibliographic databases through an information specialist or librarian and access to a specialist in meta-analysis. Once a reviewer has all the included articles to hand, they can work

Table 10.1 Indicative of hours taken to perform a meta-analysis

Average no. of hours	1,139 (Range: 216–2,518)
Breakdown*	
588 hours	Protocol, searching, and retrieval
44 hours	Statistical analysis
206 hours	Report writing
201 hours	Administration

Note: Allen and Olkin (1999) found that the time taken to conduct a meta-analysis contained a fixed component, regardless of the size of review, and a variable component that depends on the number of citations.

through the remainder of the process at their own pace, burning the legendary 'midnight oil' if necessary. However this may be at the expense of the quality of the review. It is typically the analysis which tends to fall victim to truncated time-scales. Our own calculations are informed by early research on a series of meta-analyses which found that the average time taken for a meta-analysis was 1,139 hours (but with a range from 216 to 2,518 hours (Allen and Olkin, 1999). Typical durations of the different stages of the process are shown in Table 10.1.

When attempting to calculate the time required for a meta-analysis, you should realise that additional studies (i.e. more of the same) may not contribute too greatly to an increased workload as much of the preparatory work has already been completed. However, if the additional studies are **heterogeneous,** when compared with already included studies, particularly if they will require additional subgroup analysis or include additional groups of outcomes, they can add significantly to the overall time taken.

Allied to this discussion of time taken are questions (usually from students) relating to the minimum/maximum number of articles required for a review. Again, the response is 'it depends'. Variation is necessitated by the type of review together with the type of analysis and any educational or personal development objectives. To establish reviewer competencies as part of a master's programme we set a mini-review assignment which requires assessment, synthesis and interpretation of an arbitrary five or six studies. Other institutions set a related 'systematic search and review' type of assignment that requires specific attention to formulation of the review question and study identification, but less rigorous synthesis and summary of results. Our take-home message is that systematic approaches to the literature are flexible and varied enough to meet most educational requirements. Indeed if a specific competency is required (for example meta-analysis) students may be able to use a dataset or subset from an existing review rather than having to complete the entire process.

Qualitative evidence synthesis in particular is witnessing ongoing debate regarding the optimal number of studies to be included. Here the determinants relate to the overall approach and the accompanying type of analysis. A qualitative synthesis published in *The Lancet* included as many as 32 studies. However, where an interpretive approach is required, much smaller numbers of studies have been proposed.

If this guidance seems particularly evasive we could add (off the record, of course) that an ideal review, in an educational context and from our personal perspective, would include somewhere between 8 and 12 studies. This is large enough to provide rich data (either quantitative or qualitative) and significant variation between studies. It also offers the possibility of multiple meta-analysis displays if relevant and yet proves small enough to be feasible within a typical academic timescale. However, this is a long way from advocating reverse engineering, by which the review question is shaped by the intended number of studies. Indeed, many students have been caught out trying to arrive at a 'magic number' of included studies and either drastically underestimating the number of hits (and having thousands of references to sift through) or misjudging the effect of inclusion criteria (and pruning down to too few included studies). The integrity of the review question, to a large extent independent of the volume of the literature, remains the best single marker of systematic approaches to a successful literature review.

Costing

Our experience suggests two critical factors have a bearing on the time and cost of a review. The first of these is the **conversion ratio**, namely the number of bibliographical references and abstracts that the review team will have to sift through in order to identify one relevant potentially includable study. Experience is currently being accumulated for the different conversion rates of different types of review; so, for example, public health, management and education topics will have lower conversion ratios than drug interventions or surgical procedures. Qualitative review topics also have lower conversion ratios than those addressing more quantitative questions. Factors having a bearing on the conversion ratio include the sensitivity or specificity of the search strategy, the 'tightness' of review terminology, the diffuseness of the literature and the experience and expertise of the review team. The second critical factor relates to the absolute number of included studies. Each included study carries workload implications in terms of quality assessment, data extraction and synthesis. In addition to these variable factors, there is a fixed component that relates to the overall planning, conduct and management of the review. While calculating resources required for a review is far from an exact science, a knowledge of these components helps a review team to arrive at a ball park figure.

Communication

We have already illustrated that communication is key to the success of a review. Effective communication strategies should be planned from the outset of the project. Whether this is formalised as a documented communications plan will depend upon the scale of the review. For large-scale international reviews, such a plan will help to meet the challenges that having review authors in different time zones, distant locations, and even different languages, brings. Personal communication between collaborators, typically via email, can speed a review process beyond a regular cycle of face-to-face or virtual meetings. Nevertheless, where issues require rapid resolution it may be more effective to discuss issues synchronously. Resources that harness voice over internet protocols and video services, such as Skype video, offer an attractively cheap alternative for communication (Baker et al., 2010).

Stages of the literature review

Baker and colleagues (2010) suggest that the process of producing a review may be divided into four phases of project management:

1 concept,
2 planning and definition,
3 implementation and
4 finalisation.

These four stages may be applied more generically to any review project. The concept phase includes assembling the team (Chapter 3). The planning and definition phase of the review includes protocol development (Chapter 4) which will include specific allocation of roles and responsibilities and identification of any training and resource requirements. The implementation phase covers all the operational aspects covered in Chapters 5 to 8 of this book. The finalisation stage is the write-up and publication of the review itself (Chapter 9) and making plans for future updates (Chapter 10).

Box 10.3   Case study of a review: some lessons learnt

The Higher Education Academy in the United Kingdom invited proposals on the topic of the student experience of e-learning. A team from the School of Health and Related Research (ScHARR) at the University of Sheffield submitted a proposal specifically looking at the experience of students undertaking e-learning in the work-place, an area with which the team had expertise and practical experience. The five team members had a disciplinary background in information science but also brought other skills to the table. The project director had participated in over 30 systematic reviews for a variety of national and professional funding agencies. He had worked with the project manager on a major systematic review for the National Health Service (NHS) Service Delivery and Organisation (SDO) Programme. The project manager was therefore very familiar with all the detailed stages of the systematic review. At the time of the project, two of the remaining information specialists were working in roles that supported the review activities of others. They were to lead on the retrieval and identification of studies. The final member was serving as an intern to the information resources section while studying part-time. An internal advisory panel included multi-disciplinary experience in work psychology, distance learning, inquiry-based learning and information management. The review was proposed as a mixed methods review looking at both the effectiveness of work-place-based e-learning techniques in enhancing the student learning experience and student perceptions of such techniques. Study types would include comparative quantitative studies and qualitative data in the form of surveys, focus groups, and case studies. An intended deliverable was to develop a framework outlining best practice for delivering the optimal student experience and to validate this framework with three to four case studies.

The following timetable was proposed:

- Phase 1 – problem formulation and investigation (months 1–4)
- Phase 2 – analysis (months 5–7)
- Phase 3 – validation and dissemination (months 8–10)

The review question was mapped against the SPICE Framework (Chapter 4)

- Setting – the workplace (part-time; work experience; secondments)
- Perspective(s) – the student (acceptability) and the educator (effectiveness)
- Intervention – e-learning components
- Comparison – Alternative e-learning components
- Evaluation – effect size, student satisfaction

A comprehensive selection of keywords was developed for each of the five SPICE components (Chapter 5). Databases to be searched included the Applied Social Science Index and Abstracts, ERIC (w079), Australian Education Index, the International Bibliography of the Social Sciences, British Education Index, Index to theses, Cumulative Index of Nursing and Allied Health Literature (CINAHL), Library and Information Science Abstracts (LISA), CSA abstracts (Social Services, Sociology, Information Technology Case Studies), MEDLINE (w131), Dissertation Abstracts, PsycInfo, Emerald Management Reviews, and the Social Science Citation Index. This would be supported by handsearching of relevant journals including the *International Journal of e-Learning, Journal of Workplace Learning*, and the *Journal of Open and Distance Learning*.

The poor quality of the research meant that formal quality assessment was not attempted. An alternative approach was used based on optimising the Signal to Noise ratio of rigour versus relevance (Edwards et al., 1998; Booth, 2001). Primary sources would report the actual first-hand experiences of students. These would be supplemented by secondary (reported experiences from teaching staff/managers substantiated by data) and tertiary (reported unsubstantiated experiences from teaching staff/managers) data sources.

For inclusion, studies had to report the experience of people in formal employment (full/part-time) on a course delivered purely/primarily by e-learning. E-learning had to be a single/major component of the course. Courses had to be delivered either by a UK Higher Education or Further Education Institution, or by a UK professional body (e.g. a Royal College). In addition, the actual e-learning techniques had to be specified (e.g. case studies, discussion forums, web lectures) and the study should specifically report some aspect of the student experience (e.g. satisfaction, enjoyment, usefulness, perspectives, engagement, etc.). For practical reasons the review was limited to English-language articles only published from 1992 onwards.

(Continued)

(Continued)

Comprehensive searches of the literature resulted in 3,426 unique, potentially relevant citations. Retrieved citations were divided into four sets. Each set of citations (titles and abstracts only) was screened by a member of the project team (CC, AB, AS, DP), after a test for consistency of selection across all team members. Sifting resulted in identification of 131 unique references.

Following review of the full-text of these references, 33 studies were identified reporting experiences from 22 different UK institutions.

Comment on lessons learnt: experience with this review revealed certain limitations. First, the poor quality of indexing and abstracts in non-health databases provided a possible explanation for a disproportionately high number of health e-learning studies. Frequently study reports did not mention the student experience and it was very difficult to isolate those students who were specifically accessing e-learning from work as studies tended to accumulate the demographic details. Pragmatically, studies reporting 80 per cent or more of participants at work were included. Many studies that initially looked relevant turned out to be descriptive reports of unevaluated initiatives. Our interim findings following the formal bibliographic database searching were that the non-journal literature might prove disproportionately significant. As a consequence, the team embarked on supplementary search strategies including reference checking, citation searching (of the Web of Knowledge and Google Scholar) and citation pearl growing (see Chapter 5). Other strategies included follow-up of known projects and searching of sources specifically for dissertations, conference proceedings, and books and book chapters.

The resultant 41 studies (the original 33 plus 8 additional studies) were used to develop a framework for the development and evaluation of work-place-based e-learning. Data was extracted using a standard data extraction template (Chapter 7). Thematic analysis identified 11 themes that had a bearing on the student experience and these could be grouped within five overarching constructs (Chapter 7). Further analysis identified complex relationships between several of the factors (Chapter 8). For example, some students preferred active moderation of the e-learning by their instructors but for others this could result in student inhibition. Students required multiple sources of support for a variety of technical, pastoral, and academic purposes but this contradicted a requirement to have clearly defined channels for support. For course developers, there were tensions between what was possible technically and what was easiest procedurally. The need for formal evaluation of courses was undermined by a tendency for innovators to 'just try it'.

The resulting framework was adapted into an interview instrument and used to conduct telephone interviews with five different case study sites. In each case, the team was able to identify mechanisms of good practice for seeking to address major considerations within the student experience.

The review identified several recommendations. For example, for developers there was a need to make greater use of work-based mentors (or other mechanisms for contextualisation of knowledge within the workplace. It was also seen to be important to re-engineer course content for an e-learning environment, not simply to replicate the face-to-face experience. Course participants were encouraged to actively seek opportunities to contextualise their own learning to supplement formal provision and to develop their own skills and methods for reflective practice.

In terms of writing up and data presentation (Chapter 9) what was essentially a modestly-funded literature review project, supplemented by original data collection, was significantly prolific. In addition to the project report, the study led to four peer-reviewed publications (Booth et al., 2009; Carroll et al., 2009a, 2009b; Papaioannou et al., 2010), one book chapter and two conference presentations.

Problem solving and troubleshooting

In the following section we present seven realistic scenarios relating to problems that may be encountered while undertaking a literature review. Choose one or more scenarios of interest to you and attempt to diagnose where the problems may lie and how they might be overcome. Once you have identified some potential solutions turn to the end of the chapter to read our suggested solutions.

EXERCISE 10.1

Problem-solving scenarios

Scenario A: too wide a scope

Adebola is starting a literature review as part of a funded pilot project on the social determinants of ill-health in Sub-Saharan Africa. She is interested in the causes of mortality for mothers and infants and she feels she must definitely look at some of the leading causes of disability among adults. Then there is the increasing high profile of illness in the ageing population. In her country, there is a particular concern around HIV and AIDS. As she starts to build a list of all possible population–illness combinations she realises that her topic has started to get out of hand.

What are the root causes of this particular problem?

What strategies might you suggest to help Adebola overcome this problem?

Scenario B: too narrow a scope

Sonja is a member of a small team working on a funded review in a management topic. After spending considerable time devising comprehensive search strategies for the specific review question, using the PICOS formulation, she has completed an initial sift of retrieved titles and abstracts. She applies the rigorous inclusion criteria devised by the team and finds that not a single one of the retrieved items would make it through to the full article stage. She is concerned that the team has made their review topic too exclusive and may have only an 'empty review' to offer to the research funders.

What are the root causes of this particular problem?

What strategies might you suggest to help Sonja overcome this problem?

Scenario C: scope creep

Sanjay is a part-time student conducting a literature review for his academic thesis. He has devised a comprehensive search plan for his literature review and meets with his supervisor to discuss his next steps. His supervisor suggests that, in addition to the topics he has already identified, he needs to access some key concepts from the psychological literature. Discussing his review question with a work colleague, who has recently completed an MBA, she suggests that the management literature may also have something to contribute. Revisiting his search plan, he now finds that these suggested revisions have tripled the extent of the literature to be screened and sifted.

What are the root causes of this particular problem?

What strategies might you suggest to help Sanjay overcome this problem?

Scenario D: going over time

It is month 10 of a 12-month funded project and Eloise is worried. She has completed data extraction and quality assessment of about half of the 80 articles to be included in her literature review. She has no idea what are the main findings that are going to emerge from her review, let alone how the literature review is going to be written on time.

What are the root causes of this particular problem?

What strategies might you suggest to help Eloise overcome this problem?

Scenario E: going over budget

Sandra has just received the monthly budget report for her first ever 18-month literature review. It is month seven and she has spent well over half the budget allocation for the project. The project is proceeding on schedule but she is concerned that she is going to have to report a likely end of project overspend to her line manager at her next three-monthly review meeting. She is concerned that she has underestimated the project budget for the literature review.

What are the root causes of this particular problem?

What strategies might you suggest to help Sandra overcome this problem?

Scenario F: methodological problems

Tomas is undertaking a systematic review on attitudes to citizenship of first-generation East European migrants. He is at a crucial stage of his literature project. He has identified all the studies for likely inclusion in his review. However, he is unsure which method of synthesis he should use to summarise these qualitative research reports.

His supervisor has extensive experience of supervising systematic review projects, but they have all involved meta-analyses and he has never supervised any form of qualitative evidence synthesis.

What are the root causes of this particular problem?

What strategies might you suggest to help Tomas overcome this problem?

Scenario G: communication challenges

James is feeling frustrated. For some time now he has been sending e-mails to topic experts on the review team asking for their input. Although they are only located 40 miles (64 km) away, being based in the nearest adjacent city, they seem to have 'disappeared into a black hole in the ether'. James is concerned that, without their cooperation and input, the literature review will fall behind in its time schedule and may also lack credibility with practitioners.

What are the root causes of this particular problem?

What strategies might you suggest to help James overcome this problem?

Such decisions constitute a toolkit of 'rescue' techniques to be considered for bringing a review back on track if time, quality, money, or even methodological aspects of a literature review appear to be deviating from the original plan (see also Chapter 3).

Summary

Although this consideration of project management is placed at the end of this text, you cannot afford to underestimate the fact that preparation of any review according to systematic principles is complex and time-consuming. It is essential, therefore, that you as a reviewer pay close attention to the need for initial planning. Established project management principles provide a good basis for both planning and managing the production of the review (Baker et al., 2010). Aspects to be considered include planning, management, effective communication and stakeholder engagement. All these elements, if handled appropriately, have the potential to improve the timeliness and likelihood of success for reviews, as well as enhancing the experience of the review team and the capacity of the hosting organisation. Of course the converse is also true; a lack of planning and management, poor mechanisms for communication and inappropriate engagement of stakeholders have the considerable potential to hamstring the review project. Project management is therefore a key element of systematic approaches to a successful literature review.

Key learning points

- A literature review must be managed like any project with clear definitions of roles, expectations, and timescales.
- Reviewers must not assume that processes such as updating an existing review or converting a review to a standardised format will be less time-consuming than starting a review from the beginning.
- Many review challenges are anticipable and therefore preventable. Other post hoc strategies may require concessions to time, cost, or quality and may therefore need to be renegotiated with others.
- Software to support the review process includes both bespoke software for such procedures as meta-analysis and more generic packages that can be used for data extraction, concept mapping, etc.

Suggestions for further reading

Baker, P.R., Francis, D.P., Hall, B.J., Doyle, J., and Armstrong, R. (2010) Managing the production of a Cochrane systematic review. *Journal of Public Health*, **32**, 3, 448–50.

Tools to support the review process

Little attention has been paid in the literature to identifying tools to support the review process. Typically those articles that do cover use of these tools are focused on the requirements for literature searching, reference management and analysing quantitative or qualitative data (Box 10.4). This Tools section is extended to include tools to facilitate communication (Box 10.5) and tools to facilitate project management (Box 10.6). Many of these resources have already been covered throughout this book. This Tools section is therefore designed as a source of a possible checklist to use when planning the requirements to support your own review.

Box 10.4   Tools to support review development and analysis

Concept development (Freemind)

Data mining

Reference management (Reference Manager, w161; Endnote, w071; Refworks, w162)

Reference sharing (e.g. Citeulike, w040; Mendeley, w133)

Data extraction (Access, Excel)

Quantitative data analysis (SPSS, Stata)

Qualitative data analysis (e.g. NVivo)

Recently, a group from the Cochrane Collaboration (w042) compiled some initial suggestions from within the wider context of review management (Baker et al., 2010). Their list focuses instead on tools to facilitate communication (Box 10.5).

Box 10.5 Tools to facilitate communication

Meeting planning tools

Voice and video communication

File sharing

Remote sharing of a PC desktop

We can add to this list tools required for the management of the review project, presentation of data and subsequent reporting and dissemination (Box 10.6).

Box 10.6 Tools to facilitate review project management

Project management software (e.g. Microsoft Project)

Integrated review management software (e.g. RevMan)

Presentation software (e.g. Powerpoint; OpenOffice Impress) (w147)

Wordprocessing software (e.g. Word; OpenOffice Write) (w147)

Report conversion/distribution software (e.g. Acrobat, Winzip)

References

Allen, I.E. and Olkin, I. (1999) Estimating time to conduct a meta-analysis from number of citations retrieved. *JAMA*, **282**, 7, 634–5.

Barrowman, N.J., Fang, M., Sampson, M., and Moher, D. (2003) Identifying null meta-analyses that are ripe for updating. *BMC Medical Research Methodology*, **3**, 13. (w012)

Baker, P.R., Francis, D.P., Hall, B.J., Doyle, J., and Armstrong, R. (2010) Managing the production of a Cochrane systematic review. *Journal of Public Health*, **32**, 3, 448–50.

Booth, A. (2001) Cochrane or cock-eyed? How should we conduct systematic reviews of qualitative research? Paper presentation at the Qualitative Evidence-based Practice Conference 'Taking a Critical Stance', University of Coventry, 14–16 May. (w019)

Booth, A., Carroll, C., Papaioannou, D., Sutton, A., and Wong, R. (2009) Applying findings from a systematic review of workplace-based e-learning: implications for health information professionals. *Health Information and Libraries Journal*, **26**, 1, 4–21.

Carroll, C., Booth, A., Papaioannou, D., Sutton, A., and Wong, R. (2009a) Enhancing the experience of e-learning among working students: a systematic review with thematic analysis. *Impact: Journal of Applied Research in Workplace E-learning*, **1**, 1, 80–96.

Carroll, C., Booth, A., Papaioannou, D., Sutton, A., and Wong, R. (2009b) UK health-care professionals' experience of on-line learning techniques: A systematic review of qualitative data. *The Journal of Continuing Education in the Health Professions*, **29**, 4, 235–241.

Cleland, D., and Gareis, R. (2006) *Global Project Management Handbook: Planning, Organising and Controlling International Projects.* New York: McGraw-Hill.

Edwards, A.G., Russell, I.T., and Stott, N.C. (1998) Signal versus noise in the evidence base for medicine: an alternative to hierarchies of evidence? *Family Practice*, **15**, 4, 319–22.

French, S.D., McDonald, S., McKenzie, J.E., and Green, S.E. (2005) Investing in updating: how do conclusions change when Cochrane systematic reviews are updated? *BMC Medical Research Methodology*, **5**, 33. (w085)

Gall, M.D., Borg, W.R., and Gall, J.P. (1996) *Education Research: An Introduction*, 6th edn. White Plains, NY: Longman

Gillies, D., Maxwell, H., New, K., Pennick, V., Fedorowicz, Z., van Der Wouden, J., Oliver, J., Scholten, R., Ciapponi, A., and Verbeek, J. (2009) *A Collaboration-wide Survey of Cochrane Authors.* Oxford: The Cochrane Collaboration.

Jadad, A.R., Cook, D.J., Jones, A., Klassen, T.P., Tugwell, P., Moher, M., and Moher, D. (1998) Methodology and reports of systematic reviews and meta-analyses: a comparison of Cochrane Reviews with articles published in paper-based journals. *JAMA*, **280**, 278–80.

Mallett, S. and Clarke, M. (2002) The typical Cochrane Review. How many trials? How many participants? *International Journal of Technology Assessment in Health Care*, **18**, 4, 820–3.

Moher, D. and Tsertsvadze, A. (2006) Systematic reviews: when is an update an update? *Lancet*, **367**, 9514, 881–3.

Moher, D., Tsertsvadze, A., Tricco, A., Eccles, M., Grimshaw, J., Sampson, M., and Barrowman, N. (2008) When and how to update systematic reviews. Cochrane Database of Systematic Reviews 2008, Issue 1. Art. No.: MR000023. DOI: 10.1002/14651858.MR000023.pub3

Olsen, O., Middleton, P., Ezzo, J., Gøtzsche, P., Hadhazy, V., Herxheimer, A., Kleijnen, J., and McIntosh, H. (2001) Quality of Cochrane Reviews: assessment of sample from 1998. *BMJ*, **323**, 829–32.

Papaioannou, D., Sutton, A., Carroll, C., Booth, A., and Wong, R. (2010) Literature searching for social science systematic reviews: consideration of a range of search techniques. *Health Information and Libraries Journal*, **27**, 2, 114–22.

Piehl, J.H., Green, S., and Silagy, C. (2002) Training practitioners in preparing systematic reviews: a cross-sectional survey of participants in the Australasian Cochrane Centre training program. *BMC Health Services Research*, **2**, 1, 11. (w152)

Piehl, J.H., Green, S., and McDonald, S. (2003) Converting systematic reviews to Cochrane format: a cross-sectional survey of Australian authors of systematic reviews. *BMC Health Services Research*, **3**, 1, 2. (w153)

Prabhakar, G. (2009) Projects and their management: a literature review. *International Journal of Business and Management*, **3**, 8, 3. (w157)

Soll, R.F. (2008) Updating reviews: the experience of the Cochrane Neonatal Review Group. *Paediatric and Perinatal Epidemiology*, **22**, Suppl 1, 29–32.

Smith, L.K., Pope, C., Botha, J.L. (2005) Patients' help-seeking experiences and delay in cancer presentation: a qualitative synthesis. *Lancet*, Sept. 3–9 **366**(9488), 825–31.

Webography

This webography contains links to those references and resources that are available free-of-charge, without passwords, via the World Wide Web. All resources were accessed and checked in February 2011.

w001 ALI BABA http://alibaba.informatik.hu-berlin.de/

w002 Alias and Suradi (2008) Alias, M. and Suradi, Z (2008) Concept mapping: a tool for creating a literature review, In: *Concept Mapping: Connecting Educators*, ed. by Canas, A.J. et al. The Second International Conference on Concept Mapping. Tallinn and Helsinki. http://uthm.academia.edu/MaizamAlias/Papers/171413/CONCEPT_ MAPPING_A_TOOL_FOR_CREATING_A_LITERATURE_REVIEW

w003 Ananiadou et al. (2007) Ananiadou, S., Procter, R., Rea, B., Sasaki, Y., and Thomas, J. (2007) Supporting Systematic Reviews Using Text Mining. Proceedings of the 3rd International Conference on e-Social Science, Ann Arbor, US. http://www.ncess.ac.uk/ events/conference/2007/papers/paper208.pdf

w004 Anderson et al. (2003) Anderson, L.M., Shinn, C., Fullilove, M.T., Scrimshaw, S.C., Fielding, J.E., Normand, J., Carande-Kulis,V.G. and the Task Force on Community Preventive Services (2003) The effectiveness of early childhood development programs: a systematic review. *American Journal of Preventative Medicine*, 24, 3S, 32–46. http://www.thecommunityguide.org/social/soc-AJPM-evrev-ecd.pdf

w005 Anderson et al. (2008) Anderson, S., Allen, P., Peckham, S., and Goodwin, N. (2008) Asking the right questions: scoping studies in the commissioning of research on the organisation and delivery of health services. *Health Research Policy and Systems*, 6, 7. http://www.health-policy-systems.com/content/6/1/7.

w006 Arai et al. (2007) Arai, L., Britten, N., Popay, J., Roberts, H., Petticrew, M., Rodgers, M., and Sowden, A. (2007). Testing methodological developments in the conduct of narrative synthesis: a demonstration review of research on the implementation of smoke alarm interventions. *Evidence and Policy*, 3, 3, 361–83 http://www.lancs.ac.uk/shm/ research/nssr/research/dissemination/publications/Aria_et_al.pdf

w007 Atkins and Sampson (2002) Atkins, C. and Sampson, J. (2002) Critical appraisal guidelines for single case study research ECIS 2002, June 6–8, Gdańsk, Poland. http:// citeseerx.ist.psu.edu/viewdoc/download?doi=10.1.1.97.8700&rep=rep1&type=pdf

w008 Atkins et al. (2008) Atkins, S., Lewin, S., Smith, H., Engel, M., Fretheim, A., and Volmink, J. (2008). Conducting a meta-ethnography of qualitative literature: lessons learnt. *BMC Medical Research Methodology*, 8, 21. http://www.biomedcentral.com/1471-2288/8/21

w009 Attree (2008) Attree, P. 2008. Childhood Disadvantage and Health Inequalities: A Systematic Review of the Qualitative Evidence. Lancaster: Lancaster University. http://www.sphsu.mrc.ac.uk/Evidence/Research/Review%2007/ChildDis.pdf

w010 Australian Centre for Evidence Based Residential Aged Care (2006). Australian Centre for Evidence Based Residential Aged Care (2006) Skill mix in residential care. http://www.joannabriggs.edu.au/protocols/protsklmx.php

w011 Barnett-Page and Thomas (2009) Barnett-Page, E. and Thomas, J. (2009) Methods for the synthesis of qualitative research: a critical review. *BMC Medical Research Methodology*, 9, 59. http://www.biomedcentral.com/1471-2288/9/59

w012 Barrowman et al. (2003) Barrowman, N.J., Fang, M., Sampson, M., and Moher, D. (2003) Identifying null meta-analyses that are ripe for updating. *BMC Medical Research Methodology*, 3, 13 http://www.biomedcentral.com/1471-2288/3/13

w013 Baxter et al. (2010) Baxter, S., Killoran, A., Kelly, M.P., and Goyder, E. (2010) Synthesizing diverse evidence: the use of primary qualitative data analysis methods and logic models in public health reviews. *Public Health*, 124, 2, 99–106. http://eprints.whiterose.ac.uk/10357/

w014 Bergman and Cozon (2005) Bergman, M.M. and Coxon, A.P.M. (2005) The quality in qualitative methods. *Forum Qualitative Sozialforschung/Forum: Qualitative Social Research*, 6, 2, Art. 34. http://nbn-resolving.de/urn:nbn:de:0114-fqs0502344

w015 BestBETS BestBETs CA worksheets. http://www.bestbets.org/links/BET-CA-worksheets.php

w016 BestBETS Educational Interventions BestBets. Educational interventions checklist. http://www.bestbets.org/ca/pdf/educational_intervention.pdf

w017 BestBETS Survey worksheet. http://www.bestbets.org/ca/pdf/survey.pdf

w018 Boaz et al. (2002) Boaz, A., Ashby, D., and Young, K. (2002) Systematic reviews: What have they got to offer evidence based policy and practice? ESRC UK Centre for Evidence Based Policy and Practice. Working Paper 2. Queen Mary University of London, ESRC. http://www.kcl.ac.uk/content/1/c6/03/45/85/wp2.pdf

w019 Booth (2001) Booth, A. (2001) Cochrane or cock-eyed? How should we conduct systematic reviews of qualitative research? Paper presentation at the Qualitative Evidence-based Practice Conference 'Taking a Critical Stance', University of Coventry, 14–16 May. http://www.leeds.ac.uk/educol/documents/00001724.htm

w020 Booth et al. (2008) Booth, A., Meier, P., Stockwell, T., Sutton, A., Wilkinson, A., Wong, R., Brennan, A., O'Reilly, D., Purshouse, R., and Taylor, K. (2008) Independent review of the effects of alcohol pricing and promotion. Part A: systematic reviews. Sheffield; University of Sheffield. http://www.dh.gov.uk/prod_consum_dh/groups/dh_digitalassets/documents/digitalasset/dh_091366.pdf

w021 Booth (2009) Booth, A. (2009) Searching for studies. *Cochrane Qualitative Methods Group Handbook*. http://www.joannabriggs.edu.au/cqrmg/documents/Cochrane_Guidance/Chapter5_Searching_for_Studies.pdf

w022 Braithwaite (2010) Braithwaite, J. (2010) Between-group behaviour in healthcare: gaps, edges, boundaries, disconnections, weak ties, spaces and holes. A systematic review. *BMC Health Services Research*, 10, 330. http://www.biomedcentral.com/1472-6963/10/330

w023 Brettle and Long (2001) Brettle, A.J. and Long, A.F. (2001) Comparison of bibliographic databases for information on the rehabilitation of people with severe mental illness. *Bulletin of the Medical Library Association*, 89, 4, 353–62. http://www.ncbi.nlm.nih.gov/pmc/articles/PMC57964/

w024 Bridge and Phibbs (2003) Bridge, C. and Phibbs, P. (2003) Protocol guidelines for systematic reviews of home modification information to inform best practice. Home Modification and Maintenance Clearinghouse. http://www.homemods.info/files/SysRevProtocolJune%202k3.pdf

w025 Brunton et al. (2006) Brunton, G., Oliver, S., Oliver, K., and Lorenc, T. (2006) A synthesis of research addressing children's, young people's and parents' views of walking and cycling for Transport London, EPPI-Centre, Social Science Research Unit, Institute of Education, University of London. http://eppi.ioe.ac.uk/cms/Default.aspx?tabid=942

w026 BUBL: http://bubl.ac.uk/

w027 Burls (2009) Burls, A. (2009) What is critical appraisal? 2nd edn. http://www.medicine.ox.ac.uk/bandolier/painres/download/whatis/What_is_critical_appraisal.pdf

w028 Cabinet Office (2003) Cabinet Office. The magenta book. Guidance notes for policy evaluation and analysis. Chapter 2: What do we Already Know? July 2003. http://www.nationalschool.gov.uk/policyhub/downloads/Chapter_2.pdf

w029 Campbell Collaboration. What is a systematic review? http://www.campbellcollaboration.org/what_is_a_systematic_review/index.php

w030 Campbell Library The Campbell Collaboration Library of Systematic Reviews: http://www.campbellcollaboration.org/library.php

w031 Canadian Health Services Research Foundation Reader-Friendly Writing – 1:3:25. Communication Notes. http://www.chsrf.ca/Migrated/PDF/CommunicationNotes/cn-1325_e.pdf

w032 Carroll et al. (2007) Carroll, C., Patterson, M., Wood, S., Booth, A., Rick, J., and Balain, S. (2007) A conceptual framework for implementation fidelity. *Implementation Science*, 2, 40 .http://www.implementationscience.com/content/2/1/40

w033 Centre for Evidence Based Medicine – Study Designs. Centre for Evidence Based Medicine. Study designs (2009). http://www.cebm.net/index.aspx?o=1039

w034 Centre for Evidence Based Medicine – Levels of Evidence. Chalmers, I., Glasziou, P., Greenhalgh, T., Heneghan, C., Howick, J., Liberati, A., Moschetti, I., Phillips, B., and Thornton, H. Steps in finding evidence ('Levels') for different types of question (2009). http://www.cebm.net/mod_product/design/files/CEBM-Levels-of-Evidence-2.pdf

w035 Centre for Reviews and Dissemination Databases CRD Databases. http://www.crd.york.ac.uk/crdweb/

w036 Centre for Reviews and Dissemination (2009) Centre for Reviews and Dissemination (2009) Systematic reviews: CRD's guidance for undertaking reviews in healthcare, 3rd edn. York: Centre for Reviews and Dissemination. http://www.york.ac.uk/inst/crd/SysRev/!SSL!/WebHelp/SysRev3.htm

w037 Chartered Institute for Library and Information Professionals (CILIP) CILIP (2009) Definition of Information Literacy. http://www.cilip.org.uk/policyadvocacy/learning/informationliteracy/definition/definition.htm

w038 Chartered Society of Physiotherapists (2005) Chartered Society of Physiotherapists (2005) CSP guide to searching the literature. www.csp.org.uk/uploads/documents/csp_libraryinfo_lis15.pdf

w039 Chung et al. (2007) Chung, A., Perera, R., Brueggemann, A.B., Elamin, A.E., Harnden, A., Mayon-White, R., Smith, S., Crook, D.W., and Mant, D. (2007) Effect of antibiotic prescribing on antibiotic resistance in individual children in primary care: prospective cohort study. *BMJ*, 335, 7617, 429. http://www.bmj.com/cgi/content/full/335/7617/429

w040 CiteULike. http://www.citeulike.org/

w041 ClusterMed. http://www.clustermed.info

w042 Cochrane Collaboration http://www.cochrane.org/

w043 Cochrane Handbook (2009) Higgins, J.P.T. and Green, S (eds). *Cochrane Handbook for Systematic Reviews of Interventions*. Version 5.0.2 (updated September 2009). Oxford: Cochrane Collaboration. http://www.cochrane-handbook.org/

w044 Cochrane Library The Cochrane Library: http://www.thecochranelibrary.com

w045 Cochrane Qualitative Research Methods Group (2010) Cochrane Qualitative Research Methods Group. Chapter 6 – Critical appraisal of qualitative research (in draft) (2010). http://www.joannabriggs.edu.au/cqrmg/documents/Cochrane_Guidance/Chapter6_Guidance_Critical_Appraisal.pdf

w046 College of Emergency Medicine College of Emergency Medicine. Bias and confounding (2010). http://www.collemergencymed.ac.uk/CEM/Research/technical_guide/bias-confound.htm

w047 Connotea. http://www.connotea.org/about

w048 CONSORT Statement CONSORT Group. CONSORT Statement (2010). http://www.con-sort-statement.org/

w049 Cordingley et al. (2004) Cordingley, P., Bell, M., and Thomason, S. (2004) The impact of collaborative CPD on classroom teaching and learning. Protocol: How do collaborative and sustained CPD and sustained but not collaborative CPD affect teaching and learning? Evidence for Policy and Practice Information and Co-ordinating Centre. http://eppi.ioe.ac.uk/EPPIWebContent/reel/review_groups/CPD/cpd_protocol2.pdf

w050 Coren and Barlow (2003) Coren, E. and Barlow, J. (2003) Individual and group based parenting for improving psychosocial outcomes for teenage parents and their children. http://www2.cochrane.org/reviews/en/ab002964.html

w051 Coren and Fisher (2006) Coren, E. and Fisher, M. (2006) *The conduct of systematic research reviews for SCIE knowledge reviews*. Using knowledge in social care Research Resource 1. London: Social Care Institute of Excellence. http://www.scie.org.uk/publications/researchresources/rr01.pdf

w052 Coverdale (2009) Coverdale, A. (2009) *The use of mapping in literature review* (PhD wiki). http://sites.google.com/site/andycoverdale/texts/the-use-of-mapping-in-litera-ture-review

w053 CrimDoc: Criminology, University of Toronto, CrimDoc (Criminology Library Grey Literature). http://link.library.utoronto.ca/criminology/crimdoc/index.cfm

w054 Critical Appraisal Skills Programme (CASP): http://www.sph.nhs.uk/what-we-do/pub-lic-health-workforce/resources/critical-appraisals-skills-programme

w055 Critical Appraisal Skills Programme (CASP) Cohort study checklistCritical Appraisal Skills Programme (2004). Twelve questions to help you make sense of cohort studies. http://www.sph.nhs.uk/sph-files/cohort%2012%20questions.pdf

w056 Critical Appraisal Skills Programme (CASP) Qualitative checklist Critical Appraisal Skills Programme (2006). Ten questions to help you make sense of qualitative research. http://www.sph.nhs.uk/sph-files/Qualitative%20Appraisal%20Tool.pdf

w057 Crombie and Davies (2009) Crombie, I.K., and Davies, H.T.O. (2009) What is meta-analysis? 2nd edn. London: Hayward Medical Communications. http://www.whatisseries.co.uk/whatis/pdfs/What_is_meta_analy.pdf

w058 Cruzes and Dybå (2010) Cruzes, D.S. and Dybå, T. (2010) Synthesizing Evidence in software engineering research. ESEM 10, Proceedings of the 2010 ACM-IEEE International Symposium on Empirical Software Engineering and Measurement. Association for Computing Machinery New York, NY, USA. http://www.idi.ntnu.no/grupper/su/publ/daniela/esem2010_69_cruzes_dyba.pdf

w059 Current Controlled Trials. http://www.controlled-trials.com/

w060 Damschroder et al. (2009) Damschroder, L.J., Aron, D.C., Keith, R.E., Kirsh, S.R., Alexander, J.A., and Lowery, J.C. (2009) Fostering implementation of health services research findings into practice: a consolidated framework for advancing implementation science. *Implementation Science*, 4, 50. http://www.implementationscience.com/content/4/1/50

w061 Davies et al. (2010) Davies, P., Walker, A.E., and Grimshaw, J.M. (2010) A systematic review of the use of theory in the design of guideline dissemination and implementation strategies and interpretation of the results of rigorous evaluations. *Implementation Science*, 5, 14. http://www.implementationscience.com/content/5/1/14

w062 Dixon Woods et al. (2004) Dixon-Woods, M., Agarwal, S., Young, B., Jones, D., and Sutton, A. (2004) Integrative approaches to qualitative and quantitative evidence, London: Health Development Agency. http://www.nice.org.uk/niceMedia/pdf/Integrative_approaches_evidence.pdf

w063 Dixon Woods et al. (2006) Dixon-Woods, M., Cavers, D., Agarwal, S., Annandale, E., Arthur, A., Harvey, J., Hsu, R., Katbamna, S., Olsen, R., Smith, L., Riley, R., and Sutton, A.J. 2006. Conducting a critical interpretive synthesis of the literature on access to healthcare by vulnerable groups. *BMC Medical.Research Methodology*, 6, 35. http://www.biomedcentral.com/1471-2288/6/35

w064 Duggan and Banwell (2004) Duggan, F. and Banwell, L. (2004) Constructing a model of effective information dissemination in a crisis. *Information Research* 9, 3. http://informationr.net/ir/9-3/paper178.html

w065 Dumelow et al. (2000) Dumelow, C., Littlejohns, P., and Griffiths, S. (2000) Relation between a career and family life for English hospital consultants: qualitative, semi structured interview study. *BMJ*, 320, 7247, 1437–40. http://www.bmj.com/content/320/7247/1437.full.pdf

w066 Durham University Durham University (2009) Template for a Systematic Literature Review Protocol. http://www.dur.ac.uk/ebse/resources/templates/SLRTemplate.pdf

w067 Economics Research/working papers http://research.stlouisfed.org/wp/

w068 Education research: Higher Education Academy http://www.heacademy.ac.uk/

w069 Educational Research Funders' Forum (2005) Educational Research Funders' Forum (2005) Systematic literature reviews in education: advice and information for funders. Nerf Working Paper number 2.1 (January). http://www.eep.ac.uk/nerf/word/WP2.1Systematicreviewse42d.doc?version=1

w070 Edwards et al. (2002) Edwards, P., Roberts, I., Clarke, M., DiGuiseppe, C., Pratap, S., Wentz, R., and Kwan, I. (2002) Increasing response rates to postal questionnaires: systematic review. *British Medical Journal*, 324, 7347, 1183-1192. http://www.bmj.com/content/324/7347/1183.full

w071 Endnote. http://www.Endnote.com

w072 EPPI Centre. http://eppi.ioe.ac.uk

w073 EPPI Centre Keywording Sheet EPPI Centre. Eppi-Centre Educational Keywording Sheet. EPPI Centre (2003). http://eppi.ioe.ac.uk/EPPIWebContent/downloads/EPPI_keyword_sheet_0.9.7.pdf

w074 EPPI Centre. Mapping and refining the review's scope EPPI Centre (2009) Mapping and refining the review's scope. Social Science Research Unit, Institute of Education. http://eppi.ioe.ac.uk/cms/Default.aspx?tabid=175

w075 EPPI Centre. Quality and relevance assessment. http://eppi.ioe.ac.uk/cms/Default.aspx?tabid=177

w076 EPPI-Centre Searching for studies The EPPI-Centre (2010) Searching for Studies. http://eppi.ioe.ac.uk/cms/Default.aspx?tabid=172

w077 EPPI-Centre Team EPPI-Centre team (2003) A systematic map and synthesis review of the effectiveness of personal development planning for improving student learning. EPPI-Centre. http://eppi.ioe.ac.uk/EPPIWebContent/reel/review_groups/EPPI/LTSN/LTSN_June03.pdf

w078 EQUATOR Network. http://www.equator-network.org/home/

w079 ERIC database. http://www.eric.ed.gov/

w080 Evaluation Support Scotland (2009) Evaluation Support Scotland (2009) ESS Support Guide 1.2 – Developing a logic model. http://www.evaluationsupportscotland.org.uk/downloads/Supportguide1.2logicmodelsJul09.pdf

w081 Evidence Based Library and Information Practice (EBLIP) Evidence Based Library and Information Practice (EBLIP). http://ejournals.library.ualberta.ca/index.php/EBLIP

w082 Frank et al. (2006) Frank, E., Carrera, J.S., Stratton, T., Bickel, J., and Nora, L.M. (2006). Experiences of belittlement and harassment and their correlates among medical students in the United States: longitudinal survey. BMJ 333, 682-4. http://www.bmj.com/cgi/content/full/333/7570/682

w083 FreeMind. http://freemind.sourceforge.net/wiki/index.php/Main_Page

w084 Freeplane. http://freeplane.sourceforge.net/wiki/index.php/Main_Page

w085 French et al. (2005) French, S.D., McDonald, S., McKenzie, J.E., and Green, S.E. (2005) Investing in updating: how do conclusions change when Cochrane systematic reviews are updated? *BMC Medical Research Methodology*, 5, 33. http://www.biomedcentral.com/1471-2288/5/33

w086 Ganann et al. (2010) Ganann, R., Ciliska, D., and Thomas, H. (2010) Expediting systematic reviews: methods and implications of rapid reviews. *Implementation Science*, 5, 56. http://www.implementationscience.com/content/5/1/56

w087 GanttProject. http://www.ganttproject.biz/

w088 Glynn (2006) Glynn, L. (2006) A critical appraisal tool for library and information research. *Library Hi Tech*, 24, 3, 387–99. http://www.newcastle.edu.au/service/library/gosford/ebl/toolkit/docs/EBL%20Critical%20Appraisal%20Checklist.pdf

w089 Godin et al. (2008) Godin, G., Bélanger-Gravel, A., Eccles, M., and Grimshaw, J. (2008) Healthcare professionals' intentions and behaviours: a systematic review of studies based on social cognitive theories. *Implementation Science*, 3, 36. http://www.implementationscience.com/content/3/1/36

w090 Goerlich Zief et al. (2006) Goerlich Zief, S. et al. (2006) Impacts of after-school programs on student outcomes. http://www.campbellcollaboration.org/lib/download/58/

w091 Google. http://www.google.co.uk/

w092 Google Scholar. http://scholar.google.co.uk/

w093 GoPubMed. http://www.gopubmed.com/

w094 Graham-Matheson et al. (2005) Graham-Matheson, L., Connolly, T., Robson, S., and Stow, W. (2006) A systematic map into approaches to making initial teacher training flexible and responsive to the needs of trainee teachers. Technical report. In: *Research Evidence in Education Library*. London: EPPI-Centre, Social Science Research Unit, Institute of Education, University of London. http://eppi.ioe.ac.uk/cms/Default. aspx?tabid=780

w095 Grant and Booth (2009) Grant, M.J. and Booth, A. (2009) A typology of reviews: an analysis of 14 review types and associated methodologies. *Health Information and Libraries Journal*, 26, 2, 91–108 http://onlinelibrary.wiley.com/doi/10.1111/j.1471-1842.2009.00848.x/full

w096 Grayson and Gomersall (2003) Grayson, L. and Gomersall, A. (2003) A difficult business: finding the evidence for social science reviews. (Working Paper 19), Economic and Social Research Council, UK Centre for Evidence Based Policy and Practice, London. http://www.kcl.ac.uk/content/1/c6/03/46/17/wp19.pdf

w097 Greenhalgh and Peacock (2005) Greenhalgh, T. and Peacock, R. (2005) Effectiveness and efficiency of search methods in systematic reviews of complex evidence: audit of primary sources. *BM J*, 331, 1064–1065 http://www.bmj.com/content/331/7524/1064.full

w098 Greenhalgh et al. (2007) Greenhalgh, T., Kristjansson, E., and Robinson, V. (2007) Realist review to understand the efficacy of school feeding programmes. *BMJ*, 335, 7625, 858–61. http://www.bmj.com/content/335/7625/858.full

w099 GreySource http://www.greynet.org/greysourceindex.html

w100 Grimshaw et al. (2004) Grimshaw, J.M., Thomas, R.E., MacLennan, G., Fraser, C., Ramsay, C.R., Vale, L., Whitty, P., Eccles, M.P., Matowe, L., Shirran, L., Wensing, M., Dijkstra, R., and Donaldson, C. (2004) Effectiveness and efficiency of guideline dissemination and implementation strategies. *Health Technology Assessment*, 8, 6, 1 72. http://www.hta.ac.uk/fullmono/mon806.pdf

w101 Groves et al. (2006) Groves, S., Mousely, J., and Forgasz, H. (2006) Primary numeracy: a mapping, review and analysis of Australian research in numeracy learning at the primary school level. Centre for Studies in Mathematics, Science and Environmental Education, Deakin University. Commonwealth of Australia. http://www.dest.gov.au/sectors/school_education/publications_resources/profiles/documents/primary_numeracy_pdf.htm

w102 Hammersley (2002) Hammersley, M. (2002) Systematic or unsystematic, is that the question? Some reflections on the science, art, and politics of reviewing research evidence. Text of a talk given to the Public Health Evidence Steering Group of the Health Development Agency, October, 2002. http://www.nice.org.uk/niceMedia/pdf/sys_unsys_phesg_hammersley.pdf

w103 Harden et al. (2006) Harden, A., Brunton, G., Fletcher, A., and Oakley, A. (2006) Young people, pregnancy and social exclusion: a systematic synthesis of research evidence to identify effective, appropriate and promising approaches for prevention and support. London: EPPI-Centre, Social Science Research Unit, Institute of Education, University of London. http://eprints.ioe.ac.uk/5927/

w104 Health and Safety Executive (2010) Health and Safety Executive. Advice on producing HSE research reports 03/10. http://www.hse.gov.uk/research/producing-reports-advice.pdf

w105 Hind and Booth (2007) Hind, D. and Booth, A. (2007) Do health technology assess-
ments comply with QUOROM diagram guidance? An empirical study. *BMC Medical
Research Methodology*, 7, 49. http://www.ncbi.nlm.nih.gov/pmc/articles/
PMC2211304/

w106 Home Office (2008) RDS Research Reports. Guidance for authors on the reader-
friendly 1:3:25 format (revised December 2008). http://rds.homeoffice.gov.uk/rds/
pdfs08/authorguide-1325-dec08.pdf

w107 Hopewell et al. (2009) Hopewell, S., Loudon, K., Clarke, M.J., Oxman, A.D., and
Dickersin, K. (2009) Publication bias in clinical trials due to statistical significance or
direction of trial results. Cochrane Database of Systematic Reviews. http://onlineli-
brary.wiley.com/o/cochrane/clsysrev/articles/MR000006/frame.html

w108 Index to Theses. http://www.theses.com/

w109 Inglis et al. (2010) Inglis, S.C. et al. Structured telephone support or telemonitoring
programmes for patients with chronic heart failure. Cochrane Database of Systematic
Reviews 2010, Issue 8. Art. No.: CD007228. DOI: 10.1002/14651858.CD007228.
pub2. http://onlinelibrary.wiley.com/o/cochrane/clsysrev/articles/CD007228/
frame.html

w110 InterTASC Information Specialists' Sub-Group (ISSG) The InterTASC Information Specialists'
Sub-Group Search Filter Resource. http://www.york.ac.uk/inst/crd/intertasc/

w111 Jackson (2008) Jackson, S. (2008) Systematic review protocol: a systematic review of
sensemaking and disconnect between intent and action (organisational behavioural)
and the relationship between the two in the context of embedding sustainability
activities in organisations. http://www.networkedcranfield.com/cell/Assigment%20
Submissions/Final%20Scoping%20Study%20Submissions/Systematic%20
Review%20Protocol%20%20v1%20SJ%20310708.doc

w112 James Lind Library. http://www.jameslindlibrary.org

w113 Jones (2001) Jones, K. (2001) Mission drift in qualitative research, or moving toward
a systematic review of qualitative studies, moving back to a more systematic narrative
review. *The Qualitative Report*, 9, 1, 95–112. http://www.nova.edu/ssss/QR/QR9-1/
jones.pdf

w114 Joseph Rowntree Foundation http://www.jrf.org.uk/

w115 Kane et al. (2010) Kane, S.S., Gerretsen, B., Scherpbier, R., Dal Poz, M., and Dieleman,
M. (2010) A realist synthesis of randomised control trials involving use of community
health workers for delivering child health interventions in low and middle income countries. *BMC Health Services Research*, 10, 286. http://www.biomedcentral.com/1472-
6963/10/286

w116 Katrak et al. (2004) Katrak, P., Bialocerkowski, A.E., Massy-Westropp, N., Kumar,
V.S.S., and Grimmer, K. (2004) A systematic review of the content of critical appraisal
tools. *BMC Medical Research Methodology*. 4, 22. http://www.biomedcentral.
com/1471-2288/4/22

w117 Kavanagh et al. (2005) Kavanagh, J., Trouton, A., Oakley, A., and Harden, A. (2005) A
scoping review of the evidence for incentive schemes to encourage positive health and
other social behaviours in young people. London: EPPI-Centre, Social Science
Research Unit, Institute of Education, University of London. http://eppi.ioe.ac.uk/cms/
Default.aspx?tabid=248

w118 Kitchenham et al. (2002) Kitchenham, B.A., Pfleeger, S.L., Pickard, L.M., Jones, P.W.,
Hoaglin, D.C., El Emam, K., and Rosenberg, J. (2002) Preliminary guidelines for

empirical research in software engineering. *IEE Transactions on Software Engineering*, 28, 8, 721–34. http://www.computer.org/portal/web/csdl/transactions/tse;jsessioni d=95acbeb01558dffc26c5a752f0a4#4

w119 Kitchenham (2007) Kitchenham, B. (2007) Guidelines for performing systematic literature reviews in software engineering, (Version 2.3). EBSE Technical Report: EBSE-2007-01. Software Engineering Group, School of Computer Science and Mathematics, Keele University, Staffordshire. http://www.elsevier.com/framework_products/promis_misc/infsof-systematic%20reviews.pdf

w120 Kitchenham et al. (2009) Kitchenham, B., Mendes, E., and Travassos, G. (2009) Protocol for systematic review of within- and cross-company estimation models. University of Durham. http://www.dur.ac.uk/ebse/resources/studies/protocol/BetweenandWithinCompanyEstimationProtocolv14.pdf

w121 Kmet et al. (2004) Kmet, L.M., Lee, R.C. and Cook, L.S. (2004) Standard quality assessment criteria for evaluating primary research papers from a variety of fields. http://www.ihe.ca/documents/HTA-FR13.pdf

w122 Koufogiannakis and Wiebe (2006). Koufogiannakis, D. and Wiebe, N. (2006) Effective methods for teaching information literacy skills to undergraduate students: a systematic review and meta–analysis. *Evidence based Library and Information Practice*, 1, 3, 3–43. http://ejournals.library.ualberta.ca/index.php/EBLIP/article/view/76/153.

w123 Koufogiannakis et al. (2006) Koufogiannakis, D., Booth, A., and Brettle, A. (2006) ReLIANT: Reader's guide to the literature on interventions addressing the need for education and training. E-prints in Library and Information Science. http://eprints.rclis.org/7163/1/RELIANT__final_.pdf

w124 Levy and Ellis (2006) Levy, Y. and Ellis, T.J. (2006) A systems approach to conduct an effective literature review in support of information systems research. *Informing Science Journal*, 9, 181–212. http://www.scs.ryerson.ca/aferworn/courses/CP8101/CLASSES/ConductingLiteratureReview.pdf

w125 Library, Information Science and Technology Abstracts (LISTA). http://www.libraryresearch.com

w126 Lucas et al. (2007) Lucas, P.J., Baird, J., Arai, L., Law, C., and Roberts, H.M. (2007) Worked examples of alternative methods for the synthesis of qualitative and quantitative research in systematic reviews. *BMC Medical Research Methodology*, 7, 4. http://www.biomedcentral.com/1471-2288/7/4

w127 Lundh and Gotzsche (2008) Lundh, A. and Gotzsche, P.C. (2008) Recommendations by Cochrane Review groups for assessment of the risk of bias in studies. *BMC Medical Research Methodology*, 8, 22. http://www.biomedcentral.com/1471-2288/8/22/

w128 Macauley (2001) Macauley, P. *The Literature Review*. Geelong, Victoria, Australia: Deakin University. http://www.deakin.edu.au/library/findout/research/litrev.php .

w129 Mays et al. (2005) Mays, N., Pope, C., and Popay, J. (2005) Details of approaches to synthesis – a methodological appendix to the paper: systematically reviewing qualitative and quantitative evidence to inform management and policy making in the health field. Report for the National Co-ordinating Centre for NHS Service Delivery and Organisation R&D (NCCSDO), London School of Hygiene and Tropical Medicine. http://www.chsrf.ca/funding_opportunities/commissioned_research/projects/pdf/msynth_appendix_e.pdf

w130 McMaster Hedges Project. http://hiru.mcmaster.ca/hiru/HIRU_Hedges_home.aspx

w131 MEDLINE via PubMed. http://www.ncbi.nlm.nih.gov/pubmed/

w132 Mental health research – Sainsbury Centre for Mental Health. http://www.scmh.org.uk/

w133 Mendeley: https://www.mendeley.com/

w134 Microsoft Excel Microsoft. Create a Gantt chart in Excel. http://office.microsoft.com/en-us/excel-help/create-a-gantt-chart-in-excel HA001034605.aspx

w135 Microsoft Project Microsoft. http://emea.microsoftstore.com/UK/en-GB/Microsoft/Project-Standard-2010

w136 Moher et al. (2007) Moher, D., Tetzlaff, J., Tricco, A.C., Sampson, M., and Altman, D.G. (2007) Epidemiology and reporting characteristics of systematic reviews. *PLoS Medicine*, 4, 3, e78. http://www.plosmedicine.org/article/info:doi/10.1371/journal.pmed.0040078

w137 Moher et al. (2009) Moher, D., Liberati, A., Tetzlaff, J., Altman, D.G., and PRISMA Group (2009) Preferred reporting items for systematic reviews and meta-analyses: the PRISMA statement. *PLoS Medicine*, 6, 7, e1000097. http://www.plosmedicine.org/article/info:doi/10.1371/journal.pmed.1000097

w138 Moynihan (2004) Moynihan, R. (2004) *Evaluating Health Services: A Reporter Covers the Science of Research Synthesis*. New York: Milbank Memorial Fund. http://www.milbank.org/reports/2004Moynihan/040330Moynihan.html

w139 MScanner. http://mscanner.stanford.edu/

w140 Munro et al. (2007) Munro, S., Lewin, S., Swart, T., and Volmink, J. (2007) A review of health behaviour theories: how useful are these for developing interventions to promote long-term medication adherence for TB and HIV/AIDS? *BMC Public Health*, 11, 7, 104. http://www.biomedcentral.com/1471-2458/7/104

w141 National Centre for Text Mining (2010) The National Centre for Text Mining (2010) Automatic summarisation for systematic reviews using text mining (ASSERT). http://www.nactem.ac.uk/assert/

w142 National Collaborating Centre for Methods and Tools National Collaborating Centre for Methods and Tools (NCCMT) (2008) Compendium of critical appraisal tools for public health practice. McMaster University, Hamilton, Ontario – Public Health Agency of Canada. http://www.who.int/pmnch/topics/20090831_nccmt/en/index.html

w143 National Institute for Health and Clinical Excellence (NICE) http://www.nice.org.uk/

w144 Nutley et al. (2002) Nutley, S., Davies, H. and Walter, I. (2002) ESRC UK Centre for Evidence Based Policy and Practice: Working Paper 9. Evidence based policy and practice: cross sector lessons from the UK. Research Unit for Research Utilisation. Department of Management, University of St Andrews. August 2002: ESRC UK Centre for Evidence Based Policy and Practice; Research Unit for Research Utilisation. http://kcl.ac.uk/content/1/c6/03/46/00/wp9b.pdf

w145 Ogilvie et al. (2008) Ogilvie, D., Fayter, D., Petticrew, M., Sowden, A., Thomas, S., Whitehead, M., and Worthy, G. (2008) The harvest plot: a method for synthesising evidence about the differential effects of interventions. *BMC Medical Research Methodology*, 8, 8. http://www.biomedcentral.com/1471-2288/8/8

w146 Open University (nd) The Open University (n.d.) Searching the literature. http://www.open.ac.uk/infoskills-researchers/literature-introduction.htm

w147 OpenOffice. http://www.openoffice.org/

w148 Oxman et al. (2006) Oxman, A.D., Schünemann, H.J. and Fretheim, A. (2006) Improving the use of research evidence in guideline development, 8. Synthesis and presentation of evidence. *Health Research Policy Systems*, 4, 20. http://www.health-policy-systems.com/content/4/1/20

w149 Parkes et al. (2001) Parkes, J., Hyde, C., Deeks, J., and Milne, R. (2001) Teaching critical appraisal skills in healthcare settings. Cochrane Database of Systematic Reviews, Issue 3 (Art. No.: CD001270. DOI: 10.1002/14651858.CD001270). http://onlinelibrary.wiley.com/o/cochrane/clsysrev/articles/CD001270/frame.html.

w150 Pawson (2001) Pawson, R. (2001), Evidence based policy II. The promise of 'realist synthesis', ESRC UK Centre for Evidence Based Policy and Practice, Queen Mary, University of London, London. http://www.kcl.ac.uk/content/1/c6/03/45/91/wp4.pdf

w151 Pawson et al. (2004) Pawson, R., Greenhalgh, T., Harvey, G., and Walshe, K. (2004) Realist Synthesis: An Introduction. Manchester: ESRC Research Methods Programme. http://www.ccsr.ac.uk/methods/publications/RMPmethods2.pdf

w152 Piehl et al. (2002) Piehl, J.H., Green, S., and Silagy, C. (2002) Training practitioners in preparing systematic reviews: a cross-sectional survey of participants in the Australasian Cochrane Centre training program. BMC Health Services Research, 2, 1, 11. http://www.biomedcentral.com/1472-6963/2/11

w153 Piehl et al. (2003) Piehl, J.H., Green, S., and McDonald, S. (2003) Converting systematic reviews to Cochrane format: a cross-sectional survey of Australian authors of systematic reviews. BMC Health Services Research, 3, 1, 2. http://www.biomedcentral.com/1472-6963/3/2

w154 Pirzadeh (2010) Pirzadeh, L. (2010) Human factors in software development: a systematic literature review. Master's thesis, Chalmers University of Technology, Department of Computer Science and Engineering, Gothenberg, Sweden. http://publications.lib.chalmers.se/records/fulltext/126748.

w155 The PLoS Editors (2007) The PLoS Medicine Editors (2007) Many reviews are systematic but some are more transparent and completely reported than others. PLoS Medicine 4, 3, e147. http://www.plosmedicine.org/article/info:doi/10.1371/journal.pmed.0040147

w156 Popay et al. (2006) Popay, J., Roberts, H., Sowden, A., Petticrew, M., Arai, L., Rodgers, M., and Britten, N. with Roen, K. and Duffy, S. (2006) Guidance on the conduct of narrative synthesis in systematic reviews: a product from the ESRC Methods Programme. Version 1. http://www.lancs.ac.uk/shm/research/nssr/research/dissemination/publications/NS_Synthesis_Guidance_v1.pdf

w157 Prabhakar (2009) Prabhakar, G. (2009) Projects and their management: A literature review. International Journal of Business and Management, 3, 8, 3 http://www.ccsenet.org/journal/index.php/ijbm/article/view/1290/1253

w158 PRISMA Statement. http://www.prisma-statement.org/

w159 PubMed ReMiner. http://hgserver2.amc.nl/cgi-bin/miner/miner2.cgi

w160 Randolph (2009) Randolph, J. (2009) A guide to writing the dissertation literature review. Practical Assessment, Research and Evaluation, 14, 13. http://pareonline.net/getvn.asp?v=14&n=13.

w161 Reference Manager. www.refman.com

w162 RefWorks. http://www.refworks.com/

w163 Ring et al. (2010) Ring, N., Ritchie, K., Mandava, L., and Jepson R. (2010) A guide to synthesising qualitative research for researchers undertaking health technology assessments and systematic reviews. http://www.nhshealthquality.org/nhsqis/8837.html

w164 Rousseau et al. (2008) Rousseau, D.M., Manning, J. and Denyer, D. (2008) Evidence in management and organizational science: assembling the field's full weight of scientific knowledge through syntheses. *Academy of Management Annals*, 2, 475–515. http://www.tepper.cmu.edu/facultyAdmin/upload/url4_1378611195310_Evidence_2_15_08.pdf

w165 Rowley and Slack (2004) Rowley, J. and Slack, F. (2004) Conducting a literature review. *Management Research News*, 27, 4, 31–9. http://mikehart-papers.co.uk/tutorials/lit_rev/litrev.doc

w166 Ryan et al. (2009) Ryan, R.E., Kaufman, C.A., and Hill, S.J. (2009) Building blocks for meta-synthesis: data integration tables for summarising, mapping, and synthesising evidence on interventions for communicating with health consumers. *BMC Medical Research Methodology*, 9, 16. http://www.biomedcentral.com/1471-2288/9/16

w167 Saunders (2009) Saunders, L. (2009) The policy and organisational context for commissioned research. British Educational Research Association. London: TLRP. 29-11-2010. http://www.bera.ac.uk/commissioning-and-consuming-research-in-education/

w168 SciPlore MindMapping. http://www.sciplore.org/software/sciplore_mindmapping/

w169 Scirus. http://www.scirus.com/

w170 Scopus. http://www.scopus.com/home.url

w171 Scottish Intercollegiate Guidelines Network (SIGN) Search Filters. http://www.sign.ac.uk/methodology/filters.html

w172 SIGLE. http://opensigle.inist.fr/

w173 Social care online. http://www.scie-socialcareonline.org.uk/

w174 Social sciences – European Research Papers. http://eiop.or.at/erpa/

w175 Software Engineering Group Software Engineering Group, School of Computer Science and Mathematics, Keele University and Department of Computer Science, University of Durham (2007) Guidelines for performing systematic literature reviews in software engineering. http://www.elsevier.com/framework_products/promis_misc/infsof-systematic%20reviews.pdf

w176 Song et al. (2010) Song, F., Parekh, S., Hooper, L., Loke, Y.K., Ryder, J., Sutton, A.J., Hing, C., Kwok, C.S., Pang, C., and Harvey, I. (2010) Dissemination and publication of research findings: an updated review of related biases. *Health Technology Assessment*, 14, 8, 1–193. http://www.hta.ac.uk/fullmono/mon1408.pdf

w177 SOSIG. http://www.intute.ac.uk/socialsciences/

w178 STARD Statement. http://www.stard-statement.org/

w179 STARLITE Statement Booth, A. (2006) 'Brimful of STARLITE': toward standards for reporting literature searches. *Journal of the Medical Library Association*, 94, 4, 421–9. http://www.ncbi.nlm.nih.gov/pmc/articles/PMC1629442/

w180 STREGA. http://www.medicine.uottawa.ca/public-health-genomics/web/eng/strega.html

w181 STROBE Statement STROBE Group. STROBE Statement.2010. http://www.strobe-statement.org/

w182 Student BMJ. http://student.bmj.com/

w183 Student BMJ (2000) *Student BMJ* (2000) 8, 236–40. http://archive.student.bmj.com/search/pdf/00/07/ppr.pdf

w184 Student BMJ (2006) *Student BMJ* (2006), 14, 353–96. http://archive.student.bmj.com/issues/06/10/papers/372.php

w185 Student BMJ (2007) *Student BMJ* (2007) 15, 337–82. http://archive.student.bmj.com/issues/07/10/papers/377.php

w186 Suri(1999) Suri, H. (1999) The process of synthesising qualitative research: a case study. Annual Conference of the Association for Qualitative Research, Melbourne, http://www.latrobe.edu.au/aqr/offer/papers/HSuri.htm

w187 Sweet and Moynihan (2007) Sweet M. and Moynihan, R. (2007) Improving population health: the uses of systematic reviews. New York (NY): Milbank Memorial Fund. http://www.milbank.org/reports/0712populationhealth/0712populationhealth.html

w188 TERSE reports: TERSE reports at the Centre for Evaluation and Monitoring http://midyis.cem.dur.ac.uk/RenderPagePrint.asp?LinkID=30325002http://www.cemcentre.org/

w189 Thomas et al. (2003) Thomas, J., Sutcliffe, K., Harden, A., Oakley, A., Oliver, S., Rees, R., Brunton, G., and Kavanagh, J. (2003) Children and healthy eating: a systematic review of barriers and facilitators. London: EPPI-Centre, Social Science Research Unit, Institute of Education, University of London. http://eppi.ioe.ac.uk/cms/Default.aspx?tabid=246

w190 Thomas and Harden (2007) Thomas, J. and Harden, A. (2007) Methods for the thematic synthesis of qualitative research in systematic reviews. ESRC National Centre for Research Methods NCRM Working Paper Series Number (10/07). Methods for Research Synthesis Node, Evidence for Policy and Practice Information and Co-ordinating (EPPI-Centre, Social Science Research Unit), London. http://eppi.ioe.ac.uk/cms/Default.aspx?tabid=188

w191 Thomas and Harden (2008) Thomas, J. and Harden, A. (2008) Methods for the thematic synthesis of qualitative research in systematic reviews. *BMC Medical Research Methodology*, 8, 45. http://www.biomedcentral.com/1471-2288/8/45

w192 Thomas et al. (2007) Thomas, J., Kavanagh, J., Tucker, H., Burchett, H., Tripney, J., and Oakley, A. (2007) Accidental injury, risk-taking behaviour and the social circumstances in which young people live: a systematic review. London: EPPI-Centre, Social Science Research Unit, Institute of Education, University of London. http://eprints.ioe.ac.uk/5259/

w193 Touro College Libraries. http://www.touro.edu/library/grayLit/

w194 Turner and Muller (2005) Turner, J.R. and Müller, R. (2005) The project manager's leadership style as a success factor on projects: a literature review. *Project Management Journal*, 2, 36, 49–61. http://www.kth.se/polopoly_fs/1.57061!Turner_M%C3%BCller_2005.pdf

w195 UK Clinical Research (UKCRN) Study Portfolio http://public.ukcrn.org.uk/search/

w196 Umoquit et al. (2011) Umoquit, M.J., Tso, P., Burchett, H.E., and Dobrow, M.J. (2011) A multidisciplinary systematic review of the use of diagrams as a means of collecting data from research subjects: application, benefits and recommendations. *BMC Medical Research Methodology*, 11, 1, 11. http://www.biomedcentral.com/1471-2288/11/11

w197 University of Strathclyde. Module 8: Research Synthesis in Education. http://www.strath.ac.uk/aer/materials/8systematicreview/

w198 Urquhart (2010) Urquhart, C. (2010) Systematic reviewing, meta-analysis and meta-synthesis for evidence-based library and information science. *Information Research* 15, 3, colis708. http://InformationR.net/ir/15-3/colis7/colis708.html

w199 Volmink et al. (2004) Volmink, J., Siegfried, N., Robertson, K., and Gülmezoglu, A. (2004) Research synthesis and dissemination as a bridge to knowledge management: the Cochrane Collaboration. *Bulletin of the World Health Organisation*, 82, 10, 778–783. http://www.scielosp.org/scielo.php?script=sci_arttext&pid=S0042968620040010000 14&lng=en.

w200 Web of Knowledge. http://www.isiknowledge.com/

w201 Weed (2005) Weed, M. (2005) Meta interpretation: a method for the interpretive synthesis of qualitative research. Forum Qualitative Sozialforschung/Forum: Qualitative

Social Research, 6, 1, Art. 37. http://www.qualitative-research.net/index.php/fqs/article/viewArticle/508/1096.

w202 What Works Clearing House (2005) What Works Clearing House US Department for Education. Evidence Standards for Reviewing Studies (2005). http://ies.ed.gov/ncee/wwc/references/iDocViewer/Doc.aspx?docId=20&tocId=1

w203 Williams et al. (2001) Williams, D., Wavell, C., and Coles, L. (2001) Impact of school library services on achievement and learning. Department for Education and Skills and Resource: The Council for Museums, Archives and Libraries. http://rgu.biz/files/Impact of School Library Services1.pdf See appendix p82–84.

w204 Wilson et al. (2010) Wilson, P.M., Petticrew, M., Calnan, M.W., and Nazareth, I. (2010). Disseminating research findings: what should researchers do? A systematic scoping review of conceptual frameworks. *Implementation Science*, 5, 91. http://www.implementationscience.com/content/5/1/91

w205 Winokur et al. (2009) Winokur, M. et al. (2009) Kinship care for the safety, permanency, and well-Being of children removed from the home for maltreatment. http://www2.cochrane.org/reviews/en/ab006546.html

w206 Xmind. http://www.xmind.net/

Glossary

adjacency (Chapter 5) – a term relating to the searching of electronic databases. When using adjacency in a search, you are specifying that words should be searched together in a phrase (e.g. 'heart attack', 'housing market') to yield a smaller and more precise set of results.

aggregative (Chapters 2, 7, 8) – adjective relating to a type of review that is concerned with assembling and pooling data (either quantitative as with meta-analysis or qualitative as with thematic synthesis). To achieve such aggregation requires that there is basic comparability between phenomena.

analytic/analytical (Chapter 6) – the facility to use analysis to discern patterns, trends, or themes to data or the properties of tools that assist in such analysis.

AND (Chapter 5) – a Boolean operator (qv), that is syntax entered into a search engine or database, that specifically requires two or more concepts to be present in an item (e.g. an abstract) for it to be retrieved (e.g. eat AND drink).

applicability (Chapters 6, 8) – the application of the results from individual studies or from a review of studies of a study population to individual people, cases or settings in a target population.

attrition (Chapter 6) – the loss of participants during the conduct of a study.

attrition bias (Chapter 6) – a type of selection bias caused by attrition (loss of participants).

author searching (Chapter 5) – a term relating to the searching of electronic databases or internet sources for one or more authors known to be working in a review topic area.

Bayesian meta-analysis (Chapter 7) – a specific type of meta-analysis whereby statisticians express their belief about the size of an effect by specifying some prior (up front) probability distribution before seeing the data. Once they have completed the meta-analysis, they update that belief by deriving a posterior (after the fact) probability distribution, taking the data into account. Some commentators suggest that qualitative research may be used to inform the prior belief e.g. parents' attitudes to vaccination.

bias (Chapters 4, 5, 6) – systematic error in individual studies or in a review that can lead to erroneous conclusions about an intervention, programme, or policy.

bibliographic databases (Chapter 4) – a database of bibliographic records typically containing references to the published journal literature (although its scope may also include newspaper articles, conference proceedings and papers, reports, government and legal publications, patents, books, etc.).

blind (Chapter 6) – When a study design is referred to as blind, this means the treatment a person has received or, in some cases, the outcome of their treatment is not known by individuals involved in the study. This is to avoid them being influenced by this knowledge. The person who is blinded could be either the person being treated, their caregiver or the researcher assessing the effect of the treatment (single blind), two of these people (double blind) or all three of these people (triple blind).

Boolean logic (Chapter 5) – a system of logical operators (most commonly AND, OR and NOT) used for specifying information to be retrieved from a computer (bibliographic) database.

Boolean operator (Chapter 5) – a term (most commonly AND, OR and NOT) used to specify the preferred relationship between two or more concepts to be retrieved from a computer (bibliographic) database. For example (eat AND drink; train OR bus; adult NOT child).

Campbell Collaboration (Chapter 1) – a non-profit organisation that applies a rigorous, systematic process to review the effects of interventions in the social, behavioural and educational arenas, in order to provide evidence-based information in the shape of systematic reviews.

changes clause (Chapter 4) – a term originally applied to the documentation of changes to provisions in government contracts but, in this context, used to refer to documented changes to a review plan or protocol.

checklist(s) (Chapter 4) – systematised list(s) of criteria used to assess the quality of a published research study in order to ensure that a standardised approach can be used in an attempt to minimise bias.

citation searching (Chapter 5) – a term relating to the searching of electronic databases or Internet sources for items that have cited, or been cited by, an article or study known to be relevant to a review topic. This specialised function is only available on a limited number of databases such as Web of Knowledge, CINAHL, and Google Scholar.

cite-while-you-write (Chapter 3) – the facility to use a reference management package alongside a word processing package so that a reviewer can place markers (numerical document identifiers) as they write their article and then automatically generate a bibliography upon its completion.

Cochrane Collaboration (Chapters 1, 2, 7, 8, 9, 10) – An international organisation of over 10,000 volunteers in more than 90 countries that aims to help people make well-informed decisions about health by preparing, maintaining, and ensuring the accessibility of systematic reviews of the benefits and risks of healthcare interventions.

Cochrane Library (Chapter 7) – a collection of databases in medicine and other healthcare specialties, including full-text systematic reviews provided by the Cochrane Collaboration and annotated bibliographic records supplied by other organisations.

Cochrane Review (Chapters 1, 4, 5, 7, 10) – a systematic summary of evidence of the effects of healthcare interventions intended to help people make practical decisions on focused health issues.

cohort study/ies (Chapter 4) – an observational study, commonly used in medicine and social science, in which a defined group of people (the cohort) is followed over time. The outcomes of people in subsets of this cohort are compared, to examine people who were exposed or not exposed (or exposed at different levels) to a particular intervention or other factor of interest.

concept analysis (Chapters 1, 4) – a type of analysis required to identify and determine the scope of a concept designated by a given term as it is used in the literature of a particular subject field.

concept map(s) (Chapters 4, 7) – a diagram showing the relationships among concepts. Concept maps are useful graphical tools for organising and representing the knowledge covered by a review.

concept mapping (Chapter 4) – the process of using a diagram or related graphical tool to represent the knowledge covered by a review.

conceptual map (Chapter 7) – see **concept map**

confidence value (Chapter 7) – a range of values considered to represent the likely range of values (i.e. the lowest and highest values) for a given population of effect sizes within a given margin of error (e.g. 95%)

conflict of interest statement (Chapter 9) – a written declaration, typically accompanying a systematic review or a primary research study, that documents where individuals involved with the conduct, reporting, oversight or review of research also have financial or other interests, from which they can benefit, depending on the results of the research/review.

confounding (Chapter 6) – the presence of one or more variables, in addition to the variable of interest, that makes it impossible to separate their unique effects leading to incomplete or incorrect conclusions.

confounding variable (Chapter 7) – an unforeseen, and unaccounted-for variable that poses a threat to the reliability and validity of an experiment's outcome.

constant comparative method/constant comparison (Chapter 7) – a research methodology that, when applied to reviews, requires the comparison of findings from an additional study with findings from previously reviewed studies in the quest for additional insights.

content analysis (Chapter 7) – the process of organising written, audio, or visual information into categories and themes related to the central questions of a study or review.

conversion ratio (Chapter 10) – a term originally from the domain of business which, in this context, relates to the number of references that need to be examined in order to identify one study for inclusion in a review.

controlled vocabulary (Chapter 5) – a carefully selected set of terms used in a bibliographic database, such that each concept is described using only one term in the set and each term in the set describes only one concept.

critical appraisal (Chapters 3, 6, 7, 8) – the use of explicit, transparent methods to assess the data in published research, by systematically considering such factors as validity, adherence to reporting standards, methods, conclusions and generalisability.

critical interpretive synthesis (Chapters 1,7, 9) – an approach to the synthesis of qualitative and quantitative data used in situations where theorisation of the evidence is required. Critical interpretive synthesis encourages a critique of literatures and the questioning of taken-for-granted assumptions about concepts and methods.

critical path (Chapter 3) – the path through a series of activities relating to a review, taking into account interdependencies, in which late completion of activities will impact on the review end date or delay a key milestone.

cross-sectional survey(s) (Chapter 6) – a specific research design that involves observation of some subset of a population at the same point in time, looking simply at occurrence without being able to establish causation.

database bias (Chapter 8) – a specific form of location bias (q.v.) that relates to the likelihood of a particular journal being indexed in a database and therefore to the likelihood of its constituent articles being identified through systematic literature searches. This may relate to language of publication or to location of publisher or other characteristics related to the database or the publishing industry.

data dredging (Chapter 8) – is the inappropriate (sometimes deliberate) use of processes such as data mining to uncover misleading relationships in data. These relationships may be valid within the test set but are not statistically significant within the wider population.

data extraction (Chapters 4, 6) – the process of retrieving and coding relevant variables from primary studies in order to facilitate comparison and the observation of patterns, themes, or trends.

data mining (Chapter 4) – data processing using sophisticated search capabilities and statistical algorithms in large pre-existing databases as a way to facilitate the discovery of patterns, themes or trends.

data synthesis (Chapters 4, 7) – the process of summarising the contents of original studies using textual, graphical, or tabular means.

descriptive (Chapters 3, 6) – summarising data according to its patterns or characteristics as opposed to analytical which examines relationships between data.

descriptive data synthesis (Chapter 7) – summarising studies descriptively (i.e. what the literature looks like) rather than analytically (what the literature tells us).

descriptive mapping (Chapter 4) – describing the scope of a topic according to the characteristics of its constituent literature.

disconfirming case (Chapter 2) – a case or example that that does not fit emergent patterns and allows the researcher to identify and evaluate alternative explanations.

duplicate citations (Chapter 3) – the result of literature searching across multiple databases whenever there is significant overlap in journal coverage.

electronic database(s) (Chapter 5) – databases, most typically bibliographic databases, that can be used to speed up the process of study identification.

empty reviews (Chapter 9) systematic reviews around clearly focused questions that have been unable to identify any studies that fulfil the requirements for both relevance and rigour and therefore contain no included studies.

evidence base (Chapters 6, 7) – information gathered by a reviewer that characterises what is known about a topic, typically from higher quality studies.

evidence-based health policy (Chapter 1) – the application of principles from evidence-based practice to the making of decisions at a population level regarding effective programmes and policies.

evidence-based practice (Chapter 1) – the integration of individual professional expertise with the best available external evidence from systematic research.

evidence synthesis (Chapter 7) – the process of summarising the contents of original research, typically of higher quality studies.

exclusion criteria (Chapter 6) – the standards or criteria used to specify the circumstances in which a person is disqualified from being included in a trial and, by extension, the standards used to determine whether an individual paper is disqualified from inclusion in a systematic review.

exhaustivity (Chapter 2) – the extent to which all possible sources are covered in the quest to identify relevant studies for a review.

explanatory variables (Chapter 7) – variables that may be used to explain the cause of a particular result or finding.

external validity (Chapters 6, 8) – the extent to which the effect of an intervention, programme, or policy being investigated in a study or review might be expected to occur in other participants or settings.

fixed effects analysis (Chapter 7) – an analysis using a statistical model that treats all measurements as if those quantities were non-random. A fixed effects analysis is therefore more likely to underestimate the effect of variation and, correspondingly, to overestimate the effect of an intervention, programme or policy.

Forest plot (or blobbogram) (Chapters 7, 9, 10) – a graphical display designed to illustrate the relative strength of effects in multiple studies addressing, and quantifying the effects for, the same question.

formative (Chapters 7, 8) – an adjective describing those aspects of a review that appear throughout its conduct and may thus inform its ultimate form and content.

framework analysis (Chapter 7) – the process of analysing primary data using an existing framework or model as an organising structure to facilitate the analysis.

framework synthesis (Chapter 7) – a process of synthesis that is analogous to the use of framework analysis but in this case used to analyse data from multiple studies within a review.

free-text (Chapter 5) – a retrieval term referring to when a search engine examines all of the words in every stored document in an attempt to match search words supplied by the user, not just terms pre-specified as entry terms by an indexer.

funnel plot (Chapters 3, 8) – a graphical device for exploring the likelihood of publication bias by plotting a measure of study size against a measure of effect size and thereby seeking to identify any likelihood of missing populations of studies.

Gantt chart (Chapter 4) – a project management tool that seeks to convey project tasks, timescales, deliverables, and dependencies.

generalisability (Chapters 6, 8) – the extent to which findings from research conducted in one time and place can be applied to populations in another time and/or place.

gold standard (Chapters 2, 6, 9) – a metaphorical term used to describe the extent to which a particular study or characteristic may be used as a basis for comparison with other studies or characteristics.

grey literature (Chapters 5, 9) – information produced by government, academics, business and industry in electronic and print formats not controlled by commercial publishing, (i.e. where publishing is not the primary activity of the producing body).

grounded theory (Chapters 1, 7) – procedures developed within primary data analysis, and subsequently applied to secondary research, that seek to provide a method for generating theory grounded in the data in the absence of an *a priori* theory or hypothesis.

hand searching (Chapters 5, 9) – a complementary method of searching that requires systematic scanning of the contents of key journals in order to offset perceived deficiencies in database coverage or indexing.

health technology assessment (Chapter 1) – a type of review commonly conducted for health policymakers that seeks to inform decisions about the effectiveness and cost-effectiveness of a particular procedure, programme, policy or intervention, typically within a tightly constrained timeframe.

heterogeneous (Chapter 10) this refers to the extent to which studies included in a systematic review display variability. Such variability may relate to differences in the included participants, interventions and outcomes or to diversity in study design and the consequent risk of bias. These differences may in turn contribute to variability in the intervention effects being evaluated in the different studies (statistical heterogeneity).

heterogeneity (Chapter 6) – the extent to which studies demonstrate variation across a range of key variables.

hierarchy/ies of evidence (Chapter 6) – an approach to defining the quality of research studies based on their study design, favouring studies that are comparative, prospective, and protected against systematic error or bias.

homogeneity (Chapters 2, 7) – the extent to which studies exhibit shared characteristics across a range of key variables.

idea web(s)/idea webbing (Chapters 4, 7) a form of concept mapping regarded as particularly valuable in making sense of a complex phenomenon or programme.

implementation fidelity (Chapter 8) – the degree to which an intervention, programme, or policy can be seen to have been put into practice as originally intended.

incident knowledge (Chapter 2) – newly appearing knowledge that makes a contribution to an improved understanding of a particular topic area.

inclusion criteria (Chapters 4, 6) – the standards or criteria that have to be fulfilled in order for a person to be eligible to be included in a trial and, by extension, the standards used to determine whether an individual study is eligible for inclusion in a systematic review.

index paper (Chapter 7) – a paper that is regarded as being rich in content and is therefore considered an appropriate starting point for a subsequent investigation of a series of papers.

information explosion (Chapter 1) – a social phenomenon that describes the state at which information is being produced at a rate quicker than it can be identified, organised, managed, or retrieved.

information literate (Chapter 1) – the facility of an individual to be able to undertake basic information processing tasks.

information overload (Chapter 1) – the point at which an individual has too much information and is therefore unable to process it effectively.

information retrieval (Chapters 1, 2) – a set of techniques and procedures used to specify and identify relevant items from a data source such as an electronic database.

informational redundancy (Chapter 7) – a point at which further information fails to add additional value to knowledge or understanding already established from previously identified studies.

integrative review (Chapters 1, 2) – originally a type of review that sought to integrate findings from a number of research papers; nowadays more commonly used to describe a review that integrates both quantitative and qualitative data together in the same review product.

interpretive (Chapters 2, 7) – a type of review that seeks to use the process of synthesis as a means of explaining a particular phenomenon.

internal validity (Chapters 6, 8) – the extent to which the design and conduct of a study are likely to have prevented bias and therefore the results may be considered reliable.

language bias (Chapter 8) – a form of bias relating to the original language of a publication. It is characterised by a tendency for reviews to be more likely to include studies published in the language of that review.

language of publication bias (Chapter 2) – a systematic bias caused by the increased/decreased likelihood of a research paper containing positive or negative results as a function of the language in which it is being published.

law of diminishing returns (Chapter 3) – the phenomenon that, as one extends searching across more and more databases the yield becomes correspondingly less productive.

limit function (Chapter 5) – a facility on bibliographic databases that allows the searcher to restrict search results by date, language, or publication type in order to make retrieval results more manageable.

line of argument (synthesis) (Chapter 7) – a component method of meta-ethnography that seeks to organise findings from multiple studies into a single explanatory line of argument.

location bias (Chapter 8) – an umbrella term referring to any form of bias relating to the location(s) in which a study is originally conducted. Most commonly, but not necessarily, associated with language bias it may result in a review being less likely to include studies that originate from a particular region of the world (e.g. the systematic exclusion of studies from low and middle income countries).

logic model(s) (Chapters 4, 7, 8, 9) – a visual representation showing the sequence of related events connecting the need for a planned programme with the programme's desired results or short-term and long-term outcomes. A logic model may be used at the beginning of a review to plan a review strategy or towards the end as a framework for interpreting and presenting the findings.

longitudinal (Chapter 6) – study design in which the same subjects are observed repeatedly over a period of time.

lumping (Chapter 7) – the action of deciding to undertake a broad review in preference to several related, but individual, reviews on the basis of commonalities shared by the population, interventions and/or outcomes (cf. **splitting**).

mapping review (Chapters 2, 9) – a rapid search of the literature aiming to give a broad overview of the characteristics of a topic area. Mapping of existing research, identification of gaps, and a summary assessment of the quantity and quality of the available evidence help to decide future areas for research or for systematic review.

meaningfulness (Chapter 2) – the value that an individual or population ascribes to a particular intervention, programme or policy as established from the personal opinions, experiences, values, thoughts, beliefs or interpretations of the individuals themselves, their families, or significant others.

memo-ing (Chapter 7) – the process of documenting observations on a research process conducted by a researcher or reviewer as their work progresses.

meta-analysis (Chapters 1, 3, 7, 8, 9, 10) – the process of combining statistically quantitative studies that have measured the same effect using similar methods and a common outcome measure.

meta-ethnography (Chapters 1, 2, 3, 7, 8) – the most common method of synthesis of qualitative research, originally used to synthesise ethnographies but now used to refer to synthesis of other study types, typically with the objective of theory generation.

meta-method (Chapter 2) – a type of synthesis that seeks to derive insights from studying the characteristics of different methods used to investigate a shared phenomenon.

meta-narrative (Chapter 4) – a type of synthesis that seeks to explore large and heterogeneous literatures from different research traditions or disciplines by following the unfolding storyline or narrative from each.

meta-theory (Chapter 2) – a type of synthesis that seeks to synthesise multiple theories from research papers examining a shared phenomenon.

methodological filter(s) (Chapters 3, 5) – standardised search strategies designed to retrieve studies of a particular methodology type.

mind map(s) (Chapters 4, 7) – a diagram used to represent words, ideas, tasks or other concepts linked to, and arranged around, a central key word or idea.

mixed method(s) review (Chapters 2, 7) – a literature review that seeks to bring together data from quantitative and qualitative studies integrating them in a way that facilitates subsequent analysis.

narrative review (Chapter 2) – the term used to describe a conventional overview of the literature, particularly when contrasted with a systematic review.

narrative synthesis (Chapters 4, 7) – a systematic process of describing the shared properties of a group of studies included in a review primarily through text but augmented by tabular and graphical displays of data.

NOT (Chapter 5) – a Boolean operator (see above), that is syntax entered into a search engine or database, that explicitly requires that one concept is present in an item (e.g. an abstract) and the other is absent for it to be retrieved (e.g. Female NOT Male).

observational study/studies (Chapter 7) – a study that investigates the effects of an intervention or programme where the assignment of subjects is outside the control of the investigator.

open source software (Chapter 4) – a method for the distribution of software without charge which allows the source code to be modified or developed in the public domain subject to fulfilment of prespecified terms and conditions.

OR (Chapter 5) – a Boolean operator (see above), that is syntax entered into a search engine or database, that allows for the presence in a single item (e.g. an abstract) of either one concept or an alternative concept or both in order for it to be retrieved (e.g. fruit OR vegetables).

pearl growing (Chapter 5) – the process of identifying a known highly relevant article (the pearl) as a means to isolate terms on which a search can subsequently be based.

PICOC (Chapter 4) – an acronym, coined by Petticrew and Roberts, 2006, to capture a precise review question by specifying the five elements of *population-intervention-comparison-outcome-context*.

PICOS – an acronym describing an approach to formulating or specifying a review question according to the elements of Population Intervention Comparison Outcome and Study design.

point estimate (Chapter 7) – a single point or value considered to represent the most likely approximation for a given population of effect sizes (e.g. a mean value).

practically significant (Chapter 6) – a difference observed in a study or review that is considered by professionals to be important enough to be worth achieving.

prevalent knowledge (Chapter 2) – that knowledge that exists on a topic at a particular point in time.

primary study/ies (Chapter 5) – original research studies; compare secondary studies which are reviews or syntheses.

prior distribution (Chapter 7) – the specification, in advance of a test or experiment, of the distribution of an uncertain quantity.

PRISMA (*preferred reporting items for systematic reviews and meta-analyses*) (Chapters 5, 9) – a standard for the reporting of systematic reviews and meta-analyses in the published journal literature (formerly QUOROM).

probability distribution (Chapter 7) – a statistical function that identifies either the probability of each value of a random variable (when the variable is discrete), or the probability of the value falling within a particular interval (when the variable is continuous).

programme theory (Chapters 1, 7, 8) – an idealised model that shows how programme features interact to influence performance indicators, and produce desired outcomes. It comprises three components; (i) a problem definition; (ii) programme components linked together to create a programme logic, and (iii) a link between the programme logic and programme activities through the use of performance indicators.

prospective (Chapter 6) – a prospective study asks a specific study question (usually about how a particular exposure affects an outcome), recruits appropriate participants and looks at the exposures and outcomes of interest in these people over the following months or years.

proximity (Chapter 5) – the specification of two search terms to be close to each other e.g. in a phrase or within the same sentence in order for a document to be retrieved from a database.

publication bias (Chapters 2, 3, 5, 7, 8) – the tendency for researchers, editors, and pharmaceutical companies to handle the reporting of experimental results that are positive (i.e. they show a significant finding) differently from results that are negative (i.e. supporting the null hypothesis) or inconclusive. Typically this is evidenced in an increased likelihood of publication.

qualitative (Chapter 4) – adjective relating to the facility by which a phenomenon may be effectively expressed in terms of its (non-numerical) characteristics.

qualitative evidence synthesis (Chapter 7) – an umbrella term increasingly used to describe a group of review types that attempt to synthesise and analyse findings from primary qualitative research studies.

qualitative study/ies (Chapters 4, 6) – an approach to research that is concerned with eliciting the subjective experiences of participants. Qualitative research may entail a choice of methodologies such as ethnography, grounded theory, phenomenology and may use a variety of methods of which questionnaire, interview and participant observation are the most common.

quality assessment (Chapters 2, 4, 6) – the systematic process of examining the internal and external validity of studies for potential inclusion in a review so as to evaluate their individual contributions to the overall 'bottom line' of that review.

quality of conduct (Chapter 2) – that attribute of a review that relates to how well its processes and procedures have been carried out.

quality of reporting (Chapter 2) – that attribute of a review that relates to how well its processes and procedures have been documented.

quantitative (Chapter 4) – adjective relating to the facility by which a phenomenon may be effectively expressed in numerical values.

random effects analysis (Chapter 7) – an analysis using a statistical model that allows for random variation among populations. A random effects analysis therefore provides a more conservative estimate of an effect size and is less likely to overestimate the effect of an intervention.

randomised controlled trial(s) (RCT) (Chapters 1, 4, 6, 7) – a study design considered to be the most rigorous method of determining whether a cause-effect relationship exists between an intervention and an outcome. As such systematic reviews of randomised controlled trials provide the best available evidence of effectiveness. The strength of the RCT lies in the process of randomisation that should allow both intervention and comparison to be compared on an equal basis when considering the effect of an intervention.

rapid evidence assessment (Chapters 3, 7, 8) – a tool for obtaining a rapid overview of the available research evidence on a policy issue, as comprehensively as possible, within the constraints of a given timetable. It uses elements of scoping review and mapping review methodologies.

realist synthesis (Chapters 1, 2, 7, 8) – a method for studying complex interventions in response to the perceived limitations of conventional systematic review methodology. It involves identification of contexts, mechanisms and outcomes for individual programmes in order to explain differences, intended or unintended, between them.

reciprocal translation (Chapter 7) – a component technique of meta-ethnography which involves exploring the extent to which an idea or concept used by one author accurately represents use of a related idea or concepts by other authors.

reference management (Chapters 3, 5) – the management of bibliographic references, and sometimes full-text papers, typically through electronic means so that they may be identified, stored, retrieved, and used effectively.

reflexivity (Chapter 9) – the capacity of a researcher to consider the effect that their relationship to the subject or participants of a study may have on the conduct and interpretation of that study.

refutational synthesis (Chapter 8) – a stage of meta-ethnography (q.v.) where the reviewer is involved in a purposive search for phrases, metaphors and themes that refute any emerging patterns that have emerged from included data.

reliability (Chapter 6) – the extent to which a particular result measured at a particular point in time accurately captures the likely result of a similar measurement made at another point in time.

replicability (Chapters 3, 9) – the extent to which a result or measurement achieved by one researcher or reviewer could be achieved by another researcher or reviewer working independently.

replicative (Chapter 7) – the property of causing replication.

reproducibility (Chapter 9) – the property of any scientific study by which results obtained from one experiment can be reproduced, either by the same or another investigator, by repeating the method as described. In the context of systematic reviews it refers to the extent to which review methods, if followed as described, would, at least in theory, produce the same results.

research question (Chapter 4) – a precisely stated question that specifically conveys what the researcher will attempt to answer.

research synthesis (Chapter 1) – a form of synthesis that seeks to synthesise only data obtained through the medium of research.

respondent validation – (also known as member checking) (Chapters 8, 9) a technique used by researchers to help improve the accuracy, credibility, validity and transferability of a study, Typically the interpretation and report (or a portion of it) is given to members of the sample (respondents/informants) in order to check the authenticity of the work. Feedback from the members of the sample serves as a check on whether the interpretation is viable.

risk of bias tool (Chapter 8) – an instrument developed by the Cochrane Collaboration to assist in the identification and presentation of data on the likelihood of particular types of bias both in an individual study and in a group of studies.

scope creep (Chapters 3, 4, 8) – the tendency for any review to expand the work required without due consideration of the costs and the implications for timely production.

scoping (Chapter 4) – the process of identifying the characteristics of a topic and its associate literature in order to determine a feasible strategy for a subsequent review.

scoping review (Chapters 2, 5, 9) – a type of review that has as its primary objective the identification of the size and quality of research in a topic area in order to inform subsequent review.

scoping search (Chapter 5) – a type of literature search that seeks to determine rapidly and efficiently the scale of a predefined topic to inform the subsequent conduct of a review.

search filters (Chapter 5) – a generic term for any collection of search terms designed to optimise retrieval from a bibliographical database. Such terms may be topical (i.e. related to the subject content of items to be retrieved) or methodological (pertaining to the methodology of retrieved items).

search strategy (Chapters 5, 8) – the plan for retrieval of information on a chosen topic and, more specifically, the combination of search terms used to retrieve relevant items.

selection bias (Chapters 2, 6) – a systematic error in choosing subjects for a particular study that results in an uneven comparison whether such subjects represent people (for a primary research study) or papers (for a literature review).

selective reporting bias (Chapter 8) – the selection, on the basis of the results, of a subset of analyses to be reported.

sensitivity (Chapter 5) – a diagnostic term, appropriated by information retrieval, to refer to the capacity of a search strategy to identify all relevant items (i.e. not missing any relevant items) on a particular topic.

sensitivity analysis (Chapters 2, 3, 8, 9) – in this context, an analysis used to determine how sensitive the results of a systematic review are to changes in how it was done. Sensitivity analyses assess how robust the results are to assumptions made about the data and the methods that were used.

snowballing (Chapter 5) – literature-searching technique that involves locating a relevant source paper and then using this paper as a starting point for either working back from its references or for conducting additional citation searches.

snowball sampling (Chapter 1) – an epidemiological term used to describe the sampling procedure whereby sampling of a small group of subjects (or papers) helps to define an appropriate strategy and sample for further sampling.

social validity (Chapter 7) – In this context, the selection of interventions, programmes or policies on the basis that they are socially acceptable.

specificity (Chapter 5) – a diagnostic term, appropriated by information retrieval, to refer to the capacity of a search strategy to identify *only* relevant items (i.e. not retrieving any irrelevant items) on a particular topic.

SPICE – an acronym describing an approach to formulating or specifying a review question according to the elements of Setting Perspective phenomenon of Interest Comparison and Evaluation.

splitting (Chapter 7) – the action of deciding to undertake a number of narrowly-focused reviews on adjacent topics in preference to a single broad review on the basis of meaningful differences between elements of the population, interventions; and/or outcomes (cf. **lumping**).

statistically significant (Chapters 6, 8) – a measurable statistical result that is unlikely to have been achieved by chance.

study selection (Chapter 4) – the process of applying inclusion and exclusion criteria to an initial set of documents in order to arrive at a manageable set of includable studies.

subgroup analysis (Chapters 2, 6, 9) – a set of procedures that follows up analysis of an entire study population (people or papers) by looking for patterns in one or more subsets of that population.

subject index(es) (Chapter 5) – listings, either printed or electronic, that seek to provide retrieval of items in a predefined topic area or discipline.

summative (Chapter 7) – an adjective describing those aspects of a review that can only be assessed or evaluated as it approaches its completion.

synonyms (Chapter 5) – in literature searching, different words likely to be used by authors or other researchers with a similar meaning to a word that you have selected to describe your own topic e.g. car, motor vehicle and automobile.

synthesis strategy (Chapter 7) – an approach to planning the subsequent synthesis and analysis of a review by attempting to pre-specify review procedures. Typically a synthesis strategy is based on a preliminary assessment of the likely nature of the data and a knowledge of the purpose for which the review is to be used.

systematic review (Chapters 1, 4, 5, 9) – a review of a clearly formulated question that uses systematic and explicit methods to identify, select and critically appraise relevant research and to collect and analyse data from the studies that are included in the review.

test for heterogeneity (Chapter 7) – a formal statistical test used, prior to meta-analysis, to examine quantitatively the extent of variability or differences between studies in the estimates of effects.

textwords (Chapter 5) – exact words found in the title and/or abstract of an article that can be used to retrieve its details from a bibliographic database. Often called keywords.

thematic analysis (Chapter 7) – a method often used to analyse data and to identify themes in primary qualitative research.

thematic synthesis (Chapters 2, 3, 4, 7) – the use of methods, analogous to thematic analysis in primary qualitative research, in systematic reviews to bring together and integrate the findings of multiple qualitative studies.

theoretical saturation (Chapters 2, 4, 7) – the point within an interpretive review at which all data can be coded into an existing category; new categories are not emerging, and the existing category structure appears stable or secure.

thesaurus (Chapter 5) – a list of words showing similarities, differences, dependencies, and other relationships to each other and mapping words used by database users to the actual words utilised by the constructors of that database.

transferability (Chapter 3) – the ability to apply results of research in the context of one or more study populations to the context of a target population. Also, the extent to which a review invites its readers to make meaningful connections between elements of the review and their own experiences.

transparency (Chapter 3) – the use of a set of policies, practices and procedures to help to make the contents and process of a review accessible, usable, informative and auditable to its readers.

triangulation (Chapter 8) – a term from primary qualitative research that refers to the use of two or more methods or sources to collect data on a particular phenomenon. Findings established from multiple sources are more likely to be valid and discrepancies or inconsistencies across sources will merit further investigation. In the specific context of literature reviews triangulation may refer to use of findings from different study types or methods, from quantitative and qualitative research, or from different disciplines or schools of thought.

truncation (Chapter 5) – a truncation symbol is a character (determined by the database, such as an asterisk or dollar sign) which can be substituted, when searching databases or search engines, for various endings of the stem of a word (e.g. organi* for organisation, organization, organised, organized).

truth table (Chapter 8) – a matrix using binary notation to show all possible truth-values for a particular factor, derived from the truth-values of its component studies. It is particularly useful for examining the possible relationships between factors or variables.

validity (Chapters 6, 8) – the degree to which a result (of a study or a review) is likely to be true and free of bias (systematic errors).

vote-counting (Chapter 2) – a (typically derogatory) term for the process by which the likelihood of a review finding being correct is determined simply by the numbers of studies reporting a favourable or unfavourable result.

wildcard (Chapter 5) – a wildcard character is a character (typically a question mark) that may be substituted, when searching databases or search engines, for any of a defined subset of all possible characters (e.g. wom?n for woman or women).

Index

Tables and Figures are indicated by page numbers printed in bold.